19.50

Ple
star
if r

SMALL FIRMS GROWTH AND DEVELOPMENT

Small Firms Growth and Development

Edited by

MICHAEL SCOTT
ALLAN GIBB
Durham University Business School

JOHN LEWIS
Management Studies Department,
University of Glasgow

and

TERRY FAULKNER
Small Business Centre,
Trent Polytechnic

Gower

© M.G.Scott, A.A.Gibb, T.Faulkner and J.Lewis, 1986

Published by
Gower Publishing Company Limited,
Gower House, Croft Road, Aldershot, Hampshire,
  England.

and

Gower Publishing Company,
Old Post Road, Brookfield, Vermont, 05036, U.S.A.

Printed in Great Britain by Blackmore Press, Shaftesbury, Dorset

ISBN 0-566-00811-4

Contents

MARKETING

Editors and authors

ADAM ADAMS is a Researcher in the Management Sciences
  Department, University of Manchester, Institute of Science
  and Technology.
MARTIN BINKS is Lecturer in Economics, University of
  Nottingham.
DAVID BODDY is Senior Lecturer in Organisational Behaviour,
  University of Glasgow.
ELIZABETH CHELL is Lecturer in Organisational Behaviour,
  Department of Business and Administration, University of
  Salford.
JAMES CURRAN is Reader in Industrial Sociology, Kingston
  Polytechnic.
TERRY FAULKNER is Head of the Small Business Centre, Trent
  Polytechnic.
CELIA FRANK is a Senior Economic Assistant at the Department
  of Trade and Industry.
ALLAN GIBB is Professor of Small Business, Durham University
  Business School.
GAY HASKINS is Programme Manager, European Foundation for
  Management Development, Brussels.
JEAN HAWORTH is Senior Lecturer in Statistics, University of
  Salford.
ANDREW JENNINGS is Lecturer in Economics, University of
  Nottingham.
JOHN LEWIS is Senior Lecturer in Management Studies,
  University of Glasgow.

PETER LLOYD is Reader in Geography and Director of the North West Industry Research Unit, University of Manchester.

JULIAN LOWE is Senior Lecturer in Industrial Economics, School of Management, University of Bath.

COLIN MASON is Lecturer in Geography, University of Southampton.

ROBERT MIALL is an Economic Adviser at the Department of Trade and Industry.

TOM MILNE is Senior Lecturer in Management Studies, University of Glasgow.

CHARLES MONCK is Manager, Listerhills Science Park, Bradford University.

DAVID REES is Senior Economic Adviser at the Department of Trade and Industry.

PAT RICHARDSON is a Researcher in the Department of Land Management and Development, University of Reading.

JOHN RITCHIE is Senior Lecturer in Industrial Sociology, School of Occupational Studies, Newcastle Polytechnic.

MALCOLM ROBBIE is Lecturer in Banking and Finance, University of Loughborough.

MICHAEL SCOTT is Lecturer in Small Business Studies at Durham University Business School.

NICK SEGAL is a Director of Segal, Quince & Associates.

JOHN STANWORTH is Professor of Management Studies, and Director of the Small Business Unit, Polytechnic of Central London.

MARCUS THOMPSON is Research Assistant, Business Development Research Project, University of Glasgow.

MARTIN WALLBANK is Lecturer in Management Sciences Department, University of Manchester Institute of Science & Technology.

DAVID WATKINS is Director of the New Enterprise Centre, Manchester Business School.

JEAN WATKINS is a Research worker at the New Enterprise Centre, Manchester Business School.

RICHARD WHITTINGTON is a Researcher at the Manchester Business School.

Acknowledgements

The editors would like to thank all authors whose papers appear in this book for their generous contributions of time and effort, and their courteous response to editorial requests in the preparation of their papers. The preparation of the text would not have been possible without the efficiency and tolerance of Eileen Wilkinson.

The editors would also like to thank the sponsors whose support made the Conference itself possible, Barclays Bank plc, National Westminster Bank plc, and the Foundation for Management Education.

Introduction

1983 was designated the European Year of the Small and Medium
Enterprise, signifying at last the legitimacy of the S.M.E. in
social, cultural and economic terms. In the United Kingdom,
the Sixth Annual Research and Policy Conference of the Small
Business Management Teachers Association was hosted by Durham
University Business School, within the medieval splendour of
Durham's Castle, inappropriately large in scale and founded on
the proposition that Might is Right. But that is history.
E.Y.S.M.E. symbolises perhaps the hope which is now placed on
the smaller economic unit to smooth the transition from 'smoke
stack' to 'sunshine' industry, heralding indeed post industrial
society. Smoothing the transition does not mean, sadly, the
absorbtion of mass unemployment: it does however require the
growth and development of smaller enterprises, with a modest
level of employment creation, with innovation, and with
increased efficiency. These, together with recommendations for
appropriate policies, were the topics of the Research and
Policy Conference Papers, a selection of which are the material
for this book.

Section 1 is concerned broadly with studies both at the macro
level, and at the level of the firm itself, of the development
of new and existing firms, with an emphasis on the conceptuali-
sations underlying our studies of the small enterprise.

Beginning at the macro level the Chapter by Binks and
Jennings, which is based on an interview survey of one hundred
firms in the Nottingham area, considers the role of the new firm
as a response to the need for economic restructuring of the
economy in time of recession. A priori, evolutionary change
and progress arises from the death of inefficient firms and the
birth of new, innovative ones. Government statistics showing a
steady rise in the surplus of births and deaths is taken
particularly to confirm this proposition. Binks and Jennings,
on the basis of a more discriminating methodology, suggest that
it is dying firms which provide the new owner-managers, and the
cheap second-hand equipment, to incubate firms in the same
industry, typically not innovative, and often threatening
established small firms. Without an increment in efficiency
(and these Nottingham firms tended to seek neither outside
advice nor training), Binks and Jennings suggest, current
policies run the danger of simply increasing the through-put of
firms rather than the stock, and with little positive economic
regeneration.

The Chapter by Mason and Lloyd is a reminder that much of our
knowledge of the small firm comes from studies of a few
locations, typically of declining urban-industrial areas of the
North. The spatial dimension, as a part of the small firm
sector's diversity, is frequently overlooked, the authors
claim. Their study of fifty two manufacturing firms in a
prosperous area, South Hampshire, undertaken in conjunction
with a similar study in the urban North West, is able to
indicate common experiences whilst highlighting divergencies.
Broadly, the authors conclude, there is in fact a high degree
of similarity between firms in the two area: but the
differences are illuminating. The South Hampshire founders
tended to be older, with more business experience and credit
worthiness, and a greater awareness of marketing issues. In
consequence, they experienced less problems in raising finance
or in achieving market penetration beyond their immediate
locality: but they had difficulties in obtaining skilled
labour, and the major problem for these South Hampshire firms
was in obtaining suitable premises - both factors of little
significance to the North West firms partly as a consequence of
regional policy measures.

Richard Whittington provides a most useful framework within
which to consider the previous two Chapters. Building
particularly on the attempt by David Storey to construct
a regional 'index of entrepreneurship', Whittington considers
how such an index may firstly be more fruitfully
operationalised on the basis of recently published data on
formation rates, and secondly, how it may be refined. A key
finding is that 74% of the regional variance in new firm

formation rates can be 'explained' by just three variables:
specifically that regional entrepreneurship as expressed by new
firm formation rates will be low where home ownership is rare,
where manual workers are common, and where changes in the level
of unemployment are low. The key role of the middle class is
stressed, as is the implication that Government incentives to
start up are likely to be differentially taken up, with the
prosperous areas (such as that discussed by Mason and Lloyd)
able to benefit disproportionately as a quite unintended
consequence of existing policy. Whittington suggests a much
tighter targetting of regional support, to counteract the
imbalances arising from the low level of potential
entrepreneurship in peripheral regions.

The Chapter by Milne and Thompson addresses the question of
how new firms can best be helped to succeed in their early
years. It draws on their current research involving eighty new
firms selected as having, prima facie, a better than average
change of survival and growth. Only by identifying the key
success characteristics, Milne and Thompson argue, can
appropriate support strategies be developed. They have
provided an extensive review of the literature on small firms
growth, from which they derive an 'ideal' model of the
successful infant business, against which to test their
empirical data. What emerges broadly is that the key skills
required for successful start-up are those involved in winning
the confidence firstly of the market place and through that,
secondly of the financial backers: this appears to involve an
approach which is more systematic, formalised and 'organised'
than a purely personal 'initiative' approach. The implications
of this in support terms is that the new business above all
needs practical help in finding markets (market search as much
as market research), and in becoming master of its financial
management.

The next Chapter by Gibb and Scott focusses on the
development process of existing rather than brand new firms.
On the basis of action research on a small number of companies,
they attempt firstly to produce a general model of the
development process, and secondly to assess the impact of
different forms of external assistance on this process. Their
model emphasises the need for a small firm to profile its
existing performance and its potential for development: the
existence of internal and external factors which influence the
process itself; and finally the iterative nature of that
process. The model attempts to delineate and conceptually link,
all the variables which contribute to a firm's growth (and in
their absence to its decline). The limitations of external
assistance, and especially the passive provision of information,
are considered: however, one form of assistance which is

particularly helpful in enabling firms to carry out self-
profiling and in providing organisational 'slack' within which
owner-managers commitment to the growth project can develop, is
the placement of formerly redundant managers in firms under the
M.S.C. Management Extension Scheme.

Adams and Wallbank are similarly concerned with development
aspects of existing small firms, and specifically those seeking
growth through new product ventures. Their work is based on a
study of two hundred and sixty three new product ideas in sixty
three innovating companies. The problem is how to evaluate
such new products - how to pick winners. The authors contend
that current evaluation techniques tend to be based on
theoretical rather than empirical evidence, and to reflect
often out of date large company practices. They also point out
that studies tend to focus only on ideas given the go ahead and
then meeting either market success or failure: this of course
ignores those ideas (probably a majority) which were earlier
abandoned. What Adams and Wallbank propose in this Chapter is
an iterative empirical model, essentially an adaptive 'expert
system' which in a series of stages from the initial idea,
takes in data on product, technology and environment and over
time can produce a better predicter of likely success than
existing methods. Such expert systems, say the authors, will
never replace the 'illogical' human hunches that can lead to
break-throughs; rather they supplement the normal routine,
rational (if subjective), judgements by the better use and
combination of all relevant information.

The Chapter by Curran and Stanworth returns us to a
conceptual level, reminding us that much recent work on the
small firm has concentrated on internal factors, and that we
lack systematic theoretical models which relate the small firm
to its external environment and to large firms in particular.
This creates problems in attempting any comparative analysis of
small and large firms, and in seeking explanations of the ways
in which 'size' per se may be influential. Previous work has
tended to be either structuralist, i.e. based on an analysis of
correlations between quantitive indicators (workforce size,
levels of profit, asset base), or individualist seeking
explanations of size effects in terms of qualitative data
(attitudes, feelings). Curran and Stanworth in this Chapter
show how it may be possible to link these two approaches, and
bring 'people' back into a fully and explicitly structural
analysis. Drawing on the structure-meaning approach of Benson
they see organisational structure as emerging out of the
conflicts and accommodations amongst organisational members,
which reflect wider social values. Organisation-size phenomena
are to be understood as socially produced. The effect of this
is to include in comparative analysis of large and small firms

the _perceptual_ aspects of size; the role of organisational
members other than the owner-manager or top management; and the
role of external groupings. Only in this way, the authors
believe, can better comparative research be done, leading to a
greater level of realism in policy making.

 The final Chapter in Section 1 by John Ritchie asks the
intriguing question - whatever happened to the older small
firm? His answer takes two forms; firstly a discussion of the
context of changing political values about enterprise and the
assumed role of the older small firm in this; and secondly a
case study of the distintegration of such a firm. From this,
Ritchie concludes that the changing political context has
placed (or perhaps misplaced) greater faith in the new and
growing entrepreneurial firms, and created dangerous myths
about older, existing firms which may have been set up as
sacrificial lambs on the altar of newness. Such policy shifts
may ensure that the corporate life-cycle becomes a self
fulfilling prophecy. Yet we do need strategies for dealing
with older firms, and Ritchie provides us finally with a
framework for assessing such strategies.

 Section 2 comprises a series of Chapters which address the
special areas of need of the developing small company.

 The first two Chapters in this Section are concerned with the
education and training needs of small firms. The first of
these, by Boddy and Lewis, is an evaluation of the role of
action learning in small business development. It provides
firstly an overview of action learning itself. Its originator,
Reg Revons, distinguished between two kinds of learning, P and
Q. P refers to the acquisition of existing programmed
knowledge whilst Q refers to the acquisition of the ability to
ask fresh questions. Both types are needed by the owner-
managers of small firms - to keep up-to-date on technical
aspects of the business, but also to develop skills to deal
with the ambiguities and uncertainteies of innovation and
strategic thinking if the business is to grow. Conventional
training tends to address the former, whilst finding it
difficult to cope with Q type learning. Action learning is
seen as a way to deal with this and the second part of the
Chapter describes in depth the Glasgow Programme which
comprised a series of five separate courses. These were
evaluated and were broadly found to be not only cost effective
in terms such as employment generation, but led also to
learning on the part of both clients and the academic
providers.

 The Chapter by Jean and David Watkins is concerned with the
relatively unresearched area of female entrepreneurship.

Although we lack official data, one estimate suggests that 6 per cent of all small businesses may be owned and controlled by women, and there are forces in the labour market which may (and in the USA are) resulting in a steady increase in this figure. The Chapter therefore sets out to provide a picture of the current generation of female entrepreneurs, drawn from a survey of 58 women running between them 49 independent businesses, with a matched group of 43 male owner-managers. This includes their parental backgroud, age at founding, educational background and prior work experience, all of which differs significantly between the male and female samples. In particular, the women owner-managers appeared more constrained in their choice of business, forced into stereo-typically 'female' areas such as personal service, and often unprepared by both education and occupational experience. The Chapter goes on to discuss the training implications of this, and to identify key barriers likely to be encountered in the training of female entrepreneurs. These are psychological barriers - arising from the male orientation of most programmes; entry criteria barriers - the demands for technical and managerial ability, and for financial backing are often unrealistic for women; content based barriers - the need to grade content from a start point in keeping with the lower levels of management experience; and structure based barriers - associated with, for example, the intensive, residential nature of many programmes. There are however, solutions to overcome all these problems, notably by running exclusively female programmes, and by providing a cascading recruitment to compensate for initial lack of experience.

An area of need frequently cited is that of finance. The Chapter by Malcolm Robbie is concerned with bank lending. Although it is not possible to assess whether the banks are lending money to the 'right' businesses, it is certainly possible to look at some of the businesses that are refused bank finance, and to consider why they were refused. A questionnaire survey of sixty eight bank managers provided data on their recent experience of both sanctioning and declining applications for loans or overdraft facilities. (The Chapter throughout compares this survey with published analyses of the Government's Loan Guarantee Scheme.) The reasons for decline were characterised by great diversity, but Robbie has provided an analysis in terms of seven main categories: inadequate capital resources; lack of profitability; scheme viewed as unviable; insufficient information; trading difficulties; and security unacceptable. The survey suggested that the first two of these were the most important: the evaluation of the Loan Guarantee Scheme gave them a lower ranking. The Loan Guarantee Scheme may indeed have stimulated 'lending at the margin' and the Chapter is relevant to the discussion of the extent to which lending practices of bank managers may be in the process of change.

The next Chapter, by Pat Richardson, looks at another perennial problem, especially for the new firm, that of a lack of suitable factories and workshops, and is based on a detailed examination of Local Authority provision in three Inner City partnership areas (Manchester/Salford, Newcastle/Gateshead and Birmingham) including a questionnaire survey of occupants. Her findings suggest that this provision made only a marginal contribution to employment creation for inner-city residents, although other benefits could be identified as arising: incubating new firms and stimulating enterprise; assisting some firms to grow; stimulating other agencies to add to the premises supply; and generally improving the working environment.

A special aspect of premises provision is that concerned with high technology, and the following Chapter, on University Science Parks by Monck and Segal, firstly discusses the nature of the demand for space in such Parks, and secondly examines the role of the property element in Science Parks schemes in stimulating linkages between the academic world and industry. The Chapter also crucially examines the non-property aspects of Science Parks provision making the point that highly successful schemes in the U.S. and in Cambridge in the U.K., were not 'property led'. Marketing, management and the provision of external support, as well as proper financing facilities are seen as critical issues in a total package within which property provision is only one element.

The next Chapter, by Julian Lowe, is also concerned with the means for enhancing technology transfer, in this case through the mechanism of licencing. This procedure is increasingly attractive to the S.M.E., since it allows it to compete technologically with larger rivals especially when it lacks sufficient R and D resources of its own. The Chapter draws on the results of a questionnaire survey of 105 licensing and 78 non-licensing companies, and provides a comparison, for example, between those which licence both in and out, those which do one but not both, and those which do neither. For some firms, licensing can be fruitful in competitive strategy and the Chapter suggests the factors which enhance this process.

The final Chapter in this section focusses on that often neglected area, the retail small business. Chell and Haworth set themselves the task of identifying and measuring the factors affecting the performance of a sample of retail newsagents. Whilst the Chapter is useful simply as a case study of the activities of one section of the retail trade, it has a further interest in the methodology used and here described in some detail. The model of newsagent sales performance appears to have been sufficiently rigorous to allow under-achievers to be picked out by the wholesale supplier for special marketing activities.

Section 3 is concerned with wider issues of policy, and is also intended to raise questions for further research and discussion.

The Chapter by Rees, Frank and Miall begins by outlining the policy objectives of the Department of Trade and Industry towards small firms. Firstly, this seeks to promote a climate for U.K. industry which is as conducive to enterprise as that in any other industrialised country. This involves fostering more positive attitudes towards entrepreneurship, providing tax incentives and rewards to enterprise, and removing legislative and administrative burdens. A second objective is to promote industrial efficiency, which for the small firm implies the provision of various support functions of both hardware and software types, including the encouragement of private sector involvement through the enterprise agency system. A third objective is the encouragement of the transfer of technology into the small firm.

The authors use the small business Loan Guarantee Scheme as an example of the way in which research can contribute to practical policy making, and this case also illustrates two criteria which a new policy must meet; additionality and viability.

The Chapter then raises a number of issues which the authors see as being relevant for further research. These include: studies of entrepreneurship and the founders of new firms in order to obtain a better understanding of the characteristics of actual and potential entrepreneurs, and of better ways of stimulating entrepreneurship; indicators of success or failure of small firms; the availability of finance, including an evaluation of the various government measures presently in existence; the special case of Venture Capital availability; the role of the small firm in relation to the urban problem, including analyses of the types of activity which are best suited to inner city areas and the extent to which these might provide employment; the role of local government and its policies and services, including planning policies and rates, on small firm activities; the special issues of the provision of premises; the relationship between size of firm and employment generation, including the extent to which there may be regional variations; and finally, comparative studies of small firms activities in other industrialised nations, from which policy implications may flow.

Overall, policy makers, the Chapter reminds us, need to know not only where policy may be effective but also those areas where there is no scope for policy. The point is also made that knowledge of the prospective costs and benefits of particular policy responses is also crucially needed, including reference to the costs and benefits of achieving the same policy objectives in some other way. The implication of this is that evaluation of policy may be as important as the original research which suggested that policy.

Finally, the Chapter by Gay Haskins adds an international dimension, addressing as it does Europe-wide experiences in small business management training. Drawing on a variety of data sources, including a questionnaire survey of E.F.M.D. members or affiliated business schools, the Chapter describes the wide variety of provision of training, ranging from that for undergraduates, through special start-up programmes, to programmes for existing owner-managers. The diversity of this provision prompts a series of important questions: at the level of basic education are there adequate links between 'school' and 'enterprise'; at the undergraduate level, what is the actual impact of the various small business options; for the start-up, is there enough effort being put into the special needs of different 'market segments'; and for the existing firm, do we over-emphasise the under fifty employees firm at the expense of the slightly larger, is there enough for the high tech company, what indeed is being done to identify the gaps? The Chapter warns us that since small business management training is a 'dangerously sexy area - full of allure but very risky' management centres need to think hard before rushing into it, and to be sure of both faculty commitment and resources before taking the plunge. Fortunately, there are several networks in existence, notably E.F.M.D. itself, to allow the sharing of experiences, and of validated programme models.

The theme of sharing experiences is an appropriate one on which to end this book. The Conference series on which it is based exists for that purpose. Providing assisistance to a sector as diverse as that of the small firm is not the simple matter which some pundits would have us believe. Neither throwing money at symptoms, nor providing unfettered licence for the owner-manager to do as he wishes, is a substitute for truly understanding the functioning of the small firm, in all its complexity, for only this will lead to effective (as opposed to politically expedient) policies, and give us the thriving small firm sector we all wish to see.

SECTION I
EMPIRICAL AND
THEORETICAL ISSUES

New firms as a source of industrial regeneration

MARTIN BINKS AND ANDREW JENNINGS

INTRODUCTION

The present record level of new company registrations in the UK
naturally focusses attention upon the economic contribution
made by new firms. This is particularly pertinent in a period
of severe economic recession if such firms are relied upon to
provide a crucial catalyst in a process of economic recovery.
The extent to which this reliance upon new firms, and policies
designed to increase their number, is justified, can only be
fully assessed on the basis of accurate representative
information. After a brief consideration of the problems
involved in obtaining such information, this chapter presents
some of the results obtained from a recent survey of new
manufacturing firms in the Nottingham area. Given some of the
implications of these results a final question is posed; to
what extent policies which encourage more start-ups facilitate
economic recovery as opposed to fuelling the present record
level of company failures.

SMALL FIRMS RESEARCH - A NOTE ON METHODOLOGY

The analysis of any sector of the economy must be based, as
much as is practical, on rational argument and objective
information. The small firm sector has attracted much
attention over the past decade since the Bolton Committee

reported in 1971, but it still remains an area about which we have a hazy and limited understanding. The main reason why this is particularly true of small firm research is due to the difficulty of obtaining reliable, accurate information on which to base any form of analysis. Centrally published data are highly aggregated, and as a result, they conceal much of the interesting and important variations which exist both regionally and by activity.

The combination of political emphasis and limited information has prompted academics to resort to alternative methods of information collection, of which the most common have been survey based. Also popular, has been the longitudinal case study.

The survey technique is a potentially powerful tool for data collection and when properly organised, analysis of the resulting information can be very revealing. Unfortunately the survey is also one of the easiest techniques to abuse, often unknowingly.

The misuse of the survey technique in general, and within small firm research, takes two predominant forms. Firstly, surveys often suffer from inadequate design and execution. In terms of the sample itself this often means that either too few firms are roached, or the sample is unrepresentative, non-random, or both. The resulting information is biased and as a consequence misleading inferences may be drawn. It is often the case that some form of deficiency in the sample is unavoidable. Some firms in the initial sample may refuse to cooperate; if there is some common reason for this failure, that immediately introduces bias. Further, samples are often spatially biased. This is true of the sample from which the results in the rest of this chapter derive. The importance which one must attach to bias depends directly on the type and extent of the conclusions which are drawn from the survey data. For example, in the case of the authors'own survey of manufacturing firms in the Nottingham area we are not in a position to make sweeping or generalised observations. Much of the usefulness of survey information emerges when it is combined with some form of theoretical argument. The results below are used to present a possible explanation of the mechanism of firm births and their likely economic contribution in a period of recession.

The second difficulty, which stems directly from the points above is the temptation to 'over interpret' the results of a survey. This manifests itself as the desire to make numerous comparisons of different attributes of the survey and on the basis of these comparisons produce policy conclusions. All too often however, the collected data are not sufficiently robust to allow for any meaningful comparisons. This may be particularly true in the case of financial statistics such as profit, capital values or even turnover and in subjective areas like attitudes to lenders etc. The situation is accentuated by ready access to such computer software as the Statistical Package for Social Science, which allow for mass computation without sufficient prior thought as to whether the tests and comparisons being made are statistically valid rather than numerically possible.

The longitudinal case study is in many respects a special case of the survey, but with sample size 1, or at least so small as to be insignificant, e.g. a minimum of 30 is often a useful 'rule of thumb'. Studies and small sample studies may be useful in illustrating problems or providing material for 'after dinner speeches'; they are not to be relied upon to reveal or elucidate the relative impact of different problems in the small firms sector.

THE NOTTINGHAM SURVEY

This was set up to undertake a survey of 100 new small manufacturing firms in the Nottingham area in order to study the process of start-up and establishment. The main objective was to identify the relative importance of constraints upon the birth and expansion of such firms.

For the purpose of this research, new small manufacturing firms were defined as: [1]

   i. Wholly new businesses which had started trading
      after 31.12.77; which were
  ii. independent and owner managed; and were
 iii. involved primarily in manufacturing.

The sample was drawn randomly from a total population of firms collected from the following sources:

   i. Nottingham Chamber of Commerce new members list.
  ii. Telephone directory comparisons between the 1977,
      1980 and 1982 issues. (The problems experienced
      in finding 100 suitable firms implies that the
      survey covered a very high proportion of the
      total population.)

In order to ensure an overall sample of 100 firms, it was necessary to approach 112 of those which fell within the prescribed definition. The response rate of those contacted was, therefore, 89 per cent, with only twelve refusing to participate.

The number of firms studied and the obvious limitations of their spatial distribution were necessitated by the interview approach which was to be used. It was felt that the disadvantages arising from this restriction are more than offset by the advantages of greater and more accurate information, along with more reliable and internally consistent results. The interview format enables researchers to pursue points of particular interest while ensuring that each question is interpreted correctly by the interviewee. When compared to postal surveys the response rate of the interview approach is typically much higher, and therefore more representative of the population.

THE SURVEY RESULTS

While the aide-memoire used in the survey covered a wide variety of questions, consideration is given here to the main findings which are relevant to the argument presented.

   As far as this chapter is concerned, the relevant areas of concern are as follows.

Motivation

The reasons for starting a firm can be usefully divided between 'push' and 'pull' effects. Some owner managers are pushed into founding a business by redundancy, job insecurity or increasing disenchantment with their employer's attempts to 'survive' the recession. Others are attracted into entrepreneurship by a particular idea or the conviction that they can produce and sell a product more efficiently than present suppliers. Like any distinction of this kind which refers to such a heterogenous set of experiences, the dividing line is rather blurred. For example, many of those categorised as 'pulled' due to desired independence might equally well be regarded as 'pushed' due to dissatisfaction as an employee. The summary below illustrates the main motives identified by the respondents, crudely divided into those who have been pushed into entrepreneurship and those attracted to it.

Table 1
Those 'pushed'

Motive	No. of firms
Redundant	18
Job insecurity and unemployed	12
Disagreement with previous firm	11
Own previous firm's closure	5
Other	1
	47

Table 1 (cont'd)
Those 'pulled'

Motive	No. of firms
Desired independence	25
Specialist knowledge	11
Product development	8
Financial incentive	4
More efficient	2
Other	3
	53

Choice of product

It is tempting to regard new entrepreneurs as individuals who
have made a considered choice, having weighed up the advantages
and disadvantages of various alternatives as to the industry
which they should enter. In practice their product idea is
often determined largely, and not surprisingly, by their
previous experience; many drift into production as an extension
of their hobbies and working skills; they do not necessarily
consider other areas of production because the decision as to
what to produce is often made before the new entrepreneur has
actually decided to set up his own business. This is
particularly true in periods of recession for reasons that will
be discussed further below. The extent to which new firms
start up in new as opposed to established industries is also
important.

Table 2
Choice of product in relation to
previous experience of owner manager

Industry	No. of firms
Same or similar to previous employment	78
Different but expanding established	10
Different but established (had contacts)	8
Innovation of new product or technique	4
	100

Advice

Given the plethora of sources of advice to small businesses it
is interesting to consider the extent to which these serve to
prevent rather than cure the problems which new firms may
experience. This may be best judged by observing the extent to
which potential entrepreneurs seek advice prior to starting a
business. The survey revealed the following information:

structure. This will be determined to a large extent by the
motives and previous experience of the new entrepreneur.

   The innovative element reflected by the respondents'
activities was small as is clearly indicated in table 2, with
only four firms significantly involved in innovating.

Labour costs

Not surprisingly, a large proportion of the respondents worked
long hours with little remuneration in the first two years in
order to reduce variable costs and enable market penetration
through competitive pricing. In many instances employees were
also prepared to accept relatively low wages as they saw their
own fortunes as being inextricably bound up with those of the
firm. Again, in a period of recession the low level of
alternative job opportunities would be expected to enhance this
process.

THE MAIN IMPLICATIONS OF THE SURVEY RESULTS

A simple consideration of these results substantiates the view
that new small manufacturing firms are at present unlikely to
contribute greatly to economic recovery through the innovation
of new product areas or production techniques.

   The upsurge in firm births as indicated in the rise in new
company registrations does not appear to constitute a response
to recession likely to lead to structural change and recovery.
This rise could simply reflect economic recession if more firm
births are caused by lower levels of economic activity. It may,
however, result from other factors which have led to a rising
secular trend of firm births since 1950. When this question of
causality is addressed in more detail (Binks and Jennings, 1985)
it appears that throughout the 1970s economic recession had a
negative impact upon new company registrations.

The births of firms in a recession

The underlying trend of firm births has been upward since the
early 1950s and the apparent tendency for it to rise faster in
periods of recession has been proposed in several studies
(Fothergill and Gudgin, 1982, p.117-119). It might be expected
that the main reason for this rise is the larger number of new
entrepreneurs who have been 'pushed' or 'forced' into starting
their own business. In his survey of new firms in Cleveland in
the late 1970s, David Storey found that about 20 per cent of
new owner managers were 'forced' into starting their own
businesses (Storey, 1982, p.112). The summary results above

indicate a figure of around 50 per cent in the Nottingham area. There is no a priori reason why this proportion should be two and one half times as large in the Nottingham area as it is in Cleveland. The disparity in levels implies a rise in the proportion as the recession has deepened. While 'pushed' entrepreneurs are not necessarily less efficient than those attracted to owner management, the industries which they naturally choose to enter, and their desire to innovate, may differ substantially. As is clear from the evidence on choice of product, only a very small number of the respondents were naturally innovative while the vast majority chose to enter industries related to their previous experience. While it is natural for a new entrepreneur to rely, to a large extent, on their own past history, the tendency to set up in related industries is further encouraged by the larger supply of cheap second hand plant and machinery available, usually at auction, in periods of recession. Companies which have ceased trading, or which are struggling to survive, provide not only an increasing proportion of new firm owner managers, but also the plant and machinery with which to start up. This second influence upon the entrepreneur's choice of industry would tend to be stronger in a period of recession. The relatively large increase in the supply of second hand capital due to a higher rate of firm cessations provides an attractively cheap alternative to new capital, the price of which more accurately reflects its costs of production.

At a micro level there is therefore much evidence to suggest that recession causes an increase in the proportion of new firms whose owner managers have been pushed rather than attracted into starting a business. It also suggests that this response to recession will occur in established industries with little contribution to innovation and the development of young progressive industry.

Characteristics of new firms in a recession

Having considered the motivation of many new firms' managers and their typical choice of product area, it is important to observe various other aspects of their foundation.

Seventy four per cent of respondents were 'first time founders', only 4 per cent of the sample had attended any form of course aimed at training new owner managers, and as is stated in table 3, over 40 per cent took no advice prior to starting up. These points indicate a high level of inexperience and often ignorance of normal commercial costing, pricing and marketing criteria. The high proportion of new founders may reflect the increase in those pushed into independent business. The resistance to seeking comprehensive

9

advice and training arises because most new firms still tend to regard the role of such courses as one of cure rather than prevention. Many delay taking advice until specific problems have arisen rather than seeking it in order to avoid their occurrence.

In consequence, the pricing policy of many new firms will tend to be derived from their costs of production rather than an analysis of the normal market prices which they obtain. As many firms start up with abnormally cheap capital, and tend to price their labour at a rather low level, the prices which they charge may be considerably below those which an established firm could countenance. The cost structure of older firms will tend to be higher as their capital will often have been purchased at a more 'realistic' price, while their labour force is paid at higher rates. In an attempt to maximise marketing penetration, new firms may therefore threaten existing efficient firms due to their abnormal cost advantages. The extent to which this occurs is difficult to ascertain without further research into the causes of firm closure. It does suggest, however, that the pattern of new firms which start up in a period of recession could further undermine the industries which they choose to enter rather than constituting a source of industrial regeneration.

The survey results support the hypothesis that the births and deaths of firms are interrelated. In a period of recession, firm closures provide the owner managers, the labour and the capital for many new firms. These births may in turn threaten older established firms and at the margin, lead to further closures, often of other small firms. The more pervasive this process the smaller the positive economic contribution of new small firms in general.

CONCLUSION

Research at the micro level indicates a natural tendency for new firms to set up in established and often declining industries in a period of recession. While they may play an important role in sustaining established production it is unrealistic to expect them to provide a significant source of economic recovery by changing the structure of industry and thus improving its performance. Small firms may be vital in enabling recovery to continue rather than playing a major role in its inception.

Much present government policy towards the small firms sector is designed to increase the number of new firms. In the light of the above points it is questionable how much these are

likely to contribute to economic recovery and employment.
Given the present record levels of company failure such
policies may simply be increasing the throughput of firms
rather than the stock.

NOTE

[1] Recent articles by Johnson and Cathcart (1979) and Mason
    (1983) have drawn attention to the definitional problems
    which occur when carrying out research into new firms.
    While it is not appropriate to consider these problems
    further in this chapter they will be addressed in future
    working papers. Briefly, in this survey the working
    definition of 'independent' excluded any business (in the
    case of incorporated firms) which held less than 50 per
    cent of its equity internally.

REFERENCES

Binks, M.R. and Jennings, A.N., (1985 forthcoming), 'Small
  Firms as a Source of Economic Rejuvenation', in The Survival
  of the Small Firm, Curran, Stanworth and Watkins, Gower,
  Aldershot.
Fothergill, S. and Gudgin, G., (1982), Unequal Growth,
  Heinemann Educational Books, London.
Johnson, P.S. and Cathcart, D.G., (1979), 'New Manufacturing
  Firms and Regional Development: Some Evidence from the
  Northern Region', Regional Studies, vol.13, pp.269-80.
Mason, C., (1983), 'Some Definitional Difficulties in New Firm
  Research', Area, Institute of British Geographers, vol.15,
  pp.53-60.
Storey, D.J., (1982), Entrepreneurship and the New Firm, Croom
  Helm, London.

New manufacturing firms in a prosperous U.K. sub-region: the case of South Hampshire

COLIN MASON AND PETER LLOYD

INTRODUCTION

Much of the discussion about small firms is conducted at a very
generalised level despite the sector's acknowledged diversity.
In particular, the importance of the spatial dimension is
frequently overlooked, yet by no means all parts of the UK are
equally well endowed to generate or to benefit from new firm
formation. Moreover, on account of factors such as industrial
heritage, culture, socio-economic structure and environmental
conditions (both physical and economic), new businesses in
contrasting spatial contexts may well have different
characteristics, perform various roles and, more crucially,
encounter dissimilar problems and therefore have divergent
requirements for assistance. Hence, an assessment of the role
and needs of new enterprises that comes from research undertaken in the declining urban-industrial regions of northern
Britain might be unduly pessimistic, but a Thames Valley or
Cambridge perspective will be equally unrepresentative and
misleading. For a more accurate appraisal of the attributes,
roles and needs of both new and small firms it is therefore
crucial to obtain comparable evidence from a variety of urban
and regional milieu.

NEW MANUFACTURING FIRM FORMATION IN THE UK: A SPATIAL
PERSPECTIVE

It is a feature of the new firm formation process that very few
founders move their homes in order to set up a new business.
Instead, most new businesses are created close to their
founders' place of residence (Gudgin, 1978; Scott, 1980). Any
subsequent relocation of new enterprises is similarly highly
localised (Cross, 1981). Consequently, spatial variations in
new firm formation and the subsequent growth of such
enterprises will exist if individual regions and sub-regions
have a differing propensity to generate new businesses and see
them grow.

   Cross (1981) has suggested that the nature of the local
labour market, by determining the potential availability of new
firm founders, represents a major variable conditioning spatial
variations in new firm formation and development. Certainly,
in general terms rates of new firm formation tend to be
depressed in regions which specialise in traditional heavy
industries, especially where a small number of large plants
dominate the local labour market (Chinitz, 1961). The nature
of the products themselves - often of a one-off, non
standardised design - are unsuited to production in small firms,
and the large, indivisable capital requirements represent a
formidable barrier-to-entry. Emphasis in such industries is on
production rather than marketing, the management style is
frequently paternalistic, corporate organisation is often old
fashioned and consequently there is a slow adoption of modern
management methods, with little demand for specialised
management skills and limited opportunity for occupational
mobility by managers. Production technologies emphasise
traditional craft skills and demand strength and endurance from
factory-floor employees rather than problem-solving abilities.
Here too there is often only limited opportunity for individual
initiative and advancement (Segal, 1979). In areas such as
these therefore, local populations have neither the opportunity
and incentive nor do they develop the skills needed to set up
new businesses.

   Such a line of argument might be applied to heavy industrial
regions in the UK such as West Central Scotland, North East
England and South Wales to explain why during the twentieth
century they failed to generate indigenous new firms able to
offer some diversification to the regional economy. Despite
the continued contraction of these heavy industrial complexes,
their influence on local entrepreneurial climates remains
strong. Moreover, it is possible to argue that the growth of
externally-owned, assembly-line branch plant factories in
peripheral industrial regions, frequently attracted by regional

policy incentives, has had a similar effect of depressing indigenous enterprise. Certainly, there seems to be a clear relationship between an area's plant size structure and its rate of new firm formation, with employees who work in small firms more likely to set up a new business than those working in large firms (Johnson and Cathcart, 1979a; Fothergill and Gudgin, 1982). Since many of the areas which have a high proportion of employees in large plants are in peripheral regions of Britain and most areas with a high proportion of employees working in small firms are in the Midlands and South (Fothergill and Gudgin, 1982; Storey, 1982) then it would seem valid to expect that inter-regional variations in new firm formation rates in the UK will decrease with movement north of the Wash-Severn axis.

The previous work experience of the new firm founder is an important factor in the subsequent development of the enterprise. Skilled manual workers would seem better equipped than unskilled and semi-skilled workers for initiating and running a small firm because they have acquired more of the necessary problem-solving skills, while entrepreneurs with management experience are more likly to be successful than manual workers. The educational attainment of founders also appears to be linked to the growth of new enterprises, with firms started by individuals who possess degrees or professional qualifications showing the fastest rates of growth (Fothergill and Gudgin, 1982). Another variable conditioning the supply of potential new firm founders is therefore the occupational spectrum of a city or region, which is itself influenced to a large degree by the spatial division of labour within multi-site enterprises. This has resulted in many peripheral regions being dominated by externally-owned branch plants performing routine assembly operations with a truncated range of management functions. The headquarters and divisional offices as well as the R and D laboratories of multi-site companies tend to be concentrated in the South East and adjacent regions of East Anglia and the South West (Crum and Gudgin, 1977). As a result, the proportion of the regional population in those managerial, professional and technical occupations most likely to produce fast growing new firms is highest in the South East (Fothergill and Gudgin, 1982; Storey, 1982). This South East bias is further reinforced by the tendency for multi-site enterprises to manufacture new products at their headquarters location and generally close to their R & D laboratory, whereas products reaching the end of their life cycle are frequently the responsibility of peripheral region plants (Oakey et al, 1980). The stable technology associated with mature products is unlikely to provide a stimulus for the spin-off of new technology based firms (Thwaites, 1978). In contrast, the concentration of R and D laboratories in the South East (Buswell and Lewis, 1970) would tend to suggest that numbers of high technology spin-offs will be substantially higher in this region than elsewhere in the country.

Differences in the occupational composition of new firm founders are also likely to work their way forward to influence levels of launch and post launch capital in new enterprises, again to the advantage of the South East. Founders with management backgrounds will, in all probability, have access to larger amounts of start-up capital. Prior work experience may have made them aware of sources of outside finance and of the conventions necessary in presenting successful cases for loan funds. At a personal level many will have accumulated adequate collateral against which loans can be secured as well as personal savings. By contrast, new businesses which are started by individuals with basic education and manual rather than professional backgrounds frequently display low rates of growth because of the limited aspirations of their founders combined with their frequent reluctance to use outside sources of finance. Together these tend to produce chronic undercapitalisation. The use of the founder's home is frequently a vital factor in raising initial capital require-ments, either in obtaining a second mortgage or else as collateral for a loan from a bank or financial institution (Storey, 1982). Areas with low owner-occupancy levels have fewer entrepreneurs able to raise start-up capital in this way, while the value of houses determines the amount of capital which can be obtained. On both counts southern regions are generally at an advantage while peripheral regions are handicapped.

Turning to the demand side, most new firms at least initially serve local and regional market areas. Moreover, relatively few new firms are set up on the basis of a product of their own and the majority are engaged in sub-contract work for larger companies (Gudgin, 1978). The rate of new firm formation and the subsequent growth of such enterprises will therefore tend to be significantly influenced by the level of final and intermediate demand in the local and regional economy which itself will rest upon the performance of corporate 'prime movers' and public sector agencies. Local and regional market opportunities for small businesses seem likely to vary across the UK. Specifically, it can be anticipated that because of higher income levels in the South East and as a result of the relative prosperity of its key electronics and defence industries there will be greater market opportunities for the new firm than in peripheral industrial areas such as NE England and West Central Scotland. These latter areas, with their low income levels and rapidly declining shipbuilding and heavy engineering industries have tended to experience a decline in those sub-contracting opportunities available for new and small firms (Rabey, 1977; Gibb and Quince, 1980). The growth of branch plant assembly line activities in these regional economies has, in all probability, exacerbated this situation as much of their requirements are obtained from outside the region, thereby producing little local demand to stimulate the initiation and growth of local small enterprise (McDermott, 1976; Hoare, 1978).

In summary, although much of the evidence ranks as circumstantial, there would seem to be a case a priori for anticipating that the attributes of new manufacturing firms will vary across the UK space-economy. Specifically, it might be expected that on account of its socio-economic and industrial structure, South East England (especially those parts of the region which lie outside Greater London), together with parts of the adjacent regions of East Anglia and the South West will exhibit much higher rates of new firm formation and may be expected to contain substantially larger proportions of rapidly growing and innovative enterprises than northern industrial regions. The problems which new enterprises encounter might similarly be expected to display geographical variations. It is to these issues that the study of new manufacturing firms in South Hampshire is addressed. Comparison of the findings with those from studies of new firms in other parts of the UK (e.g. Johnson and Cathcart, 1979b; Lloyd, 1980; Cross, 1981; Lloyd and Dicken, 1982; Storey, 1982) provides a tentative indication of the extent to which the characteristics and needs of new enterprises in 'prosperous' areas in southern England differ from those of firms in depressed urban-industrial regions of the north. [1]

SOUTH HAMPSHIRE: BACKGROUND CONDITIONS FOR NEW FIRM FORMATION

South Hampshire, which comprises the Southampton and Portsmouth city-regions plus the New Forest, has been one of the fastest growing sub-regions in the country since 1945. Total employment increased by 10% between 1971 and 1978 compared with 3% nationally, and while much of this growth was provided by service industries, the manufacturing sector increased its workforce by 4% at a time of general decline in the country as a whole. The recession has halted employment growth in South Hampshire since 1979 but the level of redundancies has been running at only half the national rate. Unemployment is, therefore, below the national average, at just under 12% in the Portsmouth travel-to-work area and less than 9% in the Southampton travel-to-work area (December 1983).

The local economy is currently dominated by large, externally owned establishments. Plants with 500 or more employees accounted for 47% of total manufacturing employment in 1979, and around three quarters of manufacturing jobs were provided by non-local firms. However, the area does possess an indigenous small firm sector which is significant in numerical if not in employment terms. Moreover, externally owned establishments in South Hampshire bear little resemblence to those in peripheral regions. The latter are characterised by their tendency to offer a truncated range of employment opportunities and functions and consequently represent poor 'incubators' of new enterprise. By contrast, many of the externally owned establishments in South Hampshire are either a divisional head office or the headquarters of the UK subsidiary. In addition, a considerable number of the large non-locally owned establishments undertake on-site R and D activities and are frequently responsible for products at an early stage in their life cycle. These features are reflected in an occupational structure in which the full range of managerial, technical and skilled manual workers is well represented.

With approximately one in every five manufacturing jobs provided by electronics firms, South Hampshire's industrial structure would appear to offer further advantages for new firm formation and growth. Given that new firm founders generally start their businesses in the same industry in which they previously worked (Gudgin, 1978), South Hampshire would seem particularly well placed for the formation of new, high technology enterprises. In addition, the major electronics companies in the area, along with firms in its sizeable mechanical engineering and shipbuilding industries, continue to represent a major market for small firms undertaking sub-contract work.

The entrepreneurial base of South Hampshire has been further enhanced by the considerable in-migration of population to the area during the past two decades or so, a function of the combined attractions of plentiful job opportunities and the widely held perception that it offers an attractive residential environment (Gould and White, 1968; Pacione, 1982). To a large degree, population migration is selective, with skilled manual workers and management staff having the highest propensities to migrate, groups from whose ranks a large proportion of entrepreneurs are drawn. Thus, South Hampshire, along with other parts of the Outer South East, have received a large influx of that sub-set of the economically-active population which might be expected to have a high probability of forming new enterprises.

South Hampshire therefore possessed many attributes which are
likely to promote a high level of local entrepreneurship.
Aggregate data show that this has indeed been the case, with
333 new manufacturing firms created in the period 1971 to 1979
and surviving (as independent companies) to mid-1979, providing
3636 jobs in that year. This was equivalent to 21.5% of the
1979 plant population in South Hampshire but on account of
their small size (61% had less than 10 employees) new firms
accounted for only 3.5% of the area's total manufacturing
employment. The distribution of the firms within South
Hampshire has favoured locations outside the cities of
Portsmouth and Southampton (Mason, 1982). Surprisingly, in
view of the dominant position of the electronics industry in
South Hampshire, it only accounted for 11% of new enterprises.
Much more significant as sources of new firm formation have
been the mechanical engineering (21%), metal goods (18%) and
timber and furniture (13%) industries (Figure 1).

Comparing the level of new firm formation in South Hampshire
with that of other areas is problematical because of
differences between studies in terms of data sources, time-
periods, time-spans and definitions. However, it does appear
that new firm formation has been higher in South Hampshire
during the 1970s than in Scotland, North East England, the
North West, Coventry, Norfolk and Suffolk but lower than in
Cambridgeshire and the East Midlands (Gould and Keeble, 1984:
table 3).

NEW MANUFACTURING FIRMS IN SOUTH HAMPSHIRE: SURVEY RESULTS

Information on the backgrounds of the new firm founders, the
characteristics of their businesses and the problems
encountered in their formation and early development was
derived from interviews, undertaken during the first half of
1981, with the founders of 52 new manufacturing firms in South
Hampshire. This represented an 84% response rate. To be
included in the survey each enterprise had to satisfy three
criteria. First, only firms that had begun trading during or
after 1976 were included. Second, the survey was restricted to
those firms that were engaged in manufacturing at the survey
date (although they may have been started on the basis of non-
manufacturing activity). Third, only founder-based enterprises
were included, that is companies in which the founder-owner or
owners accounted for the bulk of the equity, along with
businesses operating as sole traders and partnerships.

The founders of new firms

The widely observed tendency for a majority of businesses to be

19

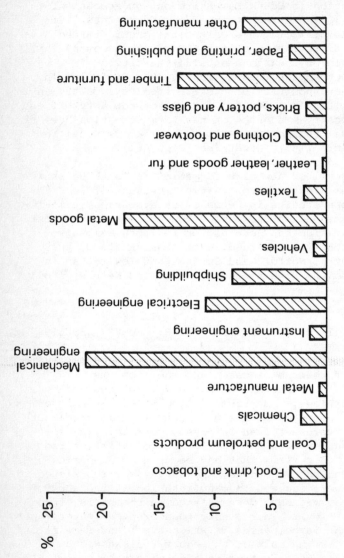

Figure 1 New Manufacturing Firms in South Hampshire 1971-79 : Industrial Distribution

initiated by two or more founders (Cross, 1981; Lloyd, 1980) was confirmed in South Hampshire where only 22 firms (42%) were started by one person. Firms started by two, three or four founders numbered twenty, six and four respectively. Partners were generally either friends or had previously worked together, although three founders did undertake a search for a suitable partner prior to launching their business. The most significant benefits derived from group founding were the creation of a management team with complimentary business skills (e.g. an ex-production manager and an ex-sales manager) and the pooling of financial resources, reflected in the larger amounts of launch capital used by firms with two or more founders compared with single-founder enterprises. Partnerships are not necessarily permanent however, and the survey identified seven firms (23% of firms with two or more founders) which had already experienced a break up of the original founding team, generally as a result of differences of opinion over business strategies.

In general terms, founder-owners of new manufacturing firms in South Hampshire were remarkably similar to those identified by survey research in other regions. A majority had some form of educational qualification, although whereas only 7% had a university/polytechnic degree (including one founder with a Ph.D) a further 55% had pursued other forms of post-school training, in some cases while in the armed forces but more commonly by undertaking an engineering appreticeship. Only 38% of founders had received no formal education since leaving school. In terms of their previous employment history, the majority of founders had manufacturing backgrounds, with three quarters having worked predominantly or exclusively in manufacturing industry. There was also a clear tendency for founders to have derived their business experience in small firms; 61% had worked in firms with less than 200 employees immediately prior to setting up on their own account while only 36% had been employed in firms with 500 or more employees. In addition, a slight majority of founders had been employed in management positions (58%), although over one third of this group had begun their working lives on the factory floor and had thus achieved considerable upward social mobility before establishing their own firm. As Cross (1981) suggests, the formation of their own business may represent a way in which such individuals were able to achieve continued career progression, particularly if their prospects of further promotion were blocked, for example by their lack of 'paper' qualifications or because they were an 'outsider' in a family owned firm.

Also consistent with evidence from other studies is that the vast majority (81%) of new firm founders had local origins in the sense that they had lived and worked in Hampshire immediately prior to establishing their new business. In only three cases (involving the setting up of two firms) did the founders move house as a direct consequence of establishing their company in South Hampshire. [2] However, almost half of the founders had moved into the area at some stage since leaving school, primarily in order to obtain a new job (typically with another company rather than in the same organisation) although in many cases the attractive residential environment was an important underlying consideration for choosing to move to South Hampshire, thus confirming the link between population migration and subsequent entrepreneurship.

Contrasts between South Hampshire and other areas were individually small but cumulatively significant. First, founder-owners in South Hampshire tended to be significantly older than their counterparts in peripheral regions. Approximately 53% of new firm founders in South Hampshire were in the 30 to 45 year age range when they set up their business, a similar proportion to that reported in surveys of new manufacturing firms in Greater Manchester and Merseyside (Lloyd, 1980) and Scotland (Cross, 1981). The differences lay in the limited representation of young founders (less than 30 years old) in South Hampshire (15%) compared with the North West conurbations (26%) and Scotland (28%) and the much greater significance of older founders (over 45 years old) who comprised 32% of the total in South Hampshire compared with 19% in the North West and 17% in Scotland. Older founders, by virtue of their age, are likely to have accumulated greater amounts of personal capital and face fewer demands on such capital from family commitments and mortgage repayments and have acquired greater business skills and contacts. This in turn suggests that the age of the founder may be an important factor in influencing the subsequent development of the firm, and if so it is likely - on this evidence - to operate to the advantage of South Hampshire's new business sector.

A second key contrast relates to the previous experience of founders in forming an independent business. Whereas 42% of founders in South Hampshire had started up a new firm before, the equivalent proportion in the North West conurbations was only 28% (Lloyd and Dicken, 1982) while in Scotland the proportion was even lower at 11.5% (Cross, 1981). [3] Moreover, no less than 60% of these 'experienced' South Hampshire founders continued as the owner-manager of the business that they had previously started, despite their involvement in a new firm. However, in the majority of such cases the 'experienced' founder acted in a part time capacity in the new enterprise, providing a source of business experience and the necessary 'track record' and security to

obtain financial backing while leaving the day-to-day
management in the hands of one or more full time co-founders.
The remaining 'experienced' founders comprised 6% whose
previous firm had been taken over, 11% who had sold out, 11%
who had closed their previous business in order to set up the
new firm and a further 11% whose earlier venture had failed.
The claim by Cross (1981, p.219), on the basis of his survey of
new firm founders in Scotland, that "it is rare for a founder
to have set up a new firm previously", while confirmed in
Manchester and Merseyside, is therefore clearly not borne out
in South Hampshire.

A third contrast relates to the motivations for establishing
a new business. While a prime motivation in South Hampshire,
as in other areas, was the desire for independence (cited by
40% of founders [4]) it is significant in view of the crucial
importance of market awareness to the success of small
businesses that 60% of founders in South Hampshire referred to
their desire to exploit a perceived market opportunity. The
equivalent proportion in Greater Manchester and Merseyside was
substantially lower at 26% (Lloyd and Dicken, 1982). Given the
relatively low level of unemployment in South Hampshire during
the second half of the 1970s, it is not unexpected that cases
where the founder was pushed into starting his own business as
a result of losing his job were most unusual, with only three
firms (6%) started for this reason. What is perhaps surprising
is that only 7% of businesses in Manchester and Merseyside were
started because of redundancy (Lloyd, 1980). However,
unemployment, or the threat of it, appears to have been a much
more potent influence on new firm formation in the Northern
Region: Storey (1982) noted that in Cleveland 26% of founders
claimed to have been out of work immediately prior to
establishing their business, while Johnson and Cathcart (1979b)
found that 35% of founders had been employed in plants which
closed either at, or subsequent to, the formation of the new
business.

In summary terms therefore, some important differences
between founder-owners in South Hampshire and those in
peripheral regions do appear to exist. Founder-owners in South
Hampshire are slightly older (and perhaps more creditworthy as
a result), slightly more experienced in business formation,
slightly more conscious of the marketing issue and less likely
to have been 'pushed' into setting up their business by
unemployment. Consequently, they do seem to have a marginal
propensity as a group to be more successful, though the average
individual founder probably differs little from his northern
counterpart.

Finance and investment

As with the characteristics of the new firm founders, it seems that the financial attributes of the average new enterprise in South Hampshire is typical of that found in other areas. However, contrasts are apparent at the margin, with the sample of new firms in South Hampshire differing in respect of the greater proportion of better performers at the top of the range.

The launch of a new business is frequently a long drawn out affair. Firms are often started on a part time basis with one or more of the founders still in full time employment and in many cases operating initially from a bedroom, garage or garden hut. Just over one quarter of new firms in South Hampshire displayed these characteristics. A further feature of the new firm formation process is the frequent transition from non-manufacturing to manufacturing at an early stage in the development of the business (Brinkley and Nicholson, 1979). Approximately one quarter of the surveyed firms in South Hampshire started on the basis of undertaking a non-manufacturing activity such as sales, repair or consultancy and only subsequently undertook manufacturing. In some cases this move into manufacturing represented a logical development of the business while in other situations a period undertaking non-manufacturing activities was necessary either to generate sufficient capital to commence manufacturing or else to finance research and development work.

The formation of a new manufacturing enterprise cannot therefore necessarily be regarded as a discrete event. This in turn creates problems in framing questions about launch capital requirements and in interpreting the responses. Bearing this caveat in mind, the median amount of start-up capital used by firms in South Hampshire was £6,000, although there was considerable variation around this figure with at one extreme three firms (6%) using in excess of £250,000 of start-up capital while at the other extreme six firms (12%) started with less than £500. For the most part, this latter group of firms were set up by skilled tradesmen undertaking sub-contract work on their own account and requiring little more than basic power tools, with the customer providing the materials on free issue and in some cases also benefitting from rent free premises or machinery. Comparison with other studies is made difficult by the highly skewed distribution, but it does appear that whereas the median amount of launch capital used by firms in South Hampshire was similar to that used by new businesses in Manchester and Merseyside, the proportion of firms with over £15,000 of launch capital was slightly higher in South Hampshire (25%) than in the North West conurbations (18%) and the proportion with less than £500 of start-up funds was lower

(11% in South Hampshire and 21% in Manchester and Merseyside) (Lloyd, 1980).

With regard to the sources of launch capital, more substantive contrasts are apparent. New manufacturing firms in South Hampshire raised launch capital primarily from two sources - personal savings and bank loan or overdraft, used by 66% and 42% of firms respectively. A total of eight new firms (15%) were at least partly financed by a founder's previous business, making it the third most significant source of launch capital. In contrast, new firms in Greater Manchester and Merseyside placed substantially less reliance on bank loans and overdrafts, with only 15% of firms raising capital in this way (Lloyd, 1980). Similarly, only 21% of new manufacturing firms in Scotland made use of banks for start-up funds (Cross, 1981), an identical proportion to that reported by Storey (1982) from his Cleveland study. Such contrasts in methods of financing can be linked back to the previously observed differences between new firm founders in South Hampshire and those in other regions, notably in terms of creditworthiness, business experience and awareness of sources of finance. Differences between new firms in South Hampshire and in Manchester and Merseyside in the use of external sources of finance were also carried over into post start-up investment where two thirds of South Hampshire firms made use of external sources (bank loans and overdrafts, finance houses), generally in conjunction with retained profits. In contrast, new businesses in the North West conurbations placed much greater reliance on internal sources of funds.

A financial profile of new firms can only be presented in very limited and approximate terms because of the difficulty of deriving consistent and relatively accurate data. An added problem was the very limited level of financial information which was easily available to most owner-managers, such matters being largely devolved to their accountants. The data which proved easiest to collect were on gross turnover; new firm founders could usually produce a fairly accurate figure, they did not regard the information as sensitive or confidential and its interpretation is generally unambiguous. The median turnover of new manufacturing firms in South Hampshire was £120,000, although the mean was almost £250,000, underlining the highly skewed distribution (Figure 2). [5] Indeed, six firms had achieved turnovers in excess of £750,000 while the two most successful firms in this respect reported turnovers of £1.3 million. Comparison with the North West England survey (Lloyd and Dicken, 1982) indicates that whereas the median turnover was similar between the studies, contrasts nevertheless existed with the upper quartile of firms in South Hampshire achieving higher turnovers than their equivalents in Manchester and

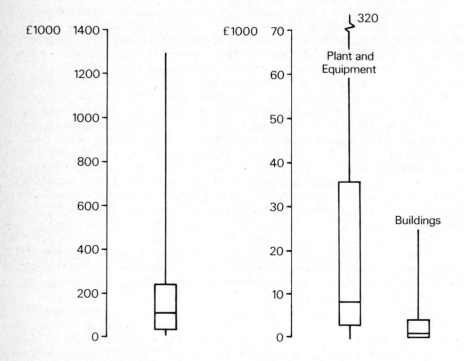

Figure 2 Gross Turnover in
New Enterprises

Figure 3 Capital Expenditure
Since Start-up

Merseyside (upper quartile values of £250,000, £210,000 and £192,000 respectively) even though the median and lower quartile values are not widely dissimilar.

On other financial indicators the pattern is maintained of broad similarity between new firms in South Hampshire and in Manchester and Merseyside but with contrasts at the upper margin of performance. Post start-up investment by South Hampshire firms was generally modest, with the median investment on plant and machinery standing at £8,000, and £700 on buildings (Figure 3). Similar values were found in the North West. Given that in both areas the majority of firms were either in rented or leased premises (51 out of 52 businesses in South Hampshire) the bias of new investment toward plant and machinery is not surprising. But there were observable differences at the top of the distribution with the upper quartile values in South Hampshire being £36,000 for investment in plant and machinery and £4,000 for investment on buildings (respective values in the North West being £20,000 and £2,000). Similarly, in respect of plant and equipment stock valuations, 31% of South Hampshire firms had plant and equipment valued in excess of £75,000 compared with only 12% of firms in Manchester and Merseyside. A smaller proportion of firms in South Hampshire relied extensively on second hand machinery - only 13% of firms had in excess of 90% of second hand plant and equipment whereas in the North West that proportion was 30%. At the other extreme just over one quarter of firms in each area had less than 15% of machinery in the second hand category. The greater creditworthiness of founders in South Hampshire is reflected in the fact that only 13% of firms reported that difficulties in obtaining outside finance had forced them to defer or abandon investment plans. The equivalent figure amongst firms in Manchester and Merseyside was 32%.

Two tentative conclusions emerge from what is admittedly patchy and incomplete financial data. First, while the average new manufacturing firm in South Hampshire is little different in its attributes from its counterparts in other parts of the country, it does contain a rather more heavily capitalised, higher turnover group of firms at the upper tail of the distribution whereas, to judge from the evidence from Manchester and Merseyside, such a dynamic group of enterprises appears to be largely absent in peripheral regions. Second, and by no means unconnected with the previous point, new firm owner-managers in South Hampshire appear to show greater willingness to gear themselves to commercial lending sources. This may arise from their product-market characteristics which enables them to gain access to favourable loan terms. Alternatively, access to loan and venture capital might itself be a function of the relative creditworthiness of entrepreneurs and could in turn provide the resources necessary to give new firms a better opportunity to develop good products and to seek out market needs.

Products and customers: the market context

New manufacturing firms in South Hampshire are very varied in terms of their activities, covering a total of 23 different MLHs, although with a bias towards engineering and metal working (42% of the surveyed firms). Significantly, 13.5% of new firms were in the high technology fields of electronics (MLHs 364 to 367) and instrument engineering. However, new manufacturing firms in South Hampshire are not, in general, innovative. Despite the presence of many high technology industries in South Hampshire only 10 firms (19%) claimed to have been set up on the basis of a new idea, seven for a product (including two firms manufacturing under licence) and three for a process. Equivalent proportions of innovative firms in Manchester and Merseyside (Lloyd and Dicken, 1982) and the Northern Region (Johnson and Cathcart, 1979b) were only a little lower at 17% and 12% respectively.

Regardless of industry, new firms in South Hampshire are primarily engaged in one-off and small batch production, frequently producing to customers' requirements. Indeed, three quarters of new firms undertook at least some sub-contract work, and for 32 firms (62%) this accounted for more than 75% of their total production. Moreover, many firms were dependent on a small number of customers: this was seen in its most extreme form in the case of nine enterprises (17%) which relied on up to four customers for over 75% of their sales.

Comparison with findings from other areas reveals little in the way of contrasts between new manufacturing firms in South Hampshire and those in peripheral regions in terms of industry type, scale of production or innovation. The propensity of South Hampshire firms to represent a more sophisticated group at the upper tail of the distribution therefore does not appear to be due to the possession of a more up-market product, customer base or technological capability. However, market characteristics may have a more significant role to play. Although most new firms in South Hampshire operated in highly competitive market environments, with two thirds of firms identifying at least ten competitors and over one third numbering their competitors in hundreds, just under one quarter of businesses have been able to identify and operate in market niches with three or fewer competitors. Not surprisingly, this small group displayed the most rapid rates of growth since start-up. It would also seem significant that whereas new manufacturing firms in South Hampshire are primarily competing

on the basis of their non-price strengths such as flexibility
and service to customer requirements (96%) and the quality of
the product or service (92%), their counterparts in Manchester
and Merseyside rank price as their most important competitive
strength (Lloyd, 1980). Nevertheless, the majority of new
firms in South Hampshire placed little effort on marketing and
typically adopted a passive attitude towards selling by relying
on orders which came their way, such as repeat orders from
their initial customers and new customers gained by personal
recommendation. In contrast, little more than one third of
firms had adopted an active marketing strategy to seek out new
customers, using such methods as advertising, mail shots and
desk research to identify potential customers.

In line with evidence from the North West (Lloyd and Dicken,
1982) and North East (Johnson and Cathcart, 1979b; Storey, 1982)
new manufacturing firms in South Hampshire were strongly tied
to local and regional markets. Half sold upwards of 50% of
their output within Hampshire, while 60% contracted in excess
of three quarters of their business within the South East
Region. Nevertheless, one quarter of new firms undertook some
direct exporting, and for five firms - each engaged in
electronics or instrument engineering - this accounted for
between 45 and 90% of their output. It would therefore appear
that the market opportunities available to new manufacturing
firms are, in general, strongly based upon the demand that is
generated by the local economy. This characteristic might
represent a further element which influences the propensity of
the South Hampshire sample of new firms to perform better than
their counterparts in the peripheral regions. The available
industrial and consumer demand within the relatively prosperous
south is likely to provide a slight widening of the market base,
allowing more local firms to survive and offering the
opportunity for each to have a slightly higher threshold of
operation in comparison with similar firms in depressed
northern regions.

The role of premises

A major element in policy initiatives to assist new and small
firms is the supply of small premises, including both the
construction of new nursery units on industrial estates and the
creation of small workshops through the renovation and sub-
division of older industrial property. This policy, which is
reflected in the actions of both central and local government
as well as by various private sector organisations, is based on
the assumption that shortages of suitable premises has been a
major constraint on the formation of new firms in the United
Kingdom. This belief has certainly been borne out in South
Hampshire where most new firms encountered severe problems in

finding suitable start-up premises, especially in the 1976 to 1978 period when most of the surveyed firms were set up. Over one quarter of firms already had suitable premises in their possession prior to start-up, either from a previous business venture of one of the founders or as a result of acquiring a defunct company. But some 70% of those firms which required to search for start-up premises reported that they had encountered difficulties (in only two cases because of restrictive requirements), and almost without exception the remainder considered that they had simply been lucky in finding suitable accommodation. In marked contrast, finding suitable premises did not represent a particularly severe constraint to new businesses in Manchester and Merseyside, with only 7% encountering real, practical difficulties (Lloyd and Dicken, 1982).

Such variations in experience between new firms in South Hampshire and those in the North West conurbations are not due to differences in premises requirements. In general, new firms in South Hampshire wanted start-up premises with less than 2,000 quare feet of floorspace, at a low rent in order to minimize their early financial overheads and on a short lease in order to keep their financial and legal commitments at a minimum. These represented very similar initial premises requirements to those of new firms in Manchester and Merseyside (Lloyd and Dicken, 1982), although there was some suggestion that firms in the North West obtained slightly larger premises; the median floorspace occupied by such firms when surveyed was 4,000 square feet (with quartile values of 2,000 square feet and 8,000 square feet), compared with 3,100 square feet in South Hampshire (quartiles of 1,500 square feet and 5,000 square feet), no doubt at least in part a function of the much cheaper cost of industrial floorspace in the North West. In both areas new firm founders generally undertook a limited spatial search for premises, with the majority in South Hampshire looking no further afield than the neighbourhood or local authority area in which the founders lived or previously worked. The founders of only two firms looked outside Hamshire for premises.

Contrasts between South Hampshire and peripheral regions in terms of the severity of the premises constraint are a function of differences in industrial heritage, industrial policy and planning attitudes. Unlike many peripheral regions, South Hampshire was largely by-passed by industrial development in the nineteenth centry and so it does not have a large stock of old industrial premises available at low rents and on short leases to act as a seedbed. In addition, the scenic parts of the sub-region have, at least until very recently, been subject to strict anti-industry planning regulations (as has been the

case in many other parts of the South East Region outside
Greater London) and this has both restricted the development of
new industrial sites to a small number of locations and has
also prevented new firms from occupying redundant farm
buildings or other empty non-industrial premises. Finally,
unlike the situation in many peripheral regions, local
authorities in South Hampshire have until recently shown little
interest in building small units, and because South Hampshire
is not an assisted area there has been no Department of Trade
and Industry involvement in the construction of small factory
units. This industrial background is reflected in the fact
that 52% of firms in South Hampshire occupied pre-1940 premises
and just under one quarter occupied nineteenth century
property, substantially lower proportions than in the North
West conurbations (Lloyd and Dicken, 1982). Similarly, the
proportion of South Hampshire firms occupying their start-up
premises on short leases (less than five years) was much less
than in Manchester and Merseyside (48% compared with 60%) while
those taking out initial leases of more than ten years was
considerably greater (37% compared with 23%).

   Once the problems of finding suitable premises were overcome
most new firms in South Hampshire seemed generally satisfied
that their immediate requirements were being met. The majority
of firms regarded the rent, security of tenure, physical
condition and suitability of the premises for their current
activities as satisfactory although the lack of space for
expansion and the unsuitability of the premises for future
activities were perceived as poor. This implies that many new
firms will require to relocate in order to accommodate growth
and diversification.

Employment and the new firm

The widely held belief that new firms can act as a major source
of job creation and thereby make a significant contribution to
the reduction of unemployment was not borne out in South
Hampshire. At the time of the survey the median employment
size was just eight employees. Most new firms in South
Hampshire are therefore very small. However, as with floorspace and turnover values, the employment size distribution is
positively skewed, reflected by a mean size of twelve workers,
and indicating that significant differentials in the growth
performance of new firms have emerged since start-up, with a
small proportion of new firms managing to grow very rapidly.
Nevertheless, the largest firm in the sample only employed 46
people and the 52 firms together created just 633 jobs
(including founders, self-employed and part time workers), with
males accounting for two thirds of the total.

In terms of employment size, new firms in South Hampshire are generally similar to those in Manchester and Merseyside where the median was also eight employees and the mean was eleven workers (Lloyd and Dicken, 1982). Enterprises in each area also had a comparable level of dependence of skilled workers (36% in South Hampshire, 33% on Merseyside and 37% in Greater Manchester), although problems in recuriting skilled workers were encountered by a larger proportion of firms in South Hampshire than in the North West conurbations (one half compared with one third). It may also be significant that the proportion of technical/professional workers employed by firms in South Hampshire is 9.5%, nearly three times that in Manchester and Merseyside (Lloyd and Dicken, 1982). New enterprises in South Hampshire therefore appear to have a slight edge over their northern counterparts in terms of technical expertise.

The prospects for substantial future employment growth in South Hampshire's new firm sector would also appear to be unlikely. Although two thirds of the surveyed firms anticipated increases in the size of their work force over the following two to three years (primarily by recruiting additional skilled workers), such job creation was expected to be modest. Many of the founders were unwilling to recruit extra workers unless it was absolutely necessary because of the additional costs and risks involved and the extra effort required to find work to keep them fully occupied. Other founder-owners wished to carefully limit expansion so that they could continue to exercise their manual skills and avoid being forced into a full time managerial and administrative role, as well as to preserve the informal and flexible personal relationships and 'family atmosphere' of their firms. By moving towards capital rather than labour intensive production the fastest growing firms in the sample also seemed likely to offer only limited additional employment creation.

This forecast was largely confirmed in a follow-up study undertaken in mid-1983. Of the 37 firms which survived as independent companies, just over two thirds recruited additional staff in the two years between the surveys, leading to the creation of 171 new jobs, but offset by the loss of 12 jobs in firms which shed labour. Just two firms (both in electronics), which together took on almost 100 extra workers, accounted for 56% of the gross new jobs created by expanding firms. However, twelve of the 52 firms closed before the follow-up survey (a closure rate of 23%) [6] and the resultant employment loss exceeded the net new jobs created by the surviving firms (Mason, 1984).

This evidence from South Hampshire therefore supports the findings from other parts of the country that new manufacturing firms are unlikely to make a major contribution to job generation. The typical new enterprise is very small, it provides few unskilled jobs and its growth potential is limited, not least because of the reluctance of most founder-owners to allow their businesses to expand substantially. Only a very small proportion of new firms actually achieve rapid growth and become major employers. Moreover, in many cases their employment creation simply offsets jobs lost in those new firms which fail.

CONCLUSION

The survey findings reveal that the majority of new enterprises in South Hampshire are very small, employing an average of just eight workers, occupying premises of around 3,000 square feet or less, and with a turnover of less than £150,000. Most are unsophisticated in terms of both technology and business methods, are largely geared to performing 'jobbing' activities, serve a localised market area, operate in very competitive market environments and are generally run on limited horizons. Moreover, a high proportion fail within a few years of start-up. To a substantial degree, the characteristics of these businesses reflect the nature of their founders, the majority of whom are 'craftsman-type' entrepreneurs and hence cautious and conservative in outlook, motivated by a desire to minimize their financial and contractual obligations and with limited ambitions and aspirations for their businesses. Only a minority of new enterprises - no more than 10 to 15% - could be described as potential 'high fliers', founded either by the 'boffin-businessman' or, more commonly, by the 'opportunist-type' entrepreneur, and displaying rapid growth in turnover and employment, product development, innovation and the aggressive pursuit of business opportunities.

New manufacturing firms in South Hampshire - an emerging area in the prosperous Outer South East - therefore display a high degree of similarity with those in depressed regions (Lloyd and Mason, 1984) and make an equally marginal contribution to job generation and regional economic development, despite its relatively high rate of new firm formation. However, some contrasts do exist, supporting the argument that was developed in the introduction to this chapter. For example, whereas the median new enterprise in both South Hampshire and the North West conurbations is very similar, there is a marginal positive shift on most indicators in the direction of South Hampshire. The contrasts are not individually sharp but collectively point to a population of new firms whose founders are slightly older, have marginally more business experience and creditworthiness, make more use of financial institutions and have a greater awareness of marketing issues. There was little hard evidence that the entrepreneurs in South Hampshire were, as a group, engaged in activities that were clearly more up-market but there did appear to be a somewhat greater (but still very limited) representation of 'enterprise-makers' and 'boffin-businessmen' (Belbin, 1980) whose firms were likely to display higher rates of growth.

The study has also demonstrated that although new firms in contrasting spatial environments face a common set of problems, there are nevertheless variations in emphasis which arise, in part, from differences in the attributes of the enterprises themselves. For example, firms in South Hampshire encountered relatively few problems in raising finance from external sources or in achieving sales outside the local area, but did find it difficult to recruit skilled labour. In contrast, obtaining outside finance was a problem for firms in the North West conurbations, although less so on Merseyside than in Greater Manchester because of the availability of regional development grants. Difficulties in the recruitment of skilled labour were also less prevalent, particularly on Merseyside, whereas market penetration beyond the local area did represent a constraint, notably for Merseyside's new firm sector. However, the most significant contrasts between areas in terms of the obstacles to new firm formation and growth are a function of environmental factors and involve the variety of experiences of firms in different locations in obtaining suitable start-up premises. This represented a major difficulty for new firms in South Hampshire (the situation has improved since the survey was undertaken) but was of only minor significance in the North West conurbations, although because such accommodation in Greater Manchester was largely confined to old buildings, its new enterprises did encounter problems associated with the poor physical condition of their premises, whereas firms on Merseyside had access to modern factory premises built under the auspices of regional policy. Such contrasts in the relative importance of problems encountered by new enterprises in different spatial environments therefore serves to underline the need for nationally-applied policies of assistance for the small firm sector to be complemented by measures that take account of the existence of geographical variations in the constraints on new enterprise formation and growth.

ACKNOWLEDGEMENTS

The survey of new manufacturing firms in South Hampshire was
conducted while in receipt of ESRC grant HR 6796. A modified
version of this chapter appears in Regional Studies, 18 (1984).

NOTES

[1] The most reliable comparison can be made with the results
    of a survey of new manufacturing firms in Greater
    Manchester and Merseyside (Lloyd, 1980; Lloyd and Dicken,
    1982). Both this and the South Hampshire survey used a
    common questionnaire and there was prior coordination on
    definitional issues (see Lloyd and Mason, 1984).
[2] A further three partners, two 'sleeping partners' and a co-
    founder who manages his firm's second plant, continued to
    live outside the county.
[3] Storey (1982) found that 32% of new firm founders in
    Cleveland had been in business on their own account before,
    but his survey related to all types of new business, not
    just those engaged in manufacturing.
[4] Where appropriate founders could cite more than one reason
    for setting up their firm.
[5] The data in Figures 2 and 3 are presented by means of a
    'box-and-whisker' diagram. The 'boxes' provide an
    indication of the spread of the data by describing the
    inter-quartile range, the 'cross-bar' depicts the median
    value, and the 'whiskers' mark the extreme values.
[6] In addition to the 37 surviving firms and 12 closures one
    firm was taken over and two others transferred production
    to locations in adjacent counties.

REFERENCES

Belbin, R.M., (1980), 'Launching New Enterprises: Some Fresh
   Initiatives for Tackling Unemployment', Employment Gazette,
   vol.83, pp.362-365.
Brinkley, I. and Nicholson, B., (1979), 'New Manufacturing
   Enterprises: Entry mechanisms, definitions and the
   monitoring problem', Centre for Environmental Studies,
   Working Note 542.
Buswell, R.J. and Lewis, E.W., (1970), 'The Geographical
   Distribution of Industrial Research Activity in the United
   Kingdom', Regional Studies, vol.4, pp.297-306.
Chinitz, B., (1961), 'Contrasts in Agglomeration: New York and
   Pittsburgh', American Economic Review, vol.51, pp.279-289.
Cross, M., (1981), New Firm Formation and Regional Development,
   Gower, Farnborough.

Crum, R.E. and Cudgin, G., (1979), Non-Production Activities in
UK Manufacturing Industry, Commission of the European
Communities, Brussels, Regional Policy Series No. 3.

Fothergill, S. and Gudgin, G., (1982), Unequal Growth: Urban
and Regional Employment Change in the UK, Heinemann, London.

Gibb, A. and Quince, T., (1980), 'Effects on Small Firms of
Industrial Change in a Development Area', Gibb, A. and Webb T.
(eds.), Policy Issues in Small Business Research, Saxon House,
Farnborough, pp.177-189.

Gould, A. and Keeble, D., (1984), 'New Firms and Rural
Industrialisation in East Anglia', Regional Studies, vol.18,
(Forthcoming).

Gould, P.R. and White, R.R., (1968), 'The Mental Maps of
British School-leavers', Regional Studies, vol.2, pp.161-182.

Gudgin, G.H., (1979), Industrial Location Processes and
Regional Employment Growth, Saxon House, Farnborough.

Hoare, A.G., (1978), 'Industrial Linkages and the Dual Economy:
The Case of Northern Ireland', Regional Studies, vol.12,
pp.167-180.

Johnson, P.S. and Cathcart, D.G., (1979a), 'The Founders of New
Manufacturing Firms: A Note on the Size of their "Incubator"
Plants', Journal of Industrial Economics, vol.28, pp.219-224.

Johnson, P.S. and Cathcart, D.G., (1979b), 'New Manufacturing
Firms and Regional Development: Some Evidence from the
Northern Region', Regional Studies, vol.13, pp.269-280.

Lloyd, P.E., (1980), 'New Manufacturing Enterprises in Greater
Manchester and Merseyside', North West Industry Research
Unit, University of Manchester, Working Paper No. 10.

Lloyd, P.E. and Dicken, P., (1982), Industrial Change: Local
Manufacturing Firms in Manchester and Merseyside, Department
of the Environment, London, Inner Cities Research Programme
No. 6.

Lloyd, P.E. and Mason, C.M., (1984), 'Spatial Variations in New
Firm Formation in the United Kingdom: Comparative Evidence
from Merseyside, Greater Manchester and South Hampshire',
Regional Studies, vol.18, (Forthcoming).

McDermott, P.J., (1976), 'Ownership, Organization and Regional
Dependence in the Scottish Elec-ronics Industry', Regional
Studies, vol.10, pp.319-335.

Mason, C.M., (1982), 'New Manufacturing Firms in South
Hampshire: Survey Results', Department of Geography,
University of Southampton, Discussion Paper No. 13.

Mason, C.M., (1984), 'Small Business in the Recession: A
Follow-up Study of New Manufacturing Firms in South Hampshire',
Department of Geography, University of Southampton,
Discussion Paper No. 25.

Oakey, R.P., Thwaites, A.T. and Nash, P.A., (1980), 'The
Regional Distribution of Innovative Manufacturing Establishments in Britain', Regional Studies, vol.14, pp.235-253.

Pacione, M., (1982), 'Space Preferences, Locational Behaviour and the Dispersal of Civil Servants from London', <u>Environment and Planning A</u>, vol.14, pp.323-333.

Rabey, G.F., (1977), 'Contraction Poles: An Exploratory Study of Traditional Industry Decline within a Regional Industrial Complex', <u>Centre for Urban and Regional Development Studies</u>, <u>University of Newcastle-upon-Tyne</u>, Discussion Paper No. 3.

Scott, M., (1980), 'Independence and the Flight from Large Scale: Some Sociological Factors in the Founding Process', in Gibb, A. and Webb, T. (eds.), <u>Policy Issues in Small Business Research</u>, Saxon House, Farnborough, pp.15-33.

Segal, N., (1979), 'The Limits and Means of 'Self-Reliant' Regional Economic Growth', in MacLennan, D. and Parr, J.B. (eds.), <u>Regional Policy: Past Experience and Future Directions</u>, Martin Robertson, Oxford, pp.212-224.

Storey, D.J., (1982), <u>Entrepreneurship and the New Firm</u>, Croom Helm, London.

Thwaites, A.T., (1978), 'Technological Change, Mobile Plants and Regional Development', <u>Regional Studies</u>, vol.12, pp.445-461.

Regional bias in new firm formation

RICHARD WHITTINGTON

INTRODUCTION

Since 1979, the Government has laid great stress on the
importance of small business, and particularly on the creation
of new small businesses. Aid to small business currently
amounts to £500 million per annum (British Business, 6th May,
1983), a sum frequently justified by the claimed employment
generating potential of new and small businesses. For
instance, the former Under-Secretary of State for Industry,
Mr. McGregor, as he opened the 1981 Commons debate on small
business, gave job creation as his first reason for supporting
the sector (Hansard, 1981). He cited as evidence the much
quoted MIT research, 'The Job Generation Process', conducted
by D.L. Birch (1979).

   Using data on 5.6 million business establishments between
1969 and 1976, Birch had concluded that in the American private
manufacturing and services sectors, 66 per cent of the net new
jobs generated over this period were created by firms employing
twenty or less people. On this basis he argued influentially,
that the US Government should concentrate on stimulating small
firms rather than assisting large firms, and focus on the
creation of new jobs rather than the protection of old ones.

   Several things ought to be noted about this study. Firstly,
though it is not always clear, Birch is referring to 'net

changes' in employment - i.e. the differences between gains and losses - rather than to gross job gains or losses. In other words, more new jobs overall may emerge from the large firm sector than from the small firm sector and, conversely, there may be more jobs to be saved that would otherwise be lost in the large firm sector than in the small firm sector. It should also be remembered that this is an American study, and Fothergill and Gudgin (1979) at least doubt whether the small firm sector in the United Kingdom is of the same quality. Moreover, the study was conducted during a period of relative economic prosperity, distant now, and completely ignores the job generating potential of the public sector. Lastly, Birch himself remarks upon the regional difference in job generation patterns and, acknowledging the general difficulty of stimulating small firms, warns of the dangers of 'shotgun-like policies' (i.e. tax incentives), urging instead that the Government should 'target' its incentive schemes.

As Sinfield and Showler (1981) have argued, it is important to understand how particular groups within the community suffer disproportionate unemployment. This argument poses a significant challenge to any employment creation policy. In particular, does new and small business assistance provide jobs for those groups and areas most in need?

Sinfield and Showler's (1981) concern was especially with certain social groups - the unskilled, women, blacks, the young and the old - which, according to dual or segmented labour market theory, predominantly comprise the normal labour force of the small, unstable firms that make up the 'secondary' sector (Friedman, 1977; Curran and Stanworth, 1981; Scott and Rainnie, 1982). Accordingly, it might be expected that the stimulation of new and small firms will serve to 'mop up' into employment these socially disadvantaged groups (though recent high unemployment may be leading to some displacement of normal 'secondary' workers by workers made redundant by 'primary' sector firms). However, the problem to be addressed here is regional rather than social disadvantage.

The extent to which new and small firm assistance will be taken advantage of depends largely upon the abilities of entrepreneurs and potential entrepreneurs to seize the new opportunities. Assuming for the moment that the economic demand for entrepreneurial services is equal nationwide, those regions with many active entrepreneurs and would be entrepreneurs will benefit more than those with few. Apparently the North of England is one region with few: "There is in relative terms an appreciable under representation of small firms in the North compared to the country as a whole .... a lack of entrepreneurship is one of the fundamental reasons for the Region's

longstanding economic difficulties ...." (Northern Region
Strategy Team, 1979, p.26). If this is so, the North will be
disadvantaged in two ways: firstly, it has fewer existing
small businesses which will benefit by those policies helping
small business in general: secondly, it has less entrepreneurial talent with which to respond to those policies specifically
designed to stimulate the creation of new businesses.

It is the differential abilities of regions to benefit from
new business creation incentives that is the concern here.
Other things being equal, regional economies fertile in new
firms will soon overtake infertile economies, thus exacerbating
regional differences. Since the Northern Region Strategy
Team's report, there has been considerable research on the
spatial differences in the distribution of entrepreneurship.
Thwaites (1979) made an early theoretical attempt to establish
a comprehensive set of indicators of regional entrepreneurship,
while Cross (1981) analysed entrepreneurial disparities between
Department of Employment local office areas in Scotland. In
America, Pennings (1982) has tried to associate differences in
entrepreneurship with regional differences in the 'quality of
life'.

Recently, Storey (1982) has gathered together the findings of
a wide range of research, including his own, to compile an
'Index of Regional Entrepreneurship in Britain'. This 'Index'
gave each region a simple ranking of entrepreneurship. Storey
found that the Northern Region, Wales and Northern Ireland came
lowest on the 'Index', while the South East, the South West and
East Anglia came highest. Storey wrote: "Unfortunately, with
the exception of the North West and the West Midlands of
England, those areas currently suffering the highest rates of
unemployment are also those with the lowest entrepreneurial
potential. Hence a policy of assisting the small (at the
expense of the large) firm risks being regionally divisive
since the biggest take up rates are in the areas which are
currently most prosperous" (1982, p.195).

Important though the implications of the 'Index' are, it does
need substantial amendment. Besides the inadequacy of simple
rankings, no weights are given to the variables, many of which,
it will be shown, are collinear anyway. The 'Index' was
untested because no dependent variable representing entrepreneurship was available. This chapter, therefore, is intended
to test, refine and add to the 'Index' using regression
analysis in order to arrive at an explanation for regional
differences in entrepreneurship. Such explanation will involve
the testing of various established theories about factors
conducive to entrepreneurship with nationwide data. It should
also suggest means of implementing new firm policy both more

41

effectively and more fairly.

ANALYSIS

According to Storey (1982), entrepreneurship - the dependent
variable - should be represented by the rate of new firm
formation. [1] New firm formation rates can be derived from
new VAT registrations for which regional statistics have
recently become available (Ganguly, 1982). [2] All new
registrations less voluntary registrations and those following
changes in legal identity are taken as new firm 'births'.
There are three weaknesses in this data. First, this definition of 'births' captures the small but unwanted element of
those tiny firms whose turnovers only reach registration level
some time after foundation. Second, only the 1980 and 1981
figures are available as yet, so that, with eleven UK regions,
there are just twenty two data points for analysis, and these
may not be drawn from years that are 'typical' (if such there
can be). Lastly, the 1981 figures remain provisional (though
the 1980 revised figures proved to be close to the original
provisional ones).

New firm formation rates by region will be measured, then, by
the number of new VAT registrations per head of regional
working population. As Storey (1982) predicted, formation
rates do vary around the country: see table 1.

The two regions which achieved the highest formation rates in
both years (the South West and the South East) were also areas
with relatively low unemployment rates; the two regions with
the lowest formation rates (Scotland and the North) were areas
with high unemployment. Surprising, however, are the formation
rates of Wales for both years, and Northern Ireland for 1980 -
both far better relative to the other regions than Storey's
'Index' predicted.

The task, however, is to explain these formation rate
differentials. Implicit in Storey's 'Index' are five
hypotheses: that small firms produce proportionately more
entrepreneurs than large firms; that people with managerial
experience and high educational attainment are more likely to
become successful entrepreneurs than the unskilled and ill
educated; that people with access to their own capital are more
able to set up their own businesses than those without; that it
will be easier to found a new business in local economies not
dominated by capital intensive, slow growing industries than in
those so dominated; and finally that opportunities for entrepreneurship are greater in prosperous areas than in poor ones.
Storey chose eleven variables to express these hypotheses in

Table 1
Regional new firm formation rates

Region	New VAT registrations per thousand of working population:		Unemployment rate October, 1981:*
	1980	1981	
North	3.1	3.8	16.2
Yorkshire & Humberside	3.8	4.5	13.4
East Midlands	4.3	4.6	11.0
East Anglia	4.2	5.0	9.9
South East	5.0	5.4	9.1
South West	5.5	6.2	10.8
West Midlands	4.0	4.7	15.3
North West	3.6	4.2	15.1
Wales	4.3	5.2	16.0
Scotland	3.2	3.4	14.6
Northern Ireland	4.5	3.9	19.6

* Regional Trends 1983

his 'Index': the percentage of the labour force employed in manufacturing plants with less than ten employees (SML); the percentage of the labour force employed in manufacturing plants with more than 500 employees (LGE); the percentage of school leavers going to degree courses (DEG); the percentage of school leavers without qualifications (NQL); the percentage of the labour force in administrative or managerial occupations (ADM); the percentage of the labour force in manual occupations (MAN); savings per head of population (SAV); owner occupied dwellings as a percentage of all dwellings (OWN); average dwelling prices (PRI); a compositive index representing regional barriers to entry (BNT); and disposable income per head (INC).

Table 2 gives the simple correlation matrix for ten of these variables (savings per head are excluded because there are no suitable data) and new firm formation rates (BIR). The correlation coefficients between the new firm formation rates (BIR) and the other variables are all in the directions that Storey (1982) predicted, but few of the relationships are strong. Regression analysis should reveal more.

Table 2

'Index of entrepreneurship': Correlation matrix*

	BIR	SML	LGE	BNT	NQL	DEG	ADM	MAN	OWN	PRI	INC
BIR	1.00										
SML	0.37	1.00									
LGE	-0.35	-0.19	1.00								
BNT	-0.37	-0.28	0.70	1.00							
NQL	-0.31	-0.45	-0.23	-0.18	1.00						
DEG	0.00	-0.30	-0.41	-0.40	0.87	1.00					
ADM	0.30	0.67	-0.24	-0.33	-0.49	-0.36	1.00				
MAN	-0.70	-0.52	0.11	0.29	0.19	-0.16	-0.31	1.00			
OWN	0.72	0.17	-0.29	-0.22	-0.48	-0.18	0.33	-0.42	1.00		
PRI	0.46	0.65	-0.26	-0.56	-0.06	0.10	0.48	-0.69	0.12	1.00	
INC	0.22	0.71	-0.08	-0.08	-0.65	-0.63	0.62	-0.26	0.19	0.49	1.00

Correlations between entrepreneurship (BIR) and other variables that are significant at the 5% level are underlined (F test).

* Full explanation of the variables and data are given in the Appendix.

44

However, the correlation matrix does give warning of multi-collinearity. Analysis of the correlations between partial regression coefficients for the independent variables and non-sensical results for backwards stepwise regressions both confirm the presence of multicollinearity. This is to be expected, for common sense at least suggests that the ten independent variables effectively represent only two broad factors: industrial structure as measured by plant size (SML, LGE, BNT) and, by some loose definition, class (the other variables). So long as the independent variables are measuring the same broad factors, the multicollinearity can be eliminated, without risk of specification error, by dropping some variables (Katz, 1982).

As for the first factor, industrial structure, there exists considerable local study evidence to show that small plants foster entrepreneurship more than large plants (Johnson and Cathcart, 1979; Cross, 1981; Fothergill and Gudgin, 1982). The first hypothesis to be tested by regression analysis, then, is that a region's proportion of workers in small manufacturing plants (SML) will be positively related to its new firm formation rate (BIR).

The second broad factor, identified loosely so far as class, can be broken down into two distinct variables, skill and wealth. Relevant to skill, Gudgin et al (1979) found that firms established by the highly qualified and managerially experienced tended to have the highest growth rates. This is not directly related to new firm formation rates: nevertheless, Storey does include both the proportions of both administrative and managerial workers and of manual workers as variables in his 'Index' and the correlation matrix (table 2) indicates the there is a fairly strong negative relationship between the proportion of manual workers (MAN) and new firm formation rates (BIR). There is a strong theoretical basis for including some measure of personal wealth as well, because of the common finding that personal savings, particularly in the form of home ownership are an important source of start-up capital for many entrepreneurs (Cross, 1981; Storey, 1982). The two variables measuring home ownership and the proportion of manual workers are not significantly collinear, so it is possible to include them both in regression analysis. The hypotheses, therefore, are that home ownership (OWN) will be positively related and the proportion of manual workers (MAN) will be negatively related to new firm formation rates (BIR).

The multiple regression results are given below. [3]

$$BIR = 0 + .038SML + .521OWN - .467MAN$$
$$(.258) \quad (3.776) \quad (-2.927)$$

Adjusted R^2 = .67 t statistics in parentheses

Though in the expected direction, the relationship between the proportion of small manufacturing plants (SML) and entrepreneurship (BIR) is not significant (nor, further regressions demonstrated, are the relationships with barriers to entry (BNT) or the proportion of large firm workers (LGE)). [4]

However, the relationships between the proportion of manual workers (MAN) and of home ownership (OWN) with entrepreneurship (BIR) are both in the expected direction and significant at the 1 per cent level. (None of the other class related variables show statistically significant relationships). In sum, regional entrepreneurship as expressed by new firm formation rates will be low where home ownership is rare, and manual workers are common.

Fothergill and Gudgin (1982) observed an association in the East Midlands between rises in unemployment and increases in new firm formation rates. The explanation seems to be that unemployment drives some individuals into setting up their own businesses, either because the shock of redundancy acts as a catalyst to entrepreneurship or because no alternative employment appears to be available. Thus a further hypothesis emerges: that the percentage change in regional unemployment rates (UNM) will be positively related to regional new firm formation rates (BIR).

Substituting the change in unemployment (UNM) for the measure of industrial structure (SML), the final regression against new firm formation rates (BIR) gave the results below:

$$BIR = 0 + .258UNM + .424OWN - .531MAN$$
$$(2.186) \quad (3.264) \quad (-4.276)$$

Adjusted R^2 = .74 t statistics in parentheses

The change in unemployment (UNM) is significantly related in the expected direction at the 5 per cent level. [5] The regression coefficients, given for the standardised variables, indicate that the proportion of manual workers (MAN) is the most influential variable, the change in unemployment (UNM) the least. However, together these three variables do statistically 'explain' 74 per cent of the variation in new firm formation rates.

POLICY IMPLICATIONS AND CONCLUSIONS

The regression analysis has allowed considerable refinement of Storey's 'Index': just three variables seem to account for most of the differences in levels of regional entrepreneurship. The findings that the percentage of home ownership is

positively related to entrepreneurship while the percentage of
manual workers is negatively related does give support to two
of Storey's original hypotheses. On the other hand, the
hypotheses that industrial structure, the existence of
industrial barriers to entry and level of prosperity (as
measured by disposable income) are related to entrepreneurship
do not receive support - but the relationships, though
statistically not significant, are all in the predicted
directions. One additional hypothesis has been supported,
however: that increases in the level of unemployment are
associated with increases in entrepreneurship. But what does
this all imply for policy?

Given the imperfect nature of both the measures and the data,
no definite conclusions can be drawn. However, since no better
measures and data appear to be available and since they are
consistent with much other research, these results should be
taken as suggestive. What does seem clear is that the benefits
from new firm formation incentives are unlikely to be evenly
distributed through the regions - indeed it is generally those
regions most in need of new jobs that will benefit least.

Evidence for unequal benefits is already clear in the
operation of the loan guarantee scheme: 37.9 per cent of
guarantees issued up to 30th September 1982 were made to
borrowers in the South East and East Anglia, and only 5.9 per
cent to borrowers in Scotland and Northern Ireland (Robson
Rhodes, 1983). In the short term the disadvantaged regions are
suffering because they are not receiving even their 'fair'
share of benefits; but the longer term effects may be more
important. The emphasis of many previous studies has been upon
the supply of entrepreneurs, neglecting the question of the
demand for their services. Most small firms serve local
markets (Storey, 1982). Thus those relatively prosperous
regions still enjoying some growth, have more room for new
firms to enter the market and expand within it: in the
stagnant and declining regions, many new firms will be
entering crowded markets and will survive only at the cost of
displacing existing firms. New firm incentives will therefore
create more new firms with potential for contributing to real
employment growth in the prosperous areas than in the poorer
ones (cf the chapter by Mason and Lloyd). The long term result,
particularly when the Government is giving higher priority to
the creation of new jobs rather than the protection of old ones,
will be to increase the employment disadvantage of regions such
as the North and Scotland. If the aim of regional industrial
policy has been to narrow the gap between rich and poor regions,
the effect of present new firm policies is to widen it.

The present high level of unemployment nationwide perhaps

undermines the case for regional policy: labour supply bottle-
necks are few now, even in the South East, and every region has
its long term unemployed. However, in its latest statement
'Regional Industrial Development' (Department of Trade and
Industry, 1983), the Government has reaffirmed its commitments
to at least some regional aid. Its aim is to stimulate 'self
generating growth' and this "... requires a high rate of
innovation and new firm formation" (Department of Trade and
Industry, 1983, p.8). But a high rate of new firm formation is
precisely what the depressed regions do not possess, and,
despite certain adjustments in aid mechanisms, is hardly likely
to be achieved by a reduction in planned expenditure on
regional industrial inventives by nearly one third, to £643
million in 1983-84.

Nevertheless, the divisive effects of the present reliance
upon new firms could be mitigated by the redesign or better
marketing of incentive schemes. As Birch (1979) argued new
firm policies should be 'targeted'. For instance, schemes
might be restricted to particular regions, or more funds might
be allocated to some regions than to others. Alternatively,
special marketing efforts could be made in the disadvantaged
regions to ensure that higher benefit take-up rates compensate
for their relative paucity of entrepreneurs.

The results of the regression analysis, as well as the
studies of, for instance, Gudgin et al (1979) and Storey (1982),
indicate the importance of middle class populations to
entrepreneurship. If the presence of large middle classes is a
'supply', rather than 'demand', factor, then this would
indicate that the immediate benefits of new firm formation
incentives will probably be disproportionately exploited by
middle class entrepreneurs, though the jobs their enterprises
generate may be more fairly distributed. Assuming that
marketing and other resources are limited, and that the concern
is primarily for employment rather than wealth distribution,
then the marketing of new firm incentives should be concentrated upon the middle class, especially upon owner occupiers
and the administratively or managerially experienced.
Nevertheless, in the cause of social fairness, entrepreneurship
could be encouraged amongst manual workers by targeted
marketing; the greater provision of entrepreneurial training
courses and training allowances, and easier access to finance.
The Enterprise Allowance Scheme is a small step in this
direction.

Because of the importance of middle class populations to
levels of entrepreneurship, present new firm formation incentives are biased against social groups and regions suffering
particularly high unemployment. The regional bias, in

48

opposition to the aims of established regional policy, will reinforce the advantage of the South East and the South West over the declining regions of the north. If the Government must persist with its present heavy emphasis on new and small firms, then efforts ought to be made to counter the side effects upon the regions. New firm policies should be modified so that, rather than discriminating against, as now, they discriminate in favour of those regions with low levels of entrepreneurship.

NOTES

[1] The new firm formation rate measures <u>expressed</u> entrepreneurship, not potential.
[2] Both company registrations and changes in levels of self employment would be even less satisfactory measures of entrepreneurship. Ganguly (1982) explains the appropriateness of the VAT measure.
[3] Regression coefficients are for the standardised variables.
[4] SML is a measure of manufacturing units only; a stronger relationship might have been observed if small service units were included.
[5] The explanation for this result may be that 1980 and 1981 were the years when the recession finally caught up with the more prosperous regions, so they experienced sharp <u>changes</u> in their levels of unemployment, even though their absolute levels remained relatively low. Data for new VAT registrations by region are not yet available for 1982.

REFERENCES

Birch, D.L., (1979), 'The Job Generation Process', Massachussetts Institute of Technology, MIT Programme on Neighbourhood and Regional Change.

British Business, (1983), 'Government Spending £500m p.a. to Help Small Firms', 6th May, 199.

Cross M., (1981), New Firm Formation and Regional Development, Farnborough, Gower.

Curran J. and Stanworth, J., (1981), 'The Social Dynamics of the Small Manufacturing Enterprise', Journal of Management Studies, vol.18, no.2, pp.141-158.

Department of Trade and Industry, (1983), 'Regional Industrial Development', Cmnd 9111, London, H.M.S.O.

Fothergill, S. and Gudgin, G., (1979), The Job Generation Process in Britain, Centre for Environmental Research, London.

Fothergil, S. and Gudgin, G., (1982), Unequal Growth: Urban and Regional Employment Change in the UK, Heinemann Educational Books, London.

Friedman, A.L., (1977), Industry and Labour, Macmillan, London.

Ganguly, A., (1982), 'Regional Distribution of Births and Deaths of Firms in the UK', British Business, 24th September.

Gudgin, G., Brunskill, I. and Fothergill, S., (1979), New Manufacturing Firms in Regional Employment Growth, Centre for Environmental Studies, Research Series No. 39, London.

Hansard, (1981), Parliamentary Debates, House of Commons, 6th Series, Volume 12, Session 1981-82, 4th November-13th November.

Johnson, P. and Cathcart, D.G., (1979), 'The Founders of New Manufacturing Firms: A Note on the Size of their "Incubator" Plants', Journal of Industrial Economics, vol.18, no.2, pp.219-24.

Katz, D.A., (1982), Econometric Theory and Applications, Prentice-Hall, Englewood Cliffs.

Northern Region Strategy Team, (1977), Strategic Plan for the Northern Region, vol.1, HMSO, London.

Robson, Rhodes, (1983), Small Business Loan Guarantee Scheme: Commentary on a Telephone Survey of Borrowers, Department of Industry, London.

Sinfield, A. and Showler, B., (1981), 'Unemployment and the Unemployed in 1980', in Showler, B. and Sinfield, A. (eds.), The Workless State, Martin Robertson, London.

Storey, D.J., (1982), Entrepreneurship and the New Firm, Croom Helm, London.

Thwaites, A., (1977), Indicators of Entrepreneurship in the Northern Region, Discussion Paper No. 2, Centre for Urban and Regional Development Studies, University of Newcastle upon Tyne.

The infant business development process

TOM MILNE AND MARCUS THOMPSON

INTRODUCTION

Although a massive amount of public support worldwide is now
finding its way to the creation and development of new
businesses nobody knows what sorts of support these business
actually need because there is no understanding of the infant
business development process. The lack of understanding
reflects a simple lack of research.

 We know that the vast majority of new businesses will fail to
become more than marginally established in the economy, and
indeed most will disappear within a few years of their creation.
It is possible to argue that more extensive provision of
support might improve the survival rate. It is easier, however,
to defend the position that an understanding of the needs of
the businesses most likely to survive, prosper, and grow should
lead more readily to the better provision if improved support.
We would argue that such discrimination should thereby enhance
the prospects of a truly dynamic sector of the small business
economy.

 The research from which these insights is derived, on which
the analysis is not yet complete, is based on semi-structured
interviews with just over 80 new business people who were
recommended to the research team as having better than average
chances of long term survival and successful growth. The

research is directed by Tom Milne and John Lewis, and was financed by the Social Science Research Council.

RECENT KEY LITERATURE

Background

The field of entrepreneurial research has been shaped by well known American studies including Collins and Moore (1964), McClelland (1961), Smith (1967), Mancuso (1973) and British studies emanating from the Bolton Report (1971), including Bannock (1976), Cameron (1971), Cross (1979), Curran and Stanworth (1973), Firn and Swales (1976), Fothergill and Gudgeon (1978), Howick and Key (1979), Johnson and Cathcart (1979) and Storey and Robinson (1979). These studies offer a contrasting view to that of the American literature, replacing a somewhat heroic picture with one that suggests that the roles of small businesses in our society are multifacetted, and that the interlinkages between small firms, their owners and the wider society they work in are complex and interactive. This more modest view reflects that of Liles (1974) who found that although successful entrepreneurs became men apart, at the beginning they were very much like other ambitious, striving individuals.

British work is also concerned about infrastructural support, notably addressed by the Wilson Committee (1979) and by studies prepared for the Department of Industry and various development agencies. The primary concerns are about evaluating basic business competence and devising non-bureacratic support packages involving not only hard support of finance and premises, but also soft support in areas such as training, consultancy, marketing and other advice. The remainder of this section offers a brief overview of some of the key work relating to the present research, itself only one strand in a very complex literature.

A process view

Gibb and Ritchie (1981), have offered a persuasive analysis of the process of new firm creation. They bring together several trends of thought. Entrepreneurial characteristics are seen to be emerging as a result of rational reaction to social forces including past influences and present opportunities and networks. This gives rise to a model of entrepreneurial styles which articulates the role of the business as a medium of relating changing social class, family of origin, prior education and training, job career patterns and family attach-ments on one dimension to the stage of personal and family

52

development on the other dimension, expressed in the form of a risk profile. This gives rise to a 20 cell taxonomy of the entrepreneur's motivational dilemma. The idea of stages of development is also applied to the process of start-up from the original idea, through part time trading to full time trading. Success, if it is to be achieved, will be determined by the quality of the business idea, the ability of the proposer and his backers, the resources needed and available, and the motivational determination of the sponsors.

Like many of the foregoing studies, Gibb and Ritchie's is concerned with the development of the entrepreneurial ideal up to the point of launching the full time business, and assumes that there is no inheritance of business resources, for example in a management buy-out situation. It is also more concerned with the social process of business idea development than the economic and technical (as well as social) processes of the development of the business after start-up.

Many of their assumptions and methods, have, however, been influential in the design of the present study, including a view of entrepreneurship as a development process, acceptance of multiple causality, the importance of non-monetary motivation, importance of the type of ownership and control, adaptability of the product/market idea, demands for marketing and sales expertise and the need to utilise external sources of assistance.

Their study is also one of several to use the idea of stages of start-up. There have been several attempts to conceptualise start-up as a series of stages. Cooper (1977) offers three. 'First, the start-up stage, including the strategic decisions to found a firm and to position it within a particular industry with a particular competitive strategy; second, the early growth stage, when the initial product/market strategy is being tested and when the president maintains direct contact with all major activities; third, the later growth stage, often characterised by some diversification from manufacturing firms; organisationally, the firm usually has one or more levels of middle management and some delegation of decision making.'

An alternative view based upon technology and innovation, rather than upon organisation, is offered by Abernathy and Utterback (1978) who conceptualise the following three stages: first, flexibility, characterised by early single technology, corporate activity focussed on the product, and R and D informally and entrepreneurially conducted; the second, or intermediate phase is characterised by a growing range of products being more widely used and growing corporate emphasis on marketing, although the product line will contain one stable, steady volume product; by the third stage, maturity, several products and technologies will be in evidence and emphasis will have moved to a profit orientation, backed by growing use of formal structures, goals and rules. Stanworth and Curran (1976) offer a review of a previous work on growth stages, and also suggest a three-stage model: the initial stage stresses the individual entrepreneur; the next stage is concerned with the division of managerial tasks, and any remaining stages are concerned with organisational stability and maturity.

Innovation

Innovation and entrepreneurship have been inextricably linked in the literature since Schumpeter (1934). Recent studies exploring this area have included Casson (1982) and Akhouri (1978) who present an economic profile of the entrepreneur as someone who is prepared to take innovatory risks others would not contemplace.

  Innovation is generally conceptualised as technological innovation involving products or processes. Cannon (1982), however, makes the point that innovation is the technological aspect of the more general phenomenon of adaptiveness, which has always been recognised as being at the root of entrepreneurship, as well as of business and more general economic achievement.

  The study by Utterback and Reitberger (1982), identifies a number of relationships amongst entrepreneurial qualities, innovation and commercial success at least in the medium term, including the importance of the technical and commercial abilities of the entrepreneurs, especially their ability to produce technologically differentiated products of high market acceptance, and to finance such development both through acquired and borrowed funds and through the generation of gross margins on sales. (They also make considerable use of a stages of development concept relating in particular to the needs for financing.)

  Adams and Walbank (1981) found that there were plenty of ideas for innovation, the problem being selection. The firms they studied had no organisational arrangement for selection which was an internal subjective process, conditioned by an unwillingness to consider future risks and the underestimation of the efforts and resources needed to succeed. The business-men lacked knowledge on how to present formal proposals for financial assistance, a matter on which second opinions and outside technical assistance could help. In appraising projects, 40 per cent of firms used cost-based appraisals, and 40 per cent used market-based appraisals while 20 per cent used both.

Technologically innovative development strategies are only one of a number of possible types. Other successful strategies may involve the domination of scarce resources such as skills or materials, or the creation of local monopolies in location sensitive operations such as retailing and service industries.

Commercial and organisational innovation is yet another possibility. Such ideas were addressed by Spender (1980) in terms of industry recipés where:

> The recipé implies a set of norms governing size, structure, technology, administration etc., encapsulated in the various constructs making up the recipé ... adopting a recipé involves the strategy maker in a delicate compromise between the norms implicated in the recipé, the particular policy (he has been) given and available resources.

This approach suggests that success in a small business context is dependent on generating appropriately innovative business recipés and that these recipés represent the total amalgam of strategies and resources and the way they are assembled.

Business success and strategy

The Glasgow research is designed to concentrate upon potentially successful entrepreneurs and their firms. The problems of dwelling upon success have recently been addressed by several important papers.

Sandberg and Hofer (1982) definitively break the link between entrepreneurial personal characteristics and business success with the finding that:

> Entrepreneurial performance is not clearly related to the entrepreneur's need for achievement, locus of control, risk preference, education or nonconformity. Entrepreneurial success is associated with experience in a relevant line of business.

Drawing upon the positions of Schumpeter, Knight, Kirzner and Penrose, Sandberg and Hofer find that disequilibrium is a precondition for an entrepreneur's success not a consequence of it. They use Schendel and Hofer's definition (Schender and Hofer, 1979) that:

> Strategic management is the process that deals with the entrepreneurial work of the organisation, with organisational renewal and growth, and more particularly

55

with developing and utilising the strategy which is to guide the organisation's operations.

They forge a link between entrepreneurship and strategy, consisting of four components: scope, the extent of the firm's interaction with the environment (the product/market segments); distinctive competence at which the firm is especially skilled; competitive advantages over its rivals; finally synergy, how the three coalesce.

The strategy of entering new markets, or innovating new products has long been the subject of research, especially in the area of barriers to entry. Sandberg and Hofer adopt Porter's view that there are two sets of deterrents to entry: structural barriers and the expected reaction of incumbent firms, with six sources of barriers and seven conditions associated with damaging retaliation. Entry in the face of these deterrents is attractive only if there is sufficient disequilibrium in the industry so that above normal profits will remain despite the deterrents (Porter, 1980).

Sandberg and Hofer summarise their theoretical position in the following paragraph:

> A common theme of strategy has emerged ... The economists remind us of the essence of entrepreneurship: a vision of the future which leads someone to effect a new combination of resources (means of production and credit) to exploit markets in disequilibrium. Perception, knowledge, ignorance and error necessarily play important roles. Strategic management theory enables us to flesh out the skeleton of a vision and a new combination of resources; we call the elaborated version a strategy, and we can learn which strategies work under which conditions (our emphasis). Venture capitalists evaluate a prospective investment on its planned strategy and the entrepreneur who heads it. Their apparent ability to screen likely failure suggests the merits of this approach. And new venture researchers have made mixed progress in understanding what type of person becomes an entrepreneur, and little progress in predicting whether he will succeed or fail.

Sandberg and Hofer quote Cooper's (1982) suggestions that:

> The entrepreneur's earliest decisions, including the decision to found a firm and position it within a particular industry with a particular competitive strategy, help to shape a firm's future development.

There has been little explicit research on the
relationships between characteristics of founders, the
strategies of their firms, and subsequent performance.
More needs to be learned about new firm performance and
the chosen strategy.

Important dimensions might include the product/market
choice, the basis of competition, the business strategy,
and the relationship of the industry life cycle.

Cooper thus articulates four strategic dimensions consistent
with those of Hofer and Schendel (1978), offering an approach
to potentially useful conceptual schemes for classifying new
venture strategies.

Vesper (1980) describes three main competitive entry wedges
for new ventures as well as 11 variants of these. The three
main wedges are, new product or service, parallel competition
(minor variants of product or service) and franchising. The 11
other entry wedges, which can be cross-related to the first
three, are: geographic transfer, supply shortage, tapping
unutilised resources, customer contracts, becoming a second
source, joint ventures, licensing, market relinquishment, sell
off a division, favoured purchasing and rule changes.

Using these entry wedges, Vesper suggests that the key to
high growth potential lies in a venture possessing some sort of
property that can readily be multiplied by that company but
cannot easily be duplicated by others - its distinctive
competence. Prosperity would follow from distinctive
competence and market share, the latter moving the new venture
further down the experience curve than its rivals.

Porter categorises competitive strategies as cost leadership,
differentiation and focus, which he operationalises as six
potentially successful paths to entering a market. These are:

(1) Reduce product costs through process technology,
    economies of scale, more modern equipment or shared
    facilities.
(2) Buy in at low price, gaining share at the expense
    of current returns.
(3) Offer a superior product to overcome differentiation.
(4) Discover a new niche.
(5) Introduce a marketing innovation to overcome
    differentiation on the power of distributors.
(6) Use piggyback distribution on established distributor
    relationships.

Hofer and Schendel suggest that strategy can be divided into three sub categories: investment, competitive position and policitical. Porter and Vesper's strategies consists of two of these - competitive and political. Sandberg and Hofer combine the two classification systems, using competitive and political strategies.

Competitive strategies consists of:

1. Product cost reduction
2. Buying in with low price
3. Offering superior product
4. Discovering new segment or niche
5. Marketing innovation
6. Imitative entry

While political strategies consist of:

1. Customer contracts
2. Favoured purchasing
3. Rule changes

Finally, Sandberg and Hofer take little account of invest-ment intensity as an enabling condition for the successful conduct of one of the other strategies. The scant attention paid to this area is possibly accounted for by their choice of research panel - all of whom are already 'adequately' capitalised for the position they intended to enter.

It is in its emphasis on the strategic dimensions of companies selected for development potential that the present study differs most strongly from the seminal study by Storey (1982) which was based upon a census approach and concentrated upon relations between the firms and their environment in the specific geographical area of Cleveland.

Finance and Investment

An acceptable model of the infant business development process, however, should self-evidently not underestimate the importance of the adequacy of finance in relation to required intensity of investment variable. It should hardly be necessary to stress the importance of either pre existing funds in the innovator's possession or the ability of the innovator to talk independent financiers into making available necessary funds for any venture's development.

The key research in this area has concentrated on the whole upon the supposed 'adequacy' of independent financial sources, but recently has included some work on patterns of financing conducive to rapid growth.

Binks (1979) concludes that overtrading is the equivalent of under financing and an inescapable concomitant of growth, while McCulloch (1983) is assessing the importance of adequate and relevant control systems and control advice.

Hutchinson, Piper and Ray (1975a) find that rapidly developing infant businesses have a high proportion of debtors, are short of cash and long term loans, have low current ratios, pay low dividends, and make extensive use of trade creditors. Profits are high and are not distributed. Liquidity can oscillate violently. Despite this somewhat dramatic chronicle of symptoms, finding necessary finance is not usually a problem for the successful companies, although the relative inability to attract long term credit no doubt reflects a healthy conservatism on the part of the potential lenders.

Hutchinson, Piper and Ray (1975b) also find that firms can be divided into two categories with reference to the adequacy of their financial control systems, those which have control systems and those which do not. Hankinson (1983) finds 'endemic investment weaknesses' amongst the small engineering companies he studied, consistent with the lack of financial control uncovered by Hutchinson, Piper and Ray.

Successful Entrepreneurs

This mixed financial picture may be contrasted to the six successful Canadian entrepreneurs studied by Litvak and Maule (1983) who were characterised as being:

  (i) quick to appoint professionals, especially in accounting and finance
  (ii) sensitive to the needs of money and financial markets
  (iii) able clearly to define the scope of their businesses in terms of products and markets
  (iv) able to develop marketing strategies which complemented the distinctive competence (cf Sandberg and Hofer, supra) on which the firm was based
  (v) able clearly to define the business activities in terms of the business scope
  (vi) concentrated on technical and marketing efforts relating to products in which the competitive edge could be maintained
  (vii) specialised, with deliberate limitation of the product range
  (viii) capable and desirous of becoming international almost from inception, in three major stages:
        Manufacturing through a Canadian Head Office
        Selling through a foreign sales branch
        Manufacturing by a foreign subsidiary

Litvak and Maule summarise their findings in terms of concentration on a clearly defined business, growth through acquisition and geographic diversification, emphasis on increasing efficiency and in-house research, and finally positive financial policies to utilise government and external financial assistance, eventually to go public - described in a telling phrase as the golden handcuffs.

The emphasis in all of these studies is upon strategic product/market positioning, distinctive competence and financial control. One aspect of those of specific economic interest arises in the extent to which the new business can be a positive price setter rather than a reactive price taker. The possibility that this might be a fundamental indication of potential development was investigated by Milne, Thorpe and Dyson (1981) with the conclusion that the positive ability to define the market was a better indicator of entrepreneurial confidence than the positiveness of pricing policies. Equally, however, one may argue that positive pricing policies follow from positive market positioning, which is accepted as a truism in elementary marketing.

Entrepreneurial traits

The lack of correlation between traits and long term business success is emphasised by Petrof (1980) who writes, 'This type of literature associates traits with self employment, but has little to do with business ability', and De Carlo and Lyons (1980) who find that, 'Factors supporting successful business initiations may be incompatible with those required for long run successful management of new firms'. Sandberg and Hofer's view has been mentioned. However, an aspiration-based typology has recently been published which suggests the possibility of different standards for 'success' depending on the goals of the entrepreneur (Dunkelberg and Cooper, 1983). This classification characterises the entrepreneurs as having an orientation towards growth, independence or craftsmanship. Craftsman entrepreneurs' companies grew most slowly, while independence orientated entrepreneurs appeared to do a little better than those who were growth orientated. A similar theme has been developed by Ettinger (1983) who classifies entrepreneurs according to their need for independence set against their desire to create an effective organisation in the market place. Both these classification systems enrich the insights into the independence motivation described by Michael Scott (1980).

Support Mechanisms and Outsiders

The importance of support mechanisms for the successful small business is emphasised by Robinson's study of successful small firms (Robinson, 1982), in which he found that such firms made significantly broader use of outside accounting services as part of a total planning activity, than did the average firm and they had a more positive outlook towards such services.

Firms using what he calls outsider-based strategic planning did have significantly greater effectiveness than a random sample. A commonly voiced question concerns the adequacy and appropriateness of support mechanisms for developing small businesses. Generally speaking accountants, bankers and business advisers fare poorly in popular accounts. Robinson's results taken alongside those of Gilroy (1979) suggest that the adverse comments may form a convenient smokescreen rather than be a reflection of a true inadequacy of such agencies in their capacity to support the business with demonstrable development potential.

Management competence and learning from experience

The sense that there is a managerial competence, different from the skills required to start a business, which is needed to sustain its growth and development, is reinforced by a number of recent research articles as well as some of the seminal literature.

Litvak and Maule (1982) report that: 'Inadequate performance of the management function, specifically as it relates to effective decision making and planning, is a primary cause of failure ... combined with a lack of experience coupled with psychological unpreparedness for the responsibilities of running a business'.

Probably, however, the key factor is how quickly the new entrepreneur can adapt and learn from the experience of dealing with his environment, a point made by Sandberg and Hofer (supra), Cole (1968) and Watkins (1982). Cole sees successful entrepreneurial development as involving:

> Ever expanding knowledge of the total situation surrounding him, modifying his primary objectives, thus fitting the actions of his enterprise more closely to the requirements of the economy.

Watkins noted that the owner managers studied were too close to the day to day problems, they had too narrow an educational and experience base, they were inward looking and information orientated and lacked a clear business strategy (cf Sandberg and Hofer, and Litvak and Maule). In particular, they appeared not to learn adequately from their environmental dealings

(Cole's point). As Watkins discovered, there was a correlation between the occurence of catastrophes and areas of reported weakness.

Cole goes further, however to clinch the point:

> Efforts to maximise the possibilities of the surrounding environment is (sic) as important here as in the growth of plants. Availability of capital or labour is of secondary importance.

Time horizons and information richness

Organisational adaptation to enviornmental disequilibrium has been viewed by some authors as a matter of time horizons, notably Dill (1958) who analyses the relationship of the environment and managerial autonomy in terms of short and long term horizons. This theme is developed by Goodman (1972) who crystallises the concept of an organisational domain conceptualised by Norman (1969) that is the part of the environment with which the organisation is in more or less constant interaction. He concludes that rich knowledgeability of the domain means that the organisation can sense and interpret sensitively from very few stimuli, and the maintenance of such rich knowledge factor diminishes both the time available for formal processes of looking forward and planning, and also the needs for these.

Summary

The foregoing suggests that the first stage of the process of development of a business is an important area of potential study. Successful market entry and subsequent development will arise from:

- unstable market conditions
- choice of appropriate entry wedges
- technological or organisational innovation

Successful development of the business will call for:

- technical and commercial competence
- market knowledge
- an aspiration to develop
- a viable development strategy
- a credible competitive strategy
- access to adequate finance
- ability to control the business
- adaptability: ability to learn from experience

The literature also suggests that these factors can be modelled and interrelated so as to make measurement possible.

MODELLING AND MEASUREMENT

Diagram 1 offers an idealised schematic arrangement of the infant business development process derived from the literature and our observations. The arrows are designed to indicate where the strongest linkages are likely to be. We are far from being able to specify the nature of the interactions, the weights to be assigned to any aspect of each cell, the extent to which the model may be cumulative, or the conditions which might determine the answers to those questions. For example, under what circumstances does lack of initial equity capital disqualify a project from proceeding, and what are the circumstances (e.g. technological novelty and innovative capacity) in which outside finance is readily obtained? We are concerned therefore with both cumulation and compensation.

Each cell gives rise to a number of tentative individual hypotheses which the research design enables us to investigate individually and in any grouping. What we need to seek out are effective groupings of characteristics, policies and practices, and means of evaluating their effectiveness, or criteria by which we can defend our evaluations.

Arising from the literature, and from just over 80 interviews we have conducted with potentially successful new business starts, we expect to find that the businesses which exhibit the fastest rate of soundly based growth will have the following characteristics.

Cell 1

(a) The owner manager will have training and experience in a technology or trade which equips him with the skills required to exploit an opportunity in an unstable product-market environment.

(b) The owner manager will have experience of participating in a start-up or turnaround situation, e.g. involving a small subsidiary of a larger company. Alternatively he will have combinations of sales, marketing and financial experience or training in larger organisations appropriate to the overall direction of the business.

(c) The owner manager's ambitions will be orientated towards business growth and independence rather than towards craftsmanship and technology.

Diagram 1
A conceptual structure for the infant business
development process

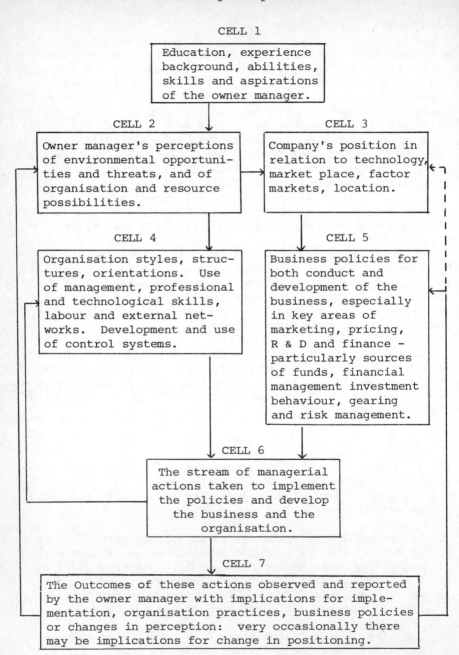

CELL 1

Education, experience
background, abilities,
skills and aspirations
of the owner manager.

CELL 2

Owner manager's perceptions
of environmental opportunities and threats, and of
organisation and resource
possibilities.

CELL 3

Company's position in
relation to technology,
market place, factor
markets, location.

CELL 4

Organisation styles, structures, orientations. Use
of management, professional
and technological skills,
labour and external net-
works. Development and use
of control systems.

CELL 5

Business policies for
both conduct and
development of the
business, especially
in key areas of
marketing, pricing,
R & D and finance -
particularly sources
of funds, financial
management investment
behaviour, gearing
and risk management.

CELL 6

The stream of managerial
actions taken to implement
the policies and develop
the business and the
organisation.

CELL 7

The Outcomes of these actions observed and reported
by the owner manager with implications for implementation, organisation practices, business policies
or changes in perception: very occasionally there
may be implications for change in positioning.

(d) The owner manager will have taken positive steps to remedy shortcomings in his educational or experience background prior to start-up, e.g. by attending a New Enterprise Programme or by seeking professional advice.

Cell 2

(e) The owner manager will have a very rich mental map of relevant environmental information - he will be an expert on market requirements, technological possibilities and other suppliers. He will also have made and be making extensive use of supporting agencies and people for information, advice or merely as sounding boards. He will actively seek and select these agencies, and will have positive attitudes towards 'outsiders'. He will make positive use of banks, local authorities, outside financiers, information sources, and resource providers. He will also have a positive awareness of environmental threats.

Cell 3

(f) The owner manager will be aware of a wide range of product-market opportunities, and will have positively vetted some of these before selecting his preferred market entry configuration. He will also be aware of a range of possibilities in factor markets which will also have been positively vetted. He will be prepared to adjust his positions in light of experience, and over the years the business will show evidence of such adjustments. These positions will reflect the distinctive competences of the business.

Cell 4

(g) The owner manager will employ open and flexible management practices internally, and will appoint subordinates with the intention that they will develop to be able to assume delegated responsibility. All members of the firms will be encouraged to undertake training and to enlarge their skills portfolios. Learning, development and adaptation will be at a premium. Subordinates will be moved to situations where they can operate most effectively. The owner manager will be ruthless in parting with subordinates who do not respond to this style of management. The pattern of appointments will be consistent with skills deficiencies in relation to the development needs of the business and key appointments will be of people whose record is already well known to the owner manager.

(h) Within the context of personal flexibility of the
    developing team, the owner manager will from the outset
    begin to create and develop financial and material con-
    trol systems which will be precise, up to the minute, and
    appropriate to the special strains of managing an over-
    geared and overtrading enterprise, so that stocks, credit
    and cash can be kept under regular (weekly or even daily)
    review. One of the earliest subordinate roles to be
    developed will be the management of the control system,
    either by a trusted employee, a financial partner, or by
    a family member, for example, the owner manager's wife.

(i) The owner manager will have formal partners, co-directors,
    or senior associates (e.g. an accountant) who will be
    involved in the strategic development aspects of the
    business. In other words, the owner manager will not be
    a 'one man band' at the strategic direction and control
    level.

Cell 5

(j) The owner manager will consciously concentrate the
    business on the chosen product-market position and
    consciously avoid distracting projects. He will develop
    a distinctive competence for the business.

(k) The owner manager will continuously adapt his product or
    service offering, in order better to serve the market by
    offering greater value.

(l) In marketing terms, the owner manager will not see him-
    self as geographically restricted and will quickly
    develop national and international marketing.

(m) The owner manager's market knowledge will enable him to
    adopt positive pricing policies which will enable him to
    earn above normal profits.

(n) The owner manager will have, and will insist upon
    implementing, a clear philosophy with regard to product
    or service quality, and product or service development.

(o) The owner manager will create and regularly update a
    credible business plan in which the financial and
    operating requirements of the business's development
    will be clearly drawn from the market and technological
    potential available. This plan will be used as a basis
    of internal control and also as a basis of communicating
    with factor suppliers, especially financial sources.

(p) The owner manager will be aware of the extent to which his firm is overgeared and overtrading, and this knowledge will be fully shared with his bankers and suppliers. He will have the active support of his bankers, and he will be able, with their support, to obtain external long term finance in a timely manner so as to be able to finance planned volume increases.

(q) The owner manager will generate a high degree of personal loyalty from a core of customers who will provide feedback on the success of the product or service in the market place.

Cell 6

(r) The owner manager will actually implement the steps necessary for the discharge of his policies. Appropriate appointments will be made at the time planned. Business plans and cash flow forecasts will be delivered to the bank when promised. Sales will be concluded, products delivered, or product developments introduced according to plan. Market development programmes will be implemented on time.

(s) Mistakes will be quickly learned from, and adaptations in operations or policies will be quickly implemented in light of them.

Cell 7

(t) The key output measure is the sustained development of wealth-creating business resources, measured by sales and market share, the asset base, value added, the size of the organisation and the strength of management in width and depth.

(u) Vulnerability to external shocks or internal development stress must be assessed in order to moderate the measures used under (t). Gearing, financial risk and balance sheet strength can all be conventionally measured. The closeness of potentially overwhelming competition is also a factor. It will only be possible to obtain meaningful measures of this variable in the event of a catastrophe involving failure or near failure overtaking a business in which none of the pre-existing conditions for failure apparently exist.

(v) The economic and social view of success embodied in variable (t) must also be supplemented by the view of the owner manager and his colleagues. Are the owner manager's

aspirations being met in terms of achievement, property
creation, technological advance, service to the market
and the community and economic reward? Are colleagues,
associates and employees being similarly rewarded?

Early evidence suggests that it will be possible to categorise
the panel into three groups - rapid developers, steady
developers, and survivors. In time, no doubt some of the firms
will discontinue trading, or will change their form through
takeover or merger. We shall be particularly interested in
analysing these events. Will there be failures attributable to
internal mismanagement or external catastrophe? Will there on
the other hand, be creative redevelopments? Will the incidence
and the predetermining mechanisms be different for different
categories of firms?

Potentially we shall have nine categories:

	Rapid Developers	Steady Developers	Survivors
Continuing in business			
Failed			
Creatively redeveloped			

PRELIMINARY INSIGHTS

What follows is necessarily impressionistic. When full
analysis has been completed it will be possible to stipulate
which of these impressions of our research panel are supported
by detailed analyses.

It is clear that the new business people who appear,
initially, to be most satisfied and most optimistic, have
certain characteristics in common.

They clearly enjoy the technological, craft or commercial
challenge in turning their skills and knowledge into marketable
proportions, through which they can ensure their living. They
are not, however, dedicated to the pursuit of craftsmanship or
technology for its own sake. This is seen clearly as being the
means to the end of profitable marketing. 'Perfection', and
many are perfectionists, lies in the match of the product to
the market need, not to an abstraction of technical quality.
The expression of this lies in a highly personalised view of
their service to their customers, rather than in formal

marketing processes. Their commitment to customer satisfaction is adamant.

Initially no one is willing to admit to aiming at the creation of a business empire. They are, initially, intent upon securing economic survival in an independent mode, more as an expression of an ideal than as an outcome of any sort of profit-maximising calculus. The ideal may perhaps be best expressed as reliance upon one's own values (not quite even self-reliance), and many of those we interviewed proved to be highly articulate in their ability to express the values which they were pursuing. Independence may be a unifying theme, but efficient use of resources (especially one's own time) recurs frequently, quality aspirations recur frequently, and gross impatience with manifestations of waste of time and other resources comes through loud and clear at all times.

They are all hyperactive, being able to find time for a stupendous range of activities each day, including time for our interviews. Their activities and interests range widely. They are not narrow minded money grubbers, although they have a very highly developed sense of economic realism, arising perhaps from their initial drive towards economic independence.

They are highly perceptive and employ an extensive contact network. The better ones do indeed appear to possess the rich mental map of the environment, described by Litvak and Maule. They use contacts. On completion of the interviews, they then interview the interviewer for all they are worth. They are plagued with self-doubts, especially when they begin to assume responsibility for employees. Like their commitment to their customers, their commitment to their employees looms large: here again practice is personalised rather than systematised. Success in the initial stages consists of proving that they can make a living out of selling the product or service they invented and they work furiously to secure a good verdict from the marketplace.

The same level of intimate commitment, however, does not appear to apply in most cases to their bankers, or to other financial suppliers. A few have a close relationship of high confidence of the sort that characterises their view of their dealings with their customers and employees, but the majority report a very nervous, and frequently dissatisfied relationship with their bankers and other agencies, as to their understanding of the business's needs and the adequacy, timing and presentation of financial or advisory packages.

They are impatient with formality including formal market research. But the successful ones are doing the research in an

extremely powerful and efficient personal contact manner. Thus
one of the more promising entry strategies may be one where the
market research can be done informally, and where trial and
error adaptation is possible before, during and after start-up.

They are not plungers. Every step is organised so that in
the event of catastrophic rejection by the market or inability,
for some reason, to deliver the situation can be retrieved
leaving everyone as little as possible worse off than before.
They are humanists, concerned to protect their associates
against the possible consequences of their own misjudgements or
mismanagements.

In short, in our study, we, unsurprisingly, came up against
no 'cowboys'.

So what do these insecure, striving, impatient, painstaking,
creative independent people do to secure their living?

First, they search, and search, and search again, to uncover
a realistic opportunity. Sometimes they commit themselves
before they have uncovered an opportunity which is good enough.

Second, they wholly underestimate the implications for
resources should the venture prove to be as successful as they
hope - even those with experience in the field.

Third, they go through traumas of trial and error, first on
paper and then in reality, as they try to match productive
resources with their perceptions of market need. Interviewers
observed much evidence of classic problem solving trial and
error behaviour.

Fourth, they continually underestimate the resources involved
in the commercial, as distinct from the technical and
organisational aspects of their business, and may well sub-
contract some of this to offload intractible and increasing
problems.

They learn rapidly from experience, and may adapt and modify
dramatically in response to it. Those who had relevant
experience of a previous start-up situation, enjoy double
benefit - first they do not have to correct nearly as many
mistakes, and second they enjoy the confidence of resource
providers from the outset of the project.

Those lacking this advantage have to recognise early, or
learn quickly, that what their success will depend upon is an
ability rapidly to gain the confidence of the two key resource
providers - customers and financial backers - both controlled
by the money nexus.

Confidence of the market is attained through the highest priority being accorded to the creation of an appropriate product or service, and intensive personal attention being paid to the demands and requirements of the customers. This intensive personalised knowledge and connections take the place of the more formal marketing techniques employed by larger businesses. It is in this way that the new business creates a competitive entry wedge to the marketplace.

Securing the confidence of financial markets requires three key elements.

First, providing evidence of the market confidence referred to above. This involves a particular skill in translating the personal knowledge possessed by the owner manager on to paper in the form of a formal business document. Whilst some market research may be incorporated into this, it would appear that the necessary conviction can be expressed more directly. Nevertheless, by no means all of our panel are able to do this, or would recognise the need to do so, or would be prepared to commit the time to this disciplined exercise. Those growing most rapidly have been able to do this, and it would seem that there are opportunities for more rapid development being fore-gone due to the reluctance to take this step. The reluctance does appear partly to follow from the personalised, and there-fore relatively unsystematic form of much of the early marketing activity, which the perpetrator would rather not commit to paper. Few of them think they do their marketing well, and would rather not open this up to the scrutiny of financial experts.

The second aspect of gaining the confidence of financiers is an ability to express realism about future prospects. This depends upon market realism, but also upon resource and development programme realism, again expressed on paper.

The final major aspect is ability to show competence in financial management. At the very least this calls for evidence of the implementation and regular utilisation of costs and cash forecasting and control mechanisms, and evidence of ability to contain financial risk. In particular it is aided by evidence of treating the banker as someone who deserves real information on which to base his lending decisions.

All this leads to the central importance of business plans, now universally sought by financing and other support agencies, but herein lies a condundrum. Two or three years ago the concept of a business plan or feasibility study was very unformed in small business circles. The MSC's New Enterprise Programmes at the leading centres of small business teaching, in search of a unifying theme for their programmes, uniformly lit upon business planning - and rightly so. A proper business plan for a new business is an intellectually demanding and convincing exercise, which carefully stipulates the realities of the opportunity and of the uncertainties, and carefully matches a flexible set of emotional, organisational and resource configurations to those, demonstrating finally that the pay offs from the venture sufficiently outweigh the risks of loss as to make the total package worth backing.

Accountancy practices, however had for years already been in business producing feasibility studies for business in which, given a sales income projection and a starting income/cost ratio, they were capable <u>ex ante</u> of rationalising any desired profit forecast, just enough to give the bank branch manager a case to put to his head office for support of the proposition. This results in a further obscuring of the problem of judging business propositions. Firms of accountants are quite willing to put the most complex analyses (easily obtained from a number of computer programmes) behind any airy-fairy sales projection for a nominal fee. It is by no means easy to distinguish the document carefully laboured over and intended as a guide and control to a conscientious entrepreneur, from the computerised work of fiction based on a set of imaginary numbers.

We are fairly confident that the detailed analysis of our data will confirm the views expressed in this chapter, that the key skills required for successful start-up are those involved in winning the confidence of the marketplace and, through that, in winning the confidence of financial backers. These skills are, in the early stages less a matter of techniques than of priorities, but there does seem to be a problem of moving from the personalised intuitive approach to more systematic processes which can be committed to paper.

WHAT HELP IS NEEDED?

One major reason for studying new businesses which are succeeding is to dispose of the alibi effect which comes so clearly through many studies of small business attitudes. As Gilroy detected, those who aren't going to succeed will find lots of forces beyond their control to account for their failure. One key question our research seeks to address is what sorts of help the successful entrepreneurs really want.

A universal characteristic is that they will adapt and get on with things under far less than ideal conditions if the ideal is out of reach, whilst nevertheless actively searching out something better. This applies particularly to premises and finance. They will not, however, compromise on people, materials or service, which directly impinge upon the heartland of their business. Most of all they are conscious that their own time is at a premium, and has to be invested carefully: it is the substitute for the financial capital which is in such short supply in an expanding situation.

The ultimate anathema in their lives appears to be a waste of their own time, and the ultimate frustration is extended negotiations with some resource providing or helping agency which abort after an extensive time commitment, or where the facility is delivered late. On the submarginal operating budgets of time and money which characterise these situations, a month or two's delay in completion of a factory, delivery of a machine, installation of a telephone or payment of a grant can have catastrophic effects on solvency, credibility with customers, or both.

A particular lesson enunciated by many of the respondents is the problem of employing other people. The entrepreneur's view of himself and his firm is of a striving, hard working and unstructured situation, calling for dedication and flexibility. They want their employees to share the same view, and the most commonly reported serious mistake they have made lies in the area of employing managers or key employees who want a structured job with conventional large firm work practices. Some reports suggest that the frustrations generated by these situations go beyond mere underperformance to implicit sabotage of the owner manager's efforts.

There is a strong preference for recruiting senior colleagues, and confidential colleagues such as secretaries or bookkeepers, from amongst former colleagues or friends whose attitudes to work can be trusted, and from recruiting other employees straight from school before they have had a chance to develop poor working practices.

Against a background in which everything is urgent, the penalties of mistakes can be fatal, extraordinarily high reliance is being placed on the performance of other people, and the priorities lie with doing the things needed to satisfy the customers now, rather than controlling and developing the business itself, what can we say about helping?

First, it must be non bureaucratic. Our respondents would rather learn half what they need on a phone call than wait a month for the survey that will tell them three quarters. They would rather be told 'NO' immediately than 'YES' after a six month delay. They would rather have a half hour meeting with an advisor who has real expertise on the problem and understands their company, than have a management consultant for a month. In situations involving an extended study, e.g. the purchase of a micro computer, they would rather deal with someone who thoroughly understands their needs, but may not thoroughly understand the computers, rather than the other way round.

This seems to provoke a problem for the support agencies, who appear not to like casual advice being thrown around by their advisers. One anecdote in particular may serve to make the point. A certain roving adviser, the employee of a public sector agency, began to figure in a few interviews as being on the ball, crisp, energetic, timely, helpful and to the point. This was mentioned in discussion with one of his superiors along the following lines:

> Well, you seem to have one very good chap out there, energetic, getting around: (Interruption) Yes, you must mean A..... B..... All the companies love him. But he's a real problem, out of control. We don't know what he'll say next. We're going to have to move him from that job.

There is an undoubted mismatch between what the bureaucracies can offer and the needs of the striving and succeeding small new businesses, often less in content than in form and presentation. The proper professional safeguards of the bureaucracies are seen often as procrastination or over-elaboration by the recipients.

As a result, there seems to be a growth in a sort of mediation function, between the immediate need and the expert response, a role which is discharged by small business clubs at the self-help end of the spectrum, courses such as Business Growth Programmes employing an action-learning format, but incorporating experts at need, and an increasing use of business development advisers by bureaucratic support agencies.

All these are clearly along the right lines. None, however, properly address two key areas.

The first is the area of market opportunity information. The most successful new businessmen clearly seem to be those who know who to call on, who to phone, what these potential buyers will be interested in, and how to find out readily the business potential for their firm. This is market search rather than formal market research. Many of our respondents have been materially helped by a small list of key names, addresses, phone numbers and interest on whom they can make a start. The best source seems to be someone 'in the know' rather than a formal reference list. It appears that many of the enterprise trusts and agencies which have sprung up in the last couple of years are now beginning to provide this resource.

The second key area is finance. Advice on financial management on a small scale seems to be hopelessly inadequately provided. Accountants are rarely consulted and even more rarely used for anything other than the production of the statutory accounts. Advice or instructions associated with externally supplied funds are often regarded as irrelevant, unhelpful, or unduly restrictive. In particular, the quality of help available from bank managers seems to be incredibly patchy. Only the best few of our respondents appeared capable of evaluating their financial risk profile, of thinking in cash flow (let alone discounted cash flow) terms, or of being in sufficient control of their financial information to enter into a meaningful negotiation with funds suppliers. Several of our better-placed people make the point that the outstanding difference between being a divisional general manager and an independent managing director is the concentration of attention on financial management. The sad thing is that many of the more modest start-ups are unaware of potential opportunities they are foregoing because of their financial naivete. Clearly the outstanding need at present is for the promising start-up to be made aware of the vital need to become a master of his financial management. There should be a provision of crash courses in this area aimed at the start-up entrepreneur, if necessary as a condition of receiving any outside funds.

A secondary, but closely related need, appears to lie in the area of effective creation and use of market intelligence. Our research panel contains numerous examples of underdevelopment of the business opportunity which can probably be related to insecurity about more rapid exploitation of the market, associated with insecurity about adding to external funding, underlain by lack of confidence about financial management and being expressed in inadequately vigorous attempts to open up and exploit markets.

The challenge to educators, trainers and consultants is the creation of formats for the efficient acquisition of this sort of material by people with urgent requirements and pressing alternative uses for their time.

REFERENCES

Abernathy, W. and Utterback, J., (1978), 'Patterns of Industrial Innovation', Technology Review, June, July.

Adams, A. and Walbank, M., (1981), New Product Introduction in Small Manufacturing Firms, U.M.I.S.T., July.

Akhouri, M.M.P., (1978), Small Entrepreneurial Development in North Eastern India, SIET Publication.

Akhouri, M.M.P., 'Entrepreneurial Economic Success Index (EESI) for Assessing Entrepreneurial Success.

Bannock, G., (1976), The Smaller Business in Britain and Germany, Witten House, London.

Binks, Martin, (1979), 'Finance for Expansion in the Small Firm', Lloyd's Bank Review, October.

Bolton, J.E., (1971), Report of the Committee of Inquiry into Small Firms, Cmnd 4811, H.M.S.O.

Boyle, R.P., (1970), 'Path Analysis and Ordinal Data', American Journal of Sociology.

Briggs, D.H. and Maclennan, D.A., (1983), 'The Prediction of Private Company Failure', European Management Journal, vol.2, no.1, Summer.

Brokhaus, Robert H., (1980), 'Risk Taking Propensity of Entrepreneurs', Academy of Management Journal, vol.23, no.3.

Brokhaus, Robert H., (1980), 'Psychological and Environmental Factors which Distinguish the Successful from the Unsuccessful Entrepreneur: A Longitudinal Study', Academy of Management Proceedings.

Burt, C., (1952), 'Tests of Significance in Factory Studies', Br. J. Psychol.

Cameron, G.C., (1971), Economic Analysis for a Declining Urban Economy, Scottish Journal of Political Economy, vol.18.

Cangelosi, Vincent E. and Dill, William R., (1965-66), 'Organisational Learning: Observations Towards a Theory', Administrative Science Quarterly, vol.10.

Cannon, T., (1982), Innovation Creativity and Small Firm Organisation, paper presented to Small Business Policy/ Research Conference, University of Glasgow.

de Carlo, J.F. and Lyons, P.R., (1980), 'Towards a Contingency Theory of Entrepreneurship', Journal of Small Business Management, July.

Casson, T., (1982), The Entrepreneur: An Economic Theory, Martin Robertson, London.

Cole, Arthur H., (1968), 'The Entrepreneur - Introductory Remarks', papers and proceedings, American Economic Review, no.58.

Collins, O.F. and Moore, D.G., (1964), The Enterprising Man, Michigan State University Business Studies, East Lancing, Michigan.

Cooper, Arnold C., (1977), 'Strategic Management, New Ventures and Small Business', paper presented at the Business Policy Conference, Pittsburgh.

Cooper, Arnold, C., (1979), 'Strategic Management: New Ventures and Small Business', in Schendel, D.E. and Hofer, C. W. (eds), Strategic Management, Little, Brown and Co., Boston.

Cross, M., (1979), <u>New Formation and the Local Labour Market</u>,
  paper presented at the Small Firms Policy and Role of
  Research Conference, Ashridge Management College,
  Berkhamstead.
Curran, J. and Stanworth, M.J., (1973), <u>Management Motivation
  in the Smaller Business</u>, London, Gower Press.
Curran, J. and Stanworth, M.J., (1981), 'The Social Dynamics of
  the Small Manufacturing Enterprise', <u>Journal of Management
  Studies</u>, no.18.
Dill, William R., (1957-58), 'Environment as an Influence on
  Managerial Autonomy', <u>Administrative Science Quarterly</u>, vol.2.
Dunkleberg, W.C. and Cooper, A.C., (1982), 'Entrepreneurial
  Typologies: An Empirical Study', paper presented to the
  Small Business Research Conference, Polytechnic of Central
  London.
Ettinger, Jean-Claude, (1983), 'Some Belgian Evidence on
  Entrepreneurial Personality', <u>European Small Business Journal</u>,
  vol.1, no.2.
Firn, J. and Swales, K., (1978), 'The Formation of New
  Manufacturing Establishments in Central Clydeside and West
  Midlands Conurbations 1963-72', <u>Regional Studies</u>. vol.12.
Fothergill, S. and Gudgin, G.H., (1978), <u>The Structural Growth
  and Decline of the U.K. Regions in its International Context</u>,
  CES WN. 495, CES, London.
Gibb, A., and Ritchie, J., (1981),'Influences on
  Entrepreneurship', a study over time, contained in
  proceedings of Small Business Research Conference.
Gilroy, Martin, H., (1979), 'Growth, The Entrepreneur and the
  Small Firm', University of Glasgow, M.Eng Dissertation.
Goodman, Richard A., (1972), 'Environmental Knowledge and
  Organisation Time Horizon: Some Functions and Disfunctions',
  <u>Human Relations</u>, vol.26, no.2.
Hankinson, Alan, (1983), <u>The Investment Problem: A study of
  Investment Behaviour of South Wessex Small Engineering Firms</u>,
  Dorset Institute of Higher Education.
Hofer, C.W. and Schendel, D.E., (1978), <u>Strategy Formulation:
  Analytical Concepts</u>, West Publishing Company, St. Paul.
Hutchinson, P.J., Piper, J.A. and Ray, G.H., (1975a) 'The
  Financing of Rapid Growth Firms up to Flotation', <u>Accounting
  and Business Research</u>, Spring.
Hutchinson, P.J., Piper, J.A. and Ray, G.H., (1975b), 'The
  Financial Control of Rapid Growth Firms up to Flotation',
  <u>Accounting and Business Research</u>, Summer.
Johnson, P.S. and Cathcart, D.G., (1979), 'The Founders of New
  Manufacturing Firms: A Note on the Size of their Incubator
  Plant', <u>Journal of Industrial Economics</u>, vol.28, no.2.
Liles, Patrick R., (1974), 'Who are the Entrepreneurs', <u>M S U
  Business Topics</u>, vol.22.
Litvak, Isiah A., and Maule, Christopher, J., (1982),
  'Successful Canadian Entrepreneurship and Innovation', paper

presented to the Babson Entrepreneurship Research Conference,
April.

Litvak, Isiah A. and Maule, Christopher J., (1980),
'Entrepreneurial Success or Failure - Ten Years Later',
Business Quarterley, Winter.

McCormick, W.T., et.al., (1972), 'Problem Decomposition and
Data Reorganisation by a Clustering Technique', Operations
Research.

McCulloch, A., (1983), Working Papers on Ph.D. Research,
University of Glasgow.

McLelland, D.C., (1961), The Achieving Society, Van Nostrand,
Princetown, New Jersey.

Mancuso, J., (1973), The Entrepreneur's Philosophy, Addison
Wesley.

Milne, T.E., Thorpe, R. and Dyson, J., (1981), 'Pricing
Policies in New Businesses', paper presented to the Small
Business Research Conference, Polytechnic of Central London.

Normann, R., (1969), 'Some Conclusions from Thirteen Case
Studies of New Product Development', report UPM-RN-100,
Swedish Institute for Administrative Research, Stockholm.

Petrof, John V., (1980), 'Entrepreneurial Profile: A
Discriminant Analysis', Journal of Small Business Management,
October.

Porter, M., (1980), Competitive Strategy, Free Press, New York.

Robinson, Richard B., (1982), 'The Importance of "Outsiders" in
Small Firm Strategic Planning', Academy of Management Journal,
vol.25, no.1.

Sandbert, W.R. and Hofer, C.W., (1982), 'A Strategic Management
Perspective on the Determinants of New Venture Success', paper
presented to the Babson Entrepreneurship Research Conference.

Schendel, D.E. and Hofer, C.W., (eds), (1979), Strategic
Management, Little, Brown and Co., Boston.

Schumpeter, J.A., (1934), The Theory of Economic Development,
Harvard University Press, Cambridge, Mass.

Scott, M.G., (1980), 'Independence and the Flight from Large
Scale: Some Sociological Factors in the Founding Process',
in Gibb, A. and Webb, T., (eds), Policy Issues in Small
Business Research, Saxon House.

Smith, N., (1967), 'The Entrepreneur and his Firm', occasional
paper, Bureau of Business and Economic Research, Michigan
State University.

Spender, J.C., (1980), Strategy-Making in Business, Ph.D.
thesis, University of Manchester.

Storey, D.J., (1982), Entrepreneurship and the New Firm, Croom
Helm.

Storey, D.J. and Robinson, J.F.F., (1979), 'Entrepreneurship,
New Firm Formation and Regional Policy: The Case of
Cleveland County', paper presented to the conference, Small
Firms Policy and the Role of Research, Ashridge Management
College, Berkhamstead.

Stanworth, M.J. and Curran, J., (1976), 'Growth and the Small Firm: An Alternative View', Journal of Management Studies, vol.13.

Tamari, M., (1982), Financial and Industrial Innovation in Sweden: A Study of New Technology-Based Firms, Centre for Policy Alternatives, Massachusetts Institute of Technology, Cambridge.

Vesper, Carl H., (1980), New Venture Strategies, Prentice Hall, Englewood Cliffs, N.J.

Watkins, David, (1982), 'Management Development and the Owner Manager', in Webb, Quince and Watkins, (eds), Small Business Research: The Development of Entrepreneurs, Gower.

Wilson Committee, (1979), The Financing of Small Firms, Interim Report of the Committee to Review the Functioning of the Financial Institutions, Cmnd 7503, H.M.S.O., London.

Understanding small firms growth

ALLAN GIBB AND MICHAEL SCOTT

INTRODUCTION

This chapter focuses on the issue of encouragement of the growth of the existing small owner managed firm. It is based on action research* which examined in detail sixteen companies over a period of up to two years and which sought to monitor and understand the impact of a range of inputs designed to enhance these companies' growth possibilities.

The research was carried out in the northern region, and its relevance initially derives from the context of the problems of that region, which are well known (see e.g. Northern Region Strategy Team, 1977; North of England County Councils Association, 1981). These can broadly be described as follows:

- A persistently higher than national level of unemployment
- Lower than average UK income levels
- Long term secular decline in old established manufacturing industries in the region
- A predominance of capital intensive industries with a high rate of replacement of labour by capital and with

* The study was commissioned and funded by the Department of Industry and the EEC Social Fund, but any opinions expressed in this paper are solely those of the authors.

some cyclical vulnerability
- . The substantial concentration of industry into large companies
- . The very high concentration of external ownership of manufacturing industry in the region
- . The weakness of the indigenous locally owned small and medium firms sector

The traditional regional policy response to these problems has been to attempt to attract foot-loose investment from elsewhere in the UK and abroad. Substantial success was achieved with this policy in job creation terms during the 1960's and early 1970's. This, however, did little to strengthen the indigenous base which remains among the weakest in the UK (British Business, 1982, p.648-9).

More recently attention has focused on ways of developing this base and considerable encouragement has been given to individuals and groups to start up their own companies. It is clear, however, that this will not in the short run generate a substantial number of jobs (although in the long run it will lead, hopefully, to a more balanced economy). It can be argued, therefore, that there is a need to address the question:

- How is it possible to enhance the growth of an under-represented small firm sector by ensuring the survival of, and encouraging the growth and competitiveness of, existing indigenous small enterprises?

Survival and growth is unlikely to come from acquisition, given the weak resource base of such firms. Nor will it come from links with the region's large companies (shipbuilding, coal, steel, heavy electrical and mechanical engineering industries) given also their decline. It can only come, we would argue, from product and market diversification engendered within the firm itself. In this respect, the problem is probably shared by other regions of the UK (and EEC): the need is for sustainable, internally generated growth.

Given a commitment to stimulate small firm development, deriving suitable policies or instruments to meet this objective poses a number of difficulties for the policy maker, in particular:

i. Who to assist? There are large numbers of widely diverse small companies with differing products, and in differing markets - too many to provide blanket assistance on any scale.

ii. What to seek to influence and how? This begs

questions of what kinds of behaviour are desirable
and how such behaviours might be brought about. Much
of existing policy is for example based on assumptions
of rationality on the part of the small firm owner
manager which may not be grounded in fact.

iii. How to achieve the best balance of support? This begs
questions about the appropriate balance between the
provision of hardware support (grants, loans, premises,
etc) and software (information, counselling, training,
etc) which in turn raises issues of their inter
relationship.

METHODOLOGICAL IMPLICATIONS

To answer these questions adequately requires an understanding
of how the process which policy is seeking to influence works.
Whether or not there is understanding, there must be, either
implicitly or explicitly, a 'model' of how companies behave in
response to certain stimuli, such as 'hardware' support. This
will be usually assumed to be rational - economic. Thus in the
take-up of an investment grant it is assumed that the equipment
acquired will have been evaluated in such a manner as to lead
to increases in productivity and that this will facilitate
competitiveness and ensure growth and survival. Behind this of
course lies assumptions about the capability of the company and
management to 'manage' the new investment in an appropriate
manner. We would argue:

i. That the assumptions behind this model may not have
been adequately tested in the context of the small
firm.

ii. That the typical methodology used for evaluating the
operation of policy instruments is of the 'black box'
variety.

At the risk of over-simplification, this envisages that in any
social situation, we can input certain activities or phenomena
and then measure the resulting outcome. We then postulate
relationships between that output and the various inputs without ever being able to say what the exact transformation
process was. For example, if the policy input were, say,
financial support for the purchase of NC machine tools, it is
possible to measure the number of grants made and new equipment
purchased at the end of the time period. By taking a previous
time period when no such policy existed, it may be possible to
regard that period as a 'control'. It is then possible to
offer explanations which causally relate the policy input to
the subsequent changed behaviour of the small firms sector.
What this 'black box' approach cannot do is answer questions
which begin with 'how ...'. To answer these kinds of questions

requires getting into the 'black box' itself and observing its internal dynamics. By definition, this cannot be achieved by methods which remain essentially external to the real activities of the subjects under study, no matter how sophisticated the measurement techniques nor how large the size of sample.

To acquire this level of understanding requires a detailed study of the process of change, as that change happens, in order to examine:

i. What actually happens within a firm over time, as it embarks on development

ii. What are the key factors which influence this process, both internally and externally

iii. Whether these factors are themselves amenable to influence during the development process itself.

The research strategy adopted was therefore 'micro'. And to enhance the possibility of gaining insights into the effectiveness and efficiency of different forms of assistance, 'action' experimentation was proposed. In this way it was hoped to gain improved understanding of just what was being influenced and what was open to influence.

The assistance provided to the research companies as action inputs was based on an examination of the literature on organisational interventions (for example, Schein, 1969) and a review of the types of assistance currently available to industry. These suggested the following categories of intervention strategy:

(a) Passive provision of information
(b) Counselling and consultancy
(c) Education and training provision
(d) Provision of additional resources

These four categories of provision relate to four potential 'gaps' which have been discussed in the literature elsewhere namely: the information gap, referred to in the Bolton Report in 1971 and which UK governments have progressively tried to fill; the problem solving and technical gap - the difficulty which the owner manager has in taking an analytical approach to his problems, therefore meriting the establishment of consulting and counselling services to help in this process; the learning gap - which has become increasingly recognised in terms of the limited knowledge and experience of the owner manager outside his own particular industry but which has, in policy terms, been particularly emphasised in the start-up situation; and the resources gap - which relates to the limited

time of the owner manager to spend on planning new developments
and the absence of technical resources to help him so to do.
(The provision of additional resources was in this case sub-
sumed under education and training, given that the training
programme used as an action input was linked to an MSC funded
retraining scheme of redundant executives, provided as extra
managerial resources.)

Sixteen locally owned companies with under 100 employees were
chosen for the research. Twelve of the companies were
allocated to the three assistance categories: education and
training, counselling, and information provision. The other
four were in some respects a 'control' group, in that measures
were taken at the beginning and end of the research period, but
no attempt was made to affect their behaviour during the
research.

In order to understand the impact of interventions it is
first necessary to understand the process. The first part of
this chapter sets out a model of the development process in the
small firm drawn from the research, and identifies the key
influences on this process. This allows an examination of the
triggers or stimuli to growth and the factors facilitating or
hindering development: finally the impact of different forms
of intervention in the process are examined and comment made on
criteria for effectiveness of different forms of intervention.

CHARACTERISING THE PROCESS OF CHANGE IN THE SMALL FIRM: A
PROPOSED MODEL

In determining the orginal parameters for the monitoring of the
small firms in the sample, the major barrier was the absence of
an established acceptable theory of small firms development
which clearly designated the relevant variables and established
the nature and weight of their influence.

Little is known about the way in which small firms develop
and grow and in particular the way that they find new products
and markets. It has, however, been recognised that small firms
face particular difficulties in applying for and obtaining
assistance under regional policy and its schemes. These have
been documented as: lack of awareness of schemes and their
applicability to small firms; impatience with the time taken to
process applications; and inability to provide the necessary
future plans and track record data as backup for the
application. Implicit in the application process for many such
schemes is the idea that the applicant can 'plan' his way ahead
in the same manner as the large company and to a similar degree
of sophistication. Thus difficulties in attracting the small

firm to the traditional incentives of regional 'hardware'
support are founded in the informality of the 'planning'
process in the small business.

   The literature search associated with the research revealed
the inadequacy of many of the planning models to the small
business and the associated absence of detailed characterisa-
tions of the development process in the firm.

   Generally the process of product and market diversification
has been discussed primarily in the context of large firms and
makes reference to: the role of research and development
departments; specific organisational forms (e.g. Venture
Groups); and the development of techniques for stimulating or
evaluating new product ideas. The 'process' of new product
development has been characterised as an idealised 'staged'
process as the firm rationally and sequentially plans its way
from an initial awareness of the need to change through to
commercial introduction (Parker, 1979; Carson and Richards,
1979). Whilst there was some evidence from earlier studies
that small firms do follow a sequential decision making process
(Cooper, 1966; Crawford and Merle, 1980), there was little in
the literature other than indications that the processes by
which the decisions are made in small firms are far more
informal and based on less sophisticated techniques than would
be common in larger firms.

   There is a vast literature on the factors which are thought
to influence the process of change in small firms. The
research attempted to draw out the major parameters, broadly
divided into external and internal factors.

   (a) The key external factors identified were:

   - The company's existing product range, and its position
     in the market.
   - The pressures for change already present in product
     (life cycle) and market (competition).
   - The range of different products and markets the
     company is involved in. Van Hoorn (1979) suggests
     this may limit the number of strategic alternatives
     open to the firm. Narrow market experience will limit
     the number and range of perceived alternatives; it
     will also limit knowledge of, and access to, informa-
     tion likely to stimulate new product development.
   - The age and development profile of the firm's major
     products, which affect the urgency with which change
     is required.
   - Environmental awareness, in terms of both 'perceived'
     and 'objective' environments. The former may be
     limited by factors such as dependency on a few

customers, leading to a 'blindness' about the real environment (Gibb et al, 1983).
- Market uncertainty and complexity and its organisational implications (Lawrence and Lorsch, 1967; Duncan, 1972).
- Rates of change in the economy as a whole.
- The existence of particular institutional or administrative blocks to progress, involving official 'permissions' for planning, standards, etc.
- Wider environmental factors, social, legal and political conditions which affect the firm's relationship with its environment.

(b) Key internal factors identified were:

- The owner manager: his personal and leadership characteristics. The following are well represented in the literature - his age and its impact on growth (Deeks, 1976); his occupational background (McGivern and Overton, 1980); personal objectives (Boswell, 1972); family influence both on his objectives and on his position within the companys' asset and decision making structures (Barry, 1975); concentration or dispersion of ownership (Saddler and Barry, 1970); management style and decision making abilities (Saddler and Barry, 1970); education and training levels (Wilkie and Young, 1971); and personal values and attitudes (Gabele, 1981).
- The presence or absence of highly qualified staff, and the extent of functional specialisation (Rothwell and Zegveld, 1980).
- The control system: how formalised.
- The managerial capability of the workforce, its flexibility and skills (Gibb, 1983).
- The financial situation of the company, with special reference to its liquidity.
- The age and quality of the physical assets of the company.
- The extent to which managerial time is available for coping with change (Gibb and Dyson, 1982).
- Levels of managerial motivation and commitment in relation to particular developments in the company, and especially the preferences between tasks (Saddler and Barry, 1970).

The monitoring process, which lasted for up to two years, was based on measures derived to test the above factors. The provision of assistance was the experimental variable: its affect on the other variables was also subject to monitoring.

DEVELOPING THE BASIC PROCESS MODEL

All the companies studied were intending one form of change,
i.e. development in product and/or market terms. Such change
may, of course, result mainly in survival and not produce any
'growth'. Furthermore, it may be more reactive to circumstance
than purely purposive. Nevertheless, there is involved a
process of movement from 'where we are now' to some future
'where we want to be', however vaguely articulated. Some
companies know more or less clearly from the outset where they
want to be: others only really know when they 'arrive'. There
may even be a range of destinations, with or without expressed
preferences. Figure 1 shows this simple first stage of
developing a model of the process.

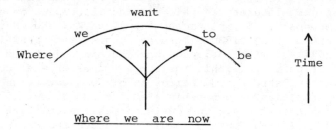

Figure 1   The basic process model

What appears in the simplified figure as a straight line
between 'present' and 'future', in reality was a complex
process with the following characteristics:

-   The firm's understanding of the potential of its ideas
    'emerges' during the process as part of its learning.
-   The process was highly iterative, and featured 'false
    starts' and 'red herrings'.
-   Evaluation of progress was largely on the basis of
    limited personal knowledge of the market, customer
    requirements and technology.
-   The information which was available was substantially
    derived from the owner manager's own contact network.

An attempt has been made (figure 2) to portray this process
in terms of 'levels'. The underlying philosophy is that after
the initiation of an idea it is subjected to progressively more
detailed testing, where success engenders further levels of
commitment.

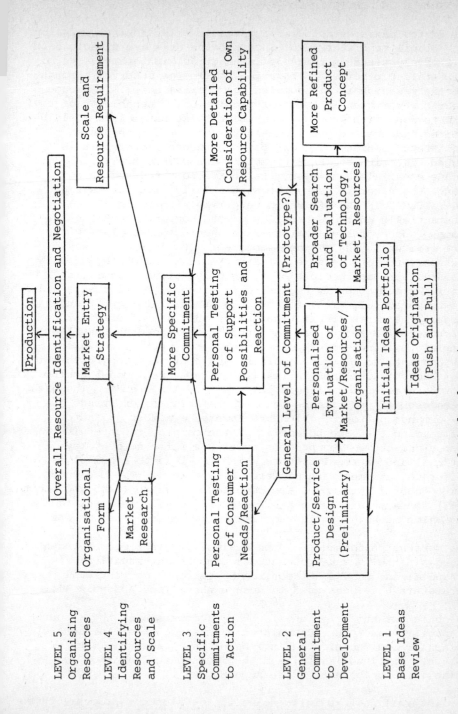

Figure 2   The stages of new product development

KEY INFLUENCES ON THE PROCESS

All of the characteristics discussed earlier as influences on
the capability of the firm to change and grow are dynamic both
in themselves and in terms of interaction with other factors.
The detailed process of their interaction as observed throughout the research is too complex to describe here. It became
clear however that in terms of prediction of capability of the
firm to cope with change a number of these parameters could be
grouped and used to profile each particular company in a
consistent fashion. The groupings of these factors, it is
argued, describe the BASE POTENTIAL FOR DEVELOPMENT. It
became clear also, however, that throughout the process of
change there were a number of particularly critical INTERNAL
and EXTERNAL INFLUENCES which were likely to impinge
substantially on the capability of the company to pursue the
process successfully. Moreover to understand completely the
base from which the company was seeking to develop it was
necessary to take measures of its EXISTING PERFORMANCE. Such
measures, perhaps because of their conventional pragmatic
nature, are frequently neglected in discussions of change and
growth potential. Yet, for example in determining attitudes of
lenders, measures of existing performance are of critical
importance. Moreover it was found in the research that lack of
complete awareness of this performance as part of the base for
development led to undue optimism and attitudes to growth which
could not be sustained in reality. The overall model posited
therefore is of the 'flower pot' variety (figure 3). The base
is made up of performance measures relating to existing
performance on top of which are layered a number of factors
influencing the base potential of the company to cope with
change and grow. The process itself is influenced by key
internal and external factors which may lead to a number of
different outcomes with different dimensions. The detailed
components of this model are reported elsewhere (Gibb and Scott,
1983) and Appendix A contains a summary of the relevant factors
for which measurement is required. In summary, these comprise:

The current performance of the business, described by recent
trends in the: market situation; production situation;
financial and management control situation. Conventional
parameters have been used to mesure these (see Appendix A1).

The base potential for development, comprising: the resource
(capacity) base; the accumulated experience base; the control
(planning and decision making) base; the leadership (style,
ownership attitude) base; and the ideas base (inventory of
ideas for development. (See Appendix A2)

Key internal factors influencing the development process; these

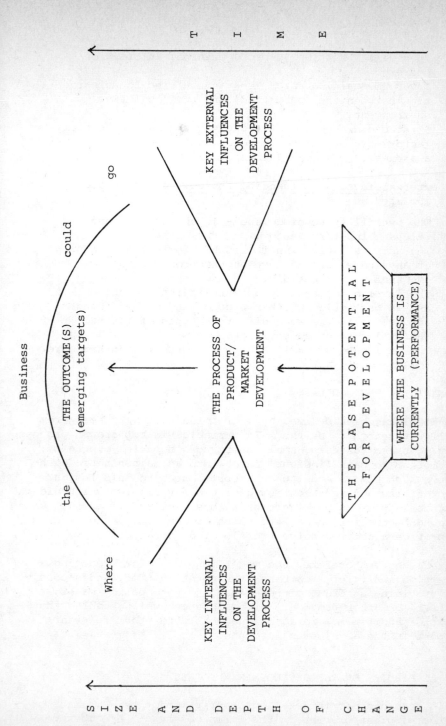

Figure 3　A model of growth through product/market development in the small firm

were isolated as:

- Management time available in the context of a lack of specialist staff, to explore external information sources.
- Environmental awareness, bearing in mind the distinction between the 'perceived' and the 'objective' environment.
- Strategic awareness, i.e. the way the base potential factors are organised in relation to the environmental awareness. (See Appendix A3)

Key external factors influencing the development process, these were isolated as:

- The overall state of demand - in the economy and relevant industry sector.
- The administrative/institutional blocks that can arise at any stage of the development process and frequently unexpectedly.
- The level of complexity and uncertainty in the market and in particular whether product and market changes involve moving between different types of market.
- The influence of competition.
- The influence of assistance both software and hardware. (See Appendix A3)

SUMMARISING THE MODEL

The model has been derived by extracting what were seen from earlier research to be the main variables in the growth process; testing these against a small number of companies over time; attempting to gain 'insight' into what was happening in each case and shaping a model which approximated to this insight. The refining and recategorising of those variables which did in practice appear to be significant, has resulted in a model with a sound theoretical base, and which pragmatically can be used to provide a comprehensive profile of a company.

In essence, therefore, the model is useful for producing a 'position audit' of a company at a point in time, and secondly for providing a 'frame of reference' for the policy maker, adviser, or other providers of assistance, which enables that position audit to be related dynamically to other relevant factors in the development process.

KEY ATTRIBUTES OF THE DEVELOPMENT PROCESS

Space does not permit detailed description of the dynamics of the development process in the firms observed. A number of

general pointers might however be made both about the overall
nature of the process and certain key attributes. These are
essentially in the nature of hypotheses given the limited size
of the sample: they do, however, receive support from other
research:

- Planning in the small business is likely to take place
  around a specific (or a number of specific) projects.
  It is unlikely to be formalised for the organisation
  as a whole in the large company planning sense.
- In the development process the firm is 'learning' all
  the time usually by coming up against problems and
  solving them rather than by anticipation (even where
  there is strategic awareness).
- This learning process often means that minor changes
  turn into major ones quite unexpectedly.
- The process is characterised by a great deal of
  personal learning by the owner manager and is influenced considerably by his personal appraisal and
  knowledge.
- The process of development is highly dynamic and
  highly iterative.
- Even when firms, measured by certain overall output
  parameters such as employment and turnover demonstrate
  little change, there may exist in fact a very high
  rate of change within the companies (which may never
  feed fully through into the conventional measures of
  growth).
- The process of development will be characterised by
  varying degrees of strategic awareness. Strategic
  awareness is defined as the ability of the owner
  manager to use a particular problem or opportunity to
  explore the wider ramifications of the new development,
  on his company and himself. Lack of such awareness is
  likely to lead the company into blind alleys.
- The absence of strategic or even simple planning
  (target) projections over several years may not
  reflect at all on the managerial capability of the
  company.

A number of further observations may be made about certain
key characteristics of the development process itself as
follows:

- There seemed to be no shortage of ideas for development
  in the companies. The triggers to development of the
  idea were however a mixture of push and pull factors.
  However it was evident that the companies with a wide
  network of contacts and previous new product/market
  development experience were more likely to be
  proactive.

- Organisational 'slack' was important in the firm taking a proactive approach.
- Spotting market gaps and indeed general market intelligence was done largely by personal contact. This was likely to pose major problems for firms moving into completely new markets.
- Ideas for new product development were very much related to the technical background of the owner manager.
- Major barriers to exploiting new ideas for development are likely to relate to inadequate awareness of the strength and weakness of the company's own current performance and base potential (and in particular its liquidity).
- There was little inclination to look actively for external assistance outside the existing personal network.
- There were difficulties in acquiring market information in the right form and at the right price. These difficulties did not altogether relate to the weakness of the company but as much to availability of adequate sources of market information.
- Shortage of finance or premises were not identified as major needs in the development process.
- There were recognised but not always completely thought out conflicts in the leadership base resulting from business/personal/family contradictions. These at times cut across professional managerial judgements.
- Lack of technical knowledge and contacts were barriers not only to the solution of problems, but to problem analysis itself. This meant that demand for technical advice was often latent and unrecognised.

THE INFLUENCE OF ASSISTANCE ON THE DEVELOPMENT PROCESS

The complexity of the development process in the companies and the numerous influences at work defies the establishment of simple one-to-one relationships between assistance inputs and outputs. It is possible however to comment upon the impact of the 'action inputs' at two levels: in terms of the impact they had upon the actions taken by the companies and the 'resultant' changes in parameters of employment, turnover, etc.; and in terms of the impact on the development process itself.

In practice a number of points can be reasonably inferred from observation of the process as follows:

- That the major impact of the sustained educational, counselling and information assistance was to encourage companies to explore more fully their base potential for development and to recognise their own strengths and weaknesses. It is firmly adduced that by this method the number of serious problems were reduced.

- In particular the more intensive assistance seemed to have an impact on the modification of the project as more advice, information and assistance was brought in to the owner manager about the environment. It is believed that such assistance leading as it did to modification of the project (sometimes substantially) was in fact anticipating the ultimate judgement of the market.

- It is recognised that major changes would probably still have taken place without the action inputs. They would probably however have been subject to a longer time scale, would have been more concerned with learning by doing and would have been based on more limited personal knowledge and awareness of the macro environment, the task environment and the assistance environment.

- Whereas it is difficult to make an overall judgement about the impact of the action inputs on major changes undertaken by the companies the research indicated that minor changes seemed to be much more linked to the support and encouragement provided by the whole range of information and counselling inputs.

- The use of the audit approach for exploring the current performance base and base potential for growth of the compnay provided a major vehicle for substantial revision of the project.

- The impact particularly of education, training and counselling assistance is to encourage the 'massaging' of the idea for development which can in itself be a 'trigger' by encouraging commitment. In this respect 'peer' support from other small businessmen can play an important role.

- The more intensive the approach the more likely it is to have an impact on environmental awareness particularly in respect of increasing the number of personal contacts.

- Intensive attempts to provide appropriate market information are likely to face limitations because of the inadequacy and irrelevance of much market data (especially in published form).

THE EFFECTIVENESS AND EFFICIENCY OF THE ACTION INPUTS

It is possible to make some statements about the relative efficiency and effectiveness of the action inputs which might be of value in redesigning assistance for small business. In particular it is important to identify the underlying assumptions which provide the rational basis for the provision of such assistance. These are set out below and contrasted with the findings of the research.

Information provision

There are several sets of assumptions underlying the provision of information as an intervention strategy as follows:

- That the client knows clearly what information is needed and can articulate it.
- That the client is aware of the sources of such information.
- That the client has motivation and ability to seek such information externally.
- That the information provision will be efficient.
- That the client knows how to use it once he has obtained it.

In practice particular problems arise in the provision of such information for the small business, which have been underlined in the research as follows:

- The low levels of awareness of the existence of information services resulting in turn from the lack of specialist and managerial time for environmental scanning.
- The inexperience of firms in defining and diagnosing problems particularly if they are moving into an unfamiliar area of experience or investigation.
- The inability of the small firm to articulate its information needs in a manner understandable to sources of outside assistance.
- The inability of the small firm to understand the information provided or to translate this information into the context of its own problems.
- The lack of resources in the small business for collecting information.

The types of information needed can be divided into two parts: that relating to the business itself; and that relating to the environment in general. The former will include information about the market, about technology, about suppliers, etc.: the latter will contain information about the various statutory and other constraints and opportunities surrounding the small business and the various forms of assistance that can be available to the firm. In the large company there is a complete line of communication involving specialists between the collection of market information, for example, and its ultimate translation into production. In the small owner managed business this process is carried on within the mind of the owner manager himself after information has been obtained on a personal contact basis. This shortens considerably the communication link, facilitates speed and, because of the absence of successive filters, limits distortion. On the other hand, because of the lack of specialist resources and the reliance on personal contact, information may be more limited and less objective. It is clear from this research that the agencies delivering information did not always take into account the difficulty of the owner manager in getting access to the information and the relevance of the information to his particular problem or circumstance. Nor did delivery systems always meet the needs of the businessman in terms of time.

Counselling provision

The differing role of the counsellor and consultant have been described elsewhere (Gibb, Scott, Webb, 1983). They may be used when there is a problem, an opportunity or an information need in the business, usually emanating from a change situation. The assumptions that underlie the provision of counselling and consulting services to small businesses may be summarised as follows:

- That the client has problems or opportunities that he cannot adequately address himself to.
- That he recognises this and therefore the need for counselling.
- That the client will look actively for assistance in this respect.
- That the client will provide open access to the counsellor and unfold truthful information.
- That the client will act on the counsellor's advice.
- That the counsellor himself/herself has adequate know-ledge, counselling skills, and relevant experience in relation to the company's problem or opportunity.

The research underlines that these assumptions are rarely fulfilled in reality in that:

- The owner manager is not always aware of his problem.
- He will rarely look outside for their solution.
- He is reluctant to provide information, particularly financial information.
- He is very price conscious in respect of paying for such services.
- He has little time either to research or implement counselling advice.

Education and training

The assumptions that underlie in the provision of education and training for owner managers can be summarised as follows:

- That the owner manager can analyse his company's problems.
- That he can in turn define his own learning needs related to these.
- That he can identify the courses or programmes required to fulfil these learning needs.
- That he has the time to attend them.
- That he has the time and commitment to apply the learning in the organisation.

The research would support the conclusion that these assumptions are not always fulfilled, in particular:

- The owner manager does not always analyse clearly the company's objectives or problems.
- He does not clearly diagnose his own knowledge need but will look around for courses that seem to offer solutions to the problems.
- The courses generally that are on offer are not particularly problem oriented and the owner manager sees little relevance in this.
- They tend to take him away from his work which creates difficulties.
- He has little time to implement knowledge inputs even when he accepts them.
- He therefore pursues his learning mainly by exposure (by doing).

SUMMARY AND CONCLUSIONS

The research has confirmed a number of previous findings about the behaviour of small firms over time, in particular: the lack of time to develop new ideas; the isolation of the owner manager and his reluctance to seek help outside of his personal contact network; the disregard of written information particularly when it is non specific; the lack of accessible and relevant market information and the reluctance to commission external market research because of its costs; the problems caused by interaction of family and business commitment; the unawareness of, and lack of concern for assistance agencies; and the deleterious effect of shortage of business skills.

The opportunity provided by the research to observe closely the behaviour of the companies over time and to experiment with action inputs has also facilitated the development of a model of the process of change and development which it has been demonstrated can be used in practice by owner managers for evaluation of their company and their development ideas. The research confirms the importance of the owner profiling his own company in the light of incomplete awareness of his own position. The research also supports the proposition that small firms learn by solving problems rather than by anticipating them. However action inputs, as provided in the research can have a number of impacts: they can provide a facility for proactive personal contact which can trigger development and reinforce the personal commitment of the owner to this; they can provide linkages for the identification and solution of technical barriers to growth; education in particular can provide a vehicle for learning from peers which can be an important motivating force; the provision of extra managerial resource creates slack within which development can take place; and supportive contact can considerably widen the environmental awareness and personal contact network of the owner.

Such conclusions are of course dependent upon the effectiveness of 'software' support systems and the research has suggested criteria for such effectiveness. For policy makers the results highlight the importance of: personal delivery systems in the provision of information; improving the specificity and relevance of information to the business; the price and resource barrier to market research; the need for counselling services to be proactive and to provide mechanisms for the owner manager better to analyse his own problems in the first instance; the need for education and training programmes to be problem/opportunity oriented to facilitate learning by exposure (which is the learning mode to which the owner is probably accustomed), to provide frameworks for the owner to diagnose the state of his own business and the validity of his business ideas, and to provide the support of his peers and resource for implementation where possible. The research also underlines the scope that there may be for 'organising' the assistance and information environment of the smaller firm in such a way that access and awareness is made easier. The importance of personal contact in the process of assistance also places a premium on the contact himself having a wide knowledge base (and personal contact with) the local assistance environment. There is considerable scope for proactive approaches to increase this awareness.

Finally the research emphasises that in the small owner managed firm the owner manager is virtually synonymous with the company. His development is the company's development. And, because of the organic nature of the development process, the resource constraints and the owner's limited horizons, assumptions of conventional rational economic behaviour in response to assistance stimuli cannot be made. This point serves to underline the importance of 'software' assistance to the small firm as opposed to 'hardware' and the potential that exists for linking both in taking an 'integrative' approach to small firms policy. (The traditional approach is very much a separatist one.) It also emphasises that in solving the 'selectivity' problem in small firms support the criteria to use might be the motivation, commitment and ability of the owner irrespective of which industry or service sector he/she is located in. Such persons will 'self-select' for support for they generally are the ones who will respond actively to 'hardware' incentives for development.

REFERENCES

Barry, B.A., (1975), 'The Development of Organisational Structure in the Family Firm', Journal of General Management, Autumn, vol.3, no.1, pp.42-60.
Boswell, J., (1972), The Rise and Decline of Small Firms, Geo. Allen & Unwin.
British Business, (1982), 'Regional Distribution of Births and Deaths of Firms in the U.K. in 1980', 2nd April, pp.648-9.
Carson, J.W. and Richards, T., (1979), Industrial New Product Development, Gower Press.
Cooper, A.C., (1966), 'Small Companies can Pioneer New Products', Harvard Business Review, September-October, pp.163-79.
Crawford, C. and Merle, (1980), 'The Idea Evaluation Function in Small Firms', Small Business Journal.
Deeks, J., (1976), The Small Firm Owner Manager: Entrepreneurial Behaviour and Management Practice, Praeger, N.Y.
Duncan, R.B., (1972), 'Characteristics of Organisational Environment and Perceived Environmental Uncertainty', Administrative Science Quarterly.
Gabele, E., (1981), Values in Small and Medium Firms, Universitat Bamberg.
Gibb, A.A. and Dyson, J., (1982), 'Stimulating the Growth of Owner Managed Firms', UK Small Business Research Conference, Glasgow.
Gibb, A.A., (1983), The Small Business Challenge to Management Education, MCB Publications.
Gibb, A.A. and Scott, M.G., (1983), 'Strategic Awareness, Personal Commitment and the Process of Planning in the Small Business', paper presented at 13th European Small Business Seminar, Hernstein Management Centre, Vienna.
Gibb, A.A., Scott, M.G. and Webb, T., (1983), 'An Action Research Approach to the Study of Small Firms and Industrial Change in a Development Area', Durham University Business School.

Lawrence, P.R. and Lorsch, J.W., (1967), 'Organisation and Environment: Managing Differentiation and Integration', Harvard Graduate School of Business Administration.

McGivern, C. and Overton, D., (1980), 'A Study of Small Firms and their Management Development Needs', in Gibb, A.A. and Webb, T., Policy Issues in Small Business Research, Saxon House.

Northern Region Strategy Team, (1977), Strategic Plan for the Northern Region, vol.1, Main Report, HMSO.

North of England County Councils Association, (1981), Third State of the Region Report.

Parker, R.C., (1979), Guidelines for Product Innovation, BIM, London.

Rothwell, R. and Zegveld, W., (1982), Innovation and the Small and Medium Sized Firm, Frances Pinter (Publishers) Ltd.

Saddler, P.J. and Barry, B.A., (1970), Organisation Development, Longmans.

Schein, E., (1969), Process Consultation: Its Role in Organisational Development.

Van Hoorn, T.P., (1979), 'Strategic Planning in Small and Medium Sized Companies', Long Range Planning, vol.12, April.

Wilkie and Young, J.N., (1971), The Owner Manager and Manager of a Small Firm, University of Strathclyde, October.

APPENDIX A1:   The current performance of the Business

THE MARKET SITUATION (Trends)	THE PRODUCTION SITUATION (Trends)	THE FINANCIAL AND MANAGEMENT CONTROL SITUATION (Trends)
Product Mix	Performance in terms of:	Net Worth
Customer Mix	Utilisation	Return on Capital Employed
Area	Efficiency	Liquidity Situation
Competition	Quality	Gearing
Channels	Wastage/Yield	Gross and Net Contribution
Sales Organisation		Product and Departmental Contribution
Marketing Mix		Net Profits
Needs met		Value Added

APPENDIX A2: The base potential for development

THE FINANCIAL AND PHYSICAL RESOURCE BASE	ACCUMULATED EXPERIENCE BASE	THE CONTROL BASE	THE LEADERSHIP BASE	THE IDEAS INVENTORY
- Liquidity and availability of finance - The technology - The physical assets - Labour skills plus standards - The product life	- Age of company - Experience of borrowing - Of product development - Of different types of markets - Of use of external agents	- The control systems - The degree of functional specialisation and responsibility - Decision making styles - Budgeting	- Ownership - Age of owner - Occupational background - Personal objectives - Education/ training background - Family influence - Attitude to change/ environment - Perceived threats and opportunities (including dependency) - Management style	- Ideas sources - Number and range of ideas - Degree of evaluation reached - Existence of prototypes and their testing - Relationship of ideas to market knowledge

APPENDIX A3: Key internal and external factors influencing the development process

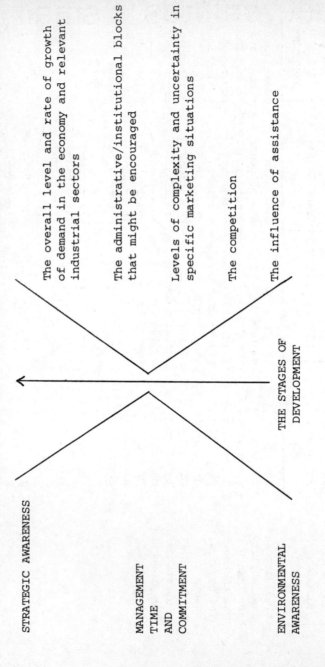

STRATEGIC AWARENESS

MANAGEMENT
TIME
AND
COMMITMENT

ENVIRONMENTAL
AWARENESS

THE STAGES OF
DEVELOPMENT

The overall level and rate of growth
of demand in the economy and relevant
industrial sectors

The administrative/institutional blocks
that might be encouraged

Levels of complexity and uncertainty in
specific marketing situations

The competition

The influence of assistance

The evaluation of new product ventures in small firms

ADAM ADAMS AND MARTIN WALLBANK

INTRODUCTION

Small firms generally operate in areas subject to many
pressures for change:

- change in customer's needs and expectations
- actions of competitors
- new technologies
- new competing products

New products may be introduced to reduce a firm's dependency
on volatile or demanding customers or markets. Investment in
new technology may be needed to meet new quality standards or
to maintain a competitive manufacturing cost performance.

In addition to such defensive strategies, new product
introductions offer a vehicle for expansion and growth into new
market areas, or for exploring new technologies offering long
term growth.

RISK IN INNOVATION

Except in a few limited and specialised areas firms failing to
introduce new products will atrophy and die.

Although new product ventures are essential for the longer term future of the business they also expose it to short term risk.

Thus the management of new products, their development and commercialisation is of critical importance to the smaller firm's future.

Each step in the venture can be thought of as a 'play'. Resources - the 'stake', are committed against an uncertain outcome - of success and gain, or of failure and loss - the 'gamble'. In a continuing game - a series of plays, the probability of ruin depends on the ratio of the stake in each play to the player's resources and on the probabilities of the failure and success for each play: the classical 'Gamblers Ruin' problem (Feller, 1969).

For low ratios of stakes to resources, such as small developments in very large firms, the probability of ruin is low and the outcome can be estimated from the probabilities and payoffs, the standard 'expectation'. When the ratio of stakes to resources becomes high the expectation may be positive but will not be reached if a series of adverse plays, failures at a number of stages, lose all the resources thus terminating the game with the ruin of the firm. The small firm may only have one chance!

To avoid high failure rates small innovating firms need to find ways of reducing the probability of ruin. The two routes to this are:

- to increase the ratio of owned resources to those hazarded in each 'play' - the Owned Funds to Stake ratio

- or to change the odds by using more effectively methods of assessing and managing the risk through each successive stage of the innovation process.

Investors organised in large funds, or large financial institutions such as the major clearing banks, can support a wider, diverse portfolio of innovative ventures with a negligible risk of ruin. They will however, not enjoy any appreciable return from their investments unless the fund managers can pick a high proportion of winners.

There are many possible ways of classifying the aspects which may determine the success or failure outcome of an innovation.

One of the simplest is to consider four key areas:

Technical Feasibility (The Idea/Product)	- can it be made, will it do what it was designed to do?
	- manufacturing processsess, operating, functioning?
Commercial Viability (The Market)	- Does anyone want what it does, who are the customers?
	- Can they be reached, competing products - firms?
Business Capability (Firm's Resources)	- Does the firm possess or can it acquire the methods, plant and people to make and distribute it at the required quantity, quality and price?
Personal Competences (Management)	- Has the management of the firm the required technical and management skills to develop and manage their venture in the firm.

When managing a new product venture the critical management activity is the making of regular and thorough reviews to update the original plan using achieved process and the latest information on future expectations, and if necessary to kill off and abandon a part completed innovation. This enables the firm to avoid the 'Concorde Syndrome' - the 'thin end of the white elephant' - continuing to pour resources into a venture which will fail for shortage of funds before development can be completed, or which will never recover the investment by commercial sales in the market.

THE EVALUATION OF NEW PRODUCT AND BUSINESS IDEAS

Wide availability of reliable evaluation techniques implemented in a cost-effective and accessible evaluation system could greatly improve the innovative and economic performance of small firms by enabling them to improve the quality of their decision making, and, by reducing some of the difficulties which currently inhibit effective venture support.

In the small firms sector very little use is made of venture capital - either as venture loans or equity investments (Adams and Walbank, 1981; Leyshon, 1983):

Venture Capital - Funds invested to back a business idea or innovation to finance research, development and design. Such essentially pre-market funding is difficult to find, seldom offered to or sought by small manufacturing firms.

Development and Expansion Capital - Most of the funds called 'venture capital' are low risk expansion, or development, funding of ideas which have completed their technical research and development stages - post market-launch funding.

Innovating firms need to be able to screen and select new ideas so that they can concentrate their efforts on those with the best potential and recognise areas of weakness or high risk for special attention during the innovation. Reliable assessment of potentials, risks and likelihoods of success can enable supporting organisations to allocate resources where they will lead to success. By reducing their risk exposure they may thus either earn higher financial returns, or extend their investment spectrum to earlier stages of innovations - to move from expansion finance toward venture finance.

Whilst a venture will fail from a failure of any one of these aspects innovative success depends on performing them all well.

Firms can minimise the risk by considering only Incremental Innovations. By staying within their existing, proven, knowledge base their estimates of times, costs and resources needs for development, manufacturing, distribution and selling activities can be based on well established current data and therefore, should be realistic.

If the idea is totally new and takes the firm into new technology, process or market areas - a Radical Innovation - the firm has little reliable information for planning the venture, they have to operate in areas of high uncertainty and thus accept high levels of risk.

Successful Radical Innovations can lead to very high growth and profits but at the expense of also accepting high risk exposure.

The successful innovation is the one that leaves the innovator richer than when he started - one that creates wealth, that adds to the innovator's resources over the life of the venture.

The two critical areas are:

- Will the combination of sales and revenue less manufacturing costs pay for the accumulated

investment in its development and lead to a positive
cash balance within the life cycle of the product?

- Can the firm afford to develop the idea - has it the
  funds to get past the peak negative balance, peak
  investment, which generally occurs during the growth
  phase some time after market launch?

A simple rule of thumb is that from 100 initial ideas only
around 10 will be developed seriously, 2 reach the market
leading to 1 commercial success (7 out of 8 new ideas never
reach the R & D stage (O'Meare, 1961)). The innovator has the
problem of managing this weeding out of ideas through the
successively more costly stages of the development (figure 1).
Surprisingly the 'abandon' decisions have seldom been studied
or reported in detail in the innovation literature.

When considering risk most organisations take a balance sheet
approach and only consider actual losses where resources have
been used and costs or investments cannot be recovered. In
decision making it is important to accept that we have to deal
with two types of error:

Type 1 Errors	-	Incorrect rejection of a correct hypothesis
	-	Incorrectly rejecting a 'good' potentially successful, idea
Type 2 Errors	-	Incorrect acceptance of an incorrect hypothesis
	-	Incorrectly backing a 'bad' idea which has to be abandoned during development or subsequently fails in the market

As the Type 2 Errors lead to actual investment in developing
a 'bad' idea and to easily quantifiable losses when it fails
most firms attempt to minimise such losses.

Assessing the 'opportunity cost' - the cash flow and profits
that would have been earned if the good product had been
developed instead of rejected by a Type 1 Error, is much more
difficult.

When attempting to pick the winners, studies of 'the ones
that got away' are rare yet the financial 'losses' may far
exceed the direct loss from a failure.

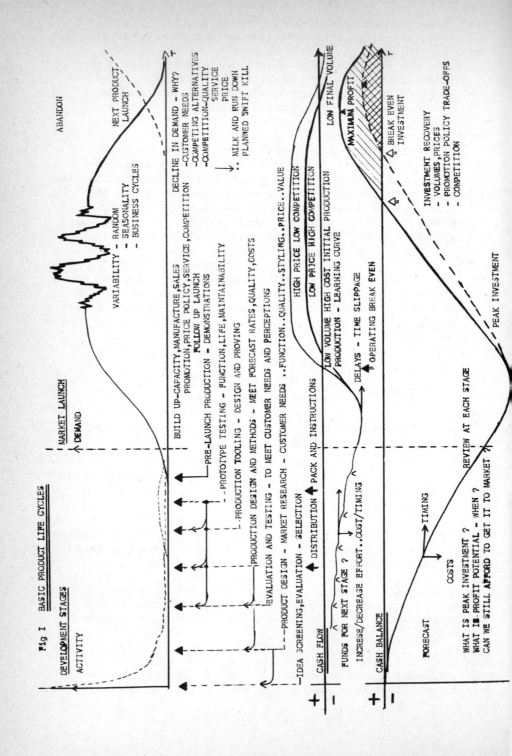

Fig I   BASIC PRODUCT LIFE CYCLES

110

The main current techniques for evaluating ideas for
screening, selecting and management of new product or business
ventures are:

Check lists   -   Lists of the aspects of the idea,
                        firm, market and environment which
                        should be considered when managing
                        the venture.

Ranking Methods   -   Comparison of two or more ideas
                        by ranking a list of aspects
                        which determine their merit. May
                        be a simple comparison or may use
                        weighted rankings.

Scoring Methods   -   Lists of key aspects with scoring
                        scales. May be simple or complex
                        models. May be used to select
                        using highest score or to screen
                        by comparison with a cut-off score.

Business   -   'Balance sheet' approaches using
Planning Models   period forecasts of sales, costs,
                        prices - discounted investments
                        and cash flows.

(Albala, 1975; Augood, 1973; Bruno and Cooper, 1974; Hart, 1960;
Mansfield and Wagner, 1975; Parker, 1974)

RECENT STUDIES

In the P.I.E.S. model developed by Baker and Udell (1980) the
applicant records his assumptions or forecasts on each of 33
factors describing the idea or product in terms of the social
impact, business risk, demand analysis, market acceptance and
competitive aspects. The completed list is then reassessed by
members of an expert panel. If the applicant and 'experts' are
in close agreement a pooled judgement can be used to make the
overall evaluation. If there is disagreement on any aspect
this may indicate an area of uncertainty and risk which should
be resolved before committing any significant resources to the
proposal.

Features leading to acceptance of the P.I.E.S. approach are:

- the simplicity of completing the questionnaire which
  uses five point scales anchored by clear verbal
  descriptions

- the provision of rapid and detailed feedback of the
    evaluation to the applicant

This is particularly important to independent inventors and
owners of very small or new businesses. By focusing on areas
of probable weakness on risk, supported by detailed comments
from the panel, an applicant or entrepreneur is given clear
guidance to concentrate his efforts on the potential problem
areas. This feedback can be used to improve the applicant's
innovative skills and may lead to successful second thoughts
when the idea in its first form would have failed.

The 'Sappho' series of studies (Rothwell, 1972) marked the
first use of the then newly practicable factor analysis methods
for detailed examination of innovative success or failure.

In his NewProd studies Cooper (1980) examined 102 successes
and 93 failures of products which had passed the normal
selection procedures in a sample of medium sized North American
firms. By using techniques for multiple regression, factor and
discriminant analysis Cooper made the most detailed examination
of the determinants of failure or success - the 'successful
dimensions'. The best combinations of discriminating factors
can then be used in the development of an empirically based
screening model.

A key point is the recognition that a factor may be highly
correlated with success, typically 'market pull' as opposed to
'technological push', yet also be nearly as highly correlated
with failure. Thus many of the factors linked with success
from earlier studies are ineffective discriminants for
screening ideas.

U.M.I.S.T. STUDIES

The initial study was of 263 new products introduced in 63
innovating small manufacturing firms with a comparison sample
of 14 non-innovating firms (Adams and Walbank, 1981).

This study indicated that:

  - a high proportion of turnover and profits came from
    products introduced within the last 5 years

  - that most firms had a backlog of ideas awaiting
    resources for development and commercialisation

  - that the failure rate of new products is high

- that nearly all the funding of new product
development was from internal sources

Obtaining venture, pre-market funding, as opposed to post-
market, development, funding was very difficult and external
funding was very seldom used in the development stages by
established smaller manufacturing firms.

A detailed follow up study of eight new products from the
sample and a further 18 from entries in a national innovation
competition provided further evidence that the venture finance
gap is a major constraint to innovation in small firms, that
judgements made by supporting and financial organisations are
often highly inconsistent and that ideas are often more readily
accepted for commercialisation overseas (Longstaff, 1981).

In the current study over 250 aspects of ideas, markets,
firms and the commercial environment were examined for 94
successful product innovations, 46 market failures and 29 ideas
abandoned in the pre-market stages.

When studying and developing screening and selection systems
we must consider all three possible outcomes. Following an
initial go-ahead decision these are:

- to abandon during the pre-market development stages
  - the abandon

- to continue - the idea then failing in the market
  - the failure

- to continue - the idea surviving in the market
  - the success

Intuitively we would expect that the factors and loadings
used in initial, or early stage, screening and selection
evaluations to commit resources to developing the idea, will be
different to those emerging from the study of eventual success
or failure in the market stage.

Factors which are highly important to the review and
management of successive stages of the venture may not emerge
from studies limited to market outcomes. Also, when making
early 'go-ahead' or 'abandon' decisions many factors which are
linked to market failures are not known and therefore, cannot
be used in early stage evaluations - screening or selection.

113

ANALYSIS

It is easy to use simple regression methods to show that correlations of specific factors with the outcomes of the ventures are highly significant. This can be of value in demonstrating that a factor increases or decreases new product success in the way predicted by a theory or model. Similarly, bivariate correlations can also be used to determine factors which show no significant correlations with the outcomes.

The problem with correlation studies is that for large samples high levels of significance can be established even when the correlations between levels of the variable and the outcome are low. Thus the mean values of the variable 'Production process totally new to the company' were 1.68 for successes and 2.95 for failures. The difference in means is significant at the 0.01 level which provides very strong support for the view that the use of new manufacturing process increase the risk of failure. The correlation coefficient however is $r = -0.22$. This implies that under 5 per cent of the variance correlates with the variable, far too low for use of the factor on a 'one-off' basis for screening or selecting new product ideas.

As our aim is to develop a practical and reliable selection system rather than to test theories, most effort has concentrated on the use of factor analysis to reduce the large number of possible factors, many of which are highly inter-correlated, to a smaller set of independent factors with a clear structure. These 'success dimensions' (Cooper, 1980) can then be used with loadings determined by stepwise multiple regression to develop reliable discriminant models.

Most of the current approaches to evaluating new products can be criticised as they lead to single 'global' models. When the wide range of types of small firm, their products and markets is considered it appears unlikely that any single model can lead to reliable screening or evaluation over the whole spectrum. The fit of a model and thus its validity and accuracy as a predictor can be improved by including and correctly using more information. Thus the use of 'Sectoral Models' based on the technology-market-environment and applied selectively should improve the performance of evaluation systems.

Earlier we implied criticism of most approaches for omitting the 'abandon' decisions. In practice the management of the aborted proposals is important as they may be more frequent than the adopted ones, and any theories based only on market failures may lead to distorted views of the sequential nature of new product management.

114

As the project develops, more information becomes available which is based on making the best use of all the information available at that stage of the venture. The study provides clear evidence that the selection and weightings of variable changes from stage to stage and so the screening and selection reliability can be improved by using both stage and sectoral models.

The programme is planned on an iterative basis working toward an adaptive expert type of evaluation system. Thus in operation the details of evaluations would be stored and periodically matched with follow-up assessments of the outcomes. Such new data can then be added to the original set and the analysis repeated to update the discriminant equations. Such adaptation in which the system evolves in response to developments, in this case the environment and economy within which small firms operate, to maintain the model's match with reality is a necessary element in any 'expert' decision support system.

STAGE MODELS

The idea of regular stage reviews for risk reduction in the management of innovative ventures has already been introduced. At each stage the investment is generally higher than for the earlier ones. At the initial decision to adopt the innovation the information is limited but the direct cost of the commitment to the first stages - to carry out a detailed evaluation - is low. At later stages - especially market research, product testing, production tooling etc. the costs are high but the manager has information from the earlier stages to improve his decision quality, and, actual appraisals can replace the estimates for activities carried out and communication variables.

By using a series of Stage Models which are structured to make the most effective use of the information available at each stage we can progressively improve the quality of the evaluations and risk exposure as the innovation progresses.

Apart from some minor statistical quirks, possibly partly explained by reduction of the 'abandoned' sample at different stages, the pattern is of the expected form and the reliability increases as more information is used. As this study is based on post-analysis with data selected to match that available at each stage we would expect that 'less time for the assumptions to change' will enhance the improvement when using stage models in real time applications.

Table 1
Performance of discriminant function

--% correct classification

STAGE	Success/ abandon	Success/ all failures	Success market failures
Screening	81.3	78.7	83.6
Prototype	84.9	80.4	83.5
Production design	87.7	86.3	86.1
Production start up	86.0	84.4	82.7
Market launch	-	-	92.7

SECTORAL MODELS

When the diversity of technology, markets and competition, sizes or firm and resources available are considered we would expect to find that these interact in different patterns and that the best evaluation model will be related to patterns of such factors as descriptor or moderating variables. Although a single 'global' screening model offers far more reliable prediction of new product outcomes than the standard check list, ranking or scoring techniques, even better performance will result from correct use of specifically developed 'Sectoral Models'.

The two main tasks when developing and using sectoral models are to decide:

1. How should the models be selected?
2. How many models should be developed? What are the trade-offs between complexity in application, increases in validity and reductions in statistical reliability?

Many aspects, technology, markets, firm etc., all appear to offer sensible bases for sectoral models. When more than one aspect is considered such partitioning leads to combinatorial problems in analysis. Thus, including three sizes: 1-20, 21-50, 51-200; three levels of technology: Lo,M,Hi; ten types of industry (S.I.C. Class); two market sectors, industrial/ consumer-leads to 180 cells. Any empirical data would then be spread very thinly and few combinations have sufficient cases for analysis.

The alternative approach is to take a completely empirical approach and derive the membership and definitions of the models by using hierarchical clustering methods. Having sorted the cases into groups with similar properties on the discriminant variables the screening models and application rules can be readily determined.

When deciding how many sectoral models should be used we have to consider two sets of trade-offs. One would expect that as the number of sectoral models increase from a single, global, broad brush approach, progressively better fits for a given proposal can be achieved and the validity of the evaluation will increase. More models imply more detailed application rules for selecting the correct model and so to more complex operating procedures (figure 2).

Increasing the number of sectoral models decreases the number of cases used in determining the discriminating screening variables - the sample is spread more thinly and the statistical reliability will decrease.

FACTOR ANALYSIS

As many of the variables are inter-correlated or have only very weak links with the outcomes, the number of variables can be reduced by using principal component analysis. The large number of variables can then be reduced to a more manageable set of principal components or dimensions which after varimax rotation are independent (orthogonal).

The factor analysis was carried out on a stage basis using only the variables which would have been available at each stage, for success/abandoned, success/market failure and success/all failures. In each case clear structures were obtained.

The best form of descriptor equations was determined at each stage by using stepwise multiple regression. This leads to a still more compact set as factors with low loadings can be dropped with little loss of power (table 2).

As many individual variables correlate highly with more than one outcome - both success and failure, they lack discriminant power for screening or selection purposes. The best combination for predicting the outcome of a venture can then be determined by discriminant analysis or by stepwise regression on the orthogonal grouped factors.

From tables 2 and 3 it can be seen that correlations and discriminating functions change progressively through each stage of the innovative process.

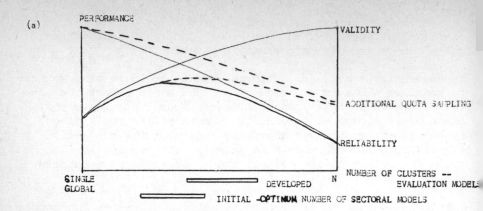

(a)

PERFORMANCE

VALIDITY

ADDITIONAL QUOTA SAMPLING

RELIABILITY

SINGLE GLOBAL

DEVELOPED

NUMBER OF CLUSTERS --
EVALUATION MODELS

INITIAL -OPTIMUM NUMBER OF SECTORAL MODELS

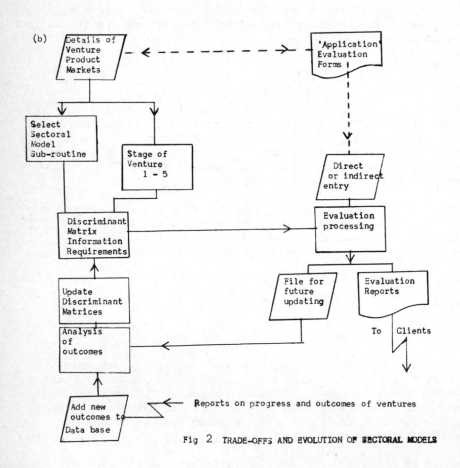

(b)

Details of Venture Product Markets

'Application' Evaluation Forms

Select Sectoral Model Sub-routine

Stage of Venture 1 - 5

Direct or indirect entry

Discriminant Matrix Information Requirements

Evaluation processing

Update Discriminant Matrices

File for future updating

Evaluation Reports

Analysis of outcomes

To Clients

Add new outcomes to Data base

Reports on progress and outcomes of ventures

Fig 2 TRADE-OFFS AND EVOLUTION OF SECTORAL MODELS

118

REGRESSION ...REGRESSSION COEFFICIENTS

TABLE 2

FACTOR NUMBER DESCRIPTION *		SCREENING		PROTOTYPE DEVELOPMENT		PRODUCTION DESIGN		PRODUCTION START UP		COMMERCIAL-ISATION
		MS/A	MS/MF	MS/A	MS/MF	MS/A	MS/MF	MS/A	MS/MF	MS/MF
1	Market Diversification	.788	-.443	-	-.335	.320	-	-	-	-
2	Technical Knowledge, Synergy of Technical Resources with Project	-	.624	.631	.579	.477	-	.869	.686	-
3	Market Dynamism	-	-	-	-	-	-	-	-	-
4	Product Differential Advantage	.453	.868	.539	.792	-	.522	-	.689	.399
5	Synergy of Resources with Project	.596	.798	-	-	.525	-	-	-	-
6	Product Visibility	.397	-	-	-	-	-	.674	-	-
7	Product Complexity	-	-.457	-.484	-.480	-.284	-.333	-.394	-.450	-.343
8	Market Growth	-	-	-	-	-	-	-	-	-
9	Project Risk Exposure	.409	.706	-	.544	-	.368	-	-	-
10	Finance Needs	-	-	-	-	-	-	-	-	-
11	Defensive Allocation of Resources	-	-	-	-	-	-	-	-.327	-
12	Regulatory Impact	-	-.299	-	-	-	-	-	-.341	-.208
13	Proficiency of Technical, Commerical & Financial Assessment	-	-	.477	.793	.338	.480	-	-	-
14	Synergy of Marketing & Managerial Resources with Project	-	-	-	.481	-	-	-	-	-
15	Technical Aid Needed & Used at Early Stages	-	-	-.553	-	-	-	-	-	-
16	Customer Involvement	-	-	.502	-	.360	-	-	-	-
17	Marketing & Management Aid Needed	-	-	-.441	-	-.443	-	-	-	-
18	Manufacturing Aid Needed and Used at Early Stage	-	-	-	-	-	-	.485	-	-
19	Finance Needed & Raised at Early Stage	-	-	-	-	-	-	-	-	-
20	Knowledge of Customers & Competitors	-	-	-	-	-	.325	-	-	-
21	Proficiency of Product Development Activities	-	-	-	-	.668	.052	-	-	-
22	Technical Aid Needed & Used	-	-	-	-	-.591	-.318	-.602	1.230	1.152
23	Marketing Knowledge, Proficiency & Resource Synergy	-	-	-	-	-	-	1.055	-	-
24	Product Safety	-	-	-	-	-	-	-	-	-
25	Marketing Aid Needed and Used	-	-	-	-	-	-	-	-	.323
26	Knowledge of Competitors	-	-	-	-	-	-	.439	-	-
27	Technical and Manufacturing Proficiency	-	-	-	-	-	-	-	-	.729
28	Technical Help Post Launch	-	-	-	-	-	-	-	-	-.546

* These are compound factors describing varying numbers of highly inter-correlated measured variables.

TABLE 3

DISCRIMINANT ..STANDARDISED FUNCTION
ANALYSIS   COEFFICIENTS

FACTOR NUMBER	DESCRIPTION *	SCREENING		PROTOTYPE DEVELOPMENT		PRODUCTION DESIGN		PRODUCTION START UP		COMMERCIAL-ISATION
		MS/A	MS/MF	MS/A	MS/MF	MS/A	MS/MF	MS/A	MS/MA	MS/MF
1	Market Diversification	-.420	-.444	-	-.409	-.191	-.320	-	-.203	-.351
2	Technical Knowledge, Synergy of Technical Resources with Project	.760	.261	.479	.298	.293	-	.617	.259	-
3	Market Dynamism	-	-	-	-	-	-	-	-	-
4	Product Differential Advantage	.456	.807	.398	.695	-	.587	.283	.615	.410
5	Synergy of Resources with Project	-	.354	-	-	.259	-	-	-	-
6	Product Visibility	.447	.263	-	-	-	-	.406	-	-
7	Product Complexity	-.655	-.283	-.528	-.409	-.353	-.279	-.493	-.414	-.298
8	Market Growth	-	-	-	-	-	-	-	-	.165
9	Project Risk Exposure	.419	.564	-	.435	.211	.334	-.264	-.216	-
10	Finance Needs	-.296	-	-	-	-.330	-	-	-.240	-.140
11	Defensive Allocation of Resources	-	-	-	-	-	-	-	-	-
12	Regulatory Impact	-	-	-	-	-	-	-	-	-
13	Proficiency of Technical, Commerical & Financial Assessment	-	-	.400	.440	.350	-	-	-	-
14	Synergy of Marketing & Managerial Resources with Project	-	-	-	.209	-	-	-	-	-
15	Technical Aid Needed & Used at Early Stages	-	-	-.621	-	-	-	-	-	-
16	Customer Involvement	-	-	.336	.160	-	-	-	-	-
17	Marketing & Management Aid Needed	-	-	-.217	-	-	-.135	-	-	-
18	Manufacturing Aid Needed and Used at Early Stage	-	-	.271	-	-	-	.307	-	-
19	Finance Needed & Raised at Early Stage	-	-	-.224	-	-	-	-	-	-
20	Knowledge of Customers & Competitors	-	-	-	-	-	.385	-	-	-
21	Proficiency of Product Development Activities	-	-	-	-	.532	.562	-	-	-
22	Technical Aid Needed & Used	-	-	-	-	-.484	-	-.512	-	-
23	Marketing Knowledge, Proficiency & Resource Synergy	-	-	-	-	-	-	.707	.669	.050
24	Product Safety	-	-	-	-	-	-	-	-.229	-.261
25	Marketing Aid Needed and Used	-	-	-	-	-	-	-	.206	.325
26	Knowledge of Competitors	-	-	-	-	-	-	-	-	-
27	Technical and Manufacturing Proficiency	-	-	-	-	-	-	-	-	.449
28	Technical Help Post Launch	-	-	-	-	-	-	-	-	-.376

* These are compound factors describing varying numbers of
highly inter-correlated measured variables.

Table 4

Comparison between NewProd and UMIST study – Multiple regression analysis:
market success/market failure

NEWPROD

FACTORS	Regression coefficients
Product superiority & uniqueness	1.744
Overall project/co.resource compatibility	1.138
Market need, growth & size	.801
Economic (dis)advantage of product	-.772
Newness to firm	-.345
Technological & resource compatibility	.342
Market competitiveness	-.301
Product customness/specialisation	-.225

Constant .328

$r^2 = .385$

UMIST

FACTORS	Regression coefficients
Marketing knowledge proficiency & synergy of marketing resources with project	1.152
Technical & manufacturing proficiency	.729
Technical help needed and used at market & post launch stages	-.546
Marketing aid needed & used pre-market launch	.323
Products differential advantage	.399
Product complexity	-.343
Defensive allocation of resources	-.208

Constant 4.50

$r^2 = .572$

As expected, the pattern and weightings of factors describing UK smaller firms differed from those found by Cooper in his study of larger firms in Canada (table 4).

DISCUSSION

The survival of many smaller manufacturing firms is at risk. This is due to their low propensity to innovate and of poor performance when they do. This poor performance is strongly linked to three aspects of current practice:

1. Lack of a reliable and easily accessible, cost-effective, technique for screening and selecting ideas - for picking the winners.

2. Inability to tap expert opinion on the technical, marketing and manufacturing features of the ideas.

3. Lack of feedback of reasons for rejection by supporting organisations or from an independent 'objective' appraisal limits their learning process and development of entrepreneurial skills.

The results of the study show that it is possible to develop evaluation techniques based on empirical evidence. The predictive performance of an overall discriminant based Global Model is much higher than current methods. By using a Stage analysis it can also be shown that the form and parameters of the discriminant model change through the successive stages of the project and that the performance can be improved by using the correct model to maximise the use of the available information at each stage. In practice this approach could also be used in periodic reviews within a risk reducing incremental project management approach.

The study also demonstrates that Sectoral Models are more reliable than single global ones. This results from the increasing validity due to the use of more information in selective application. Determining the best structure of the limited number of sectoral models which we can develop whilst maintaining statistical accuracy forms part of our current studies. As well as offering an increase in performance a great attraction of sectoral models is that they can improve their acceptability of the system to clients. Entrepreneurs tend to argue 'We are different' ... everyone is a special case! Decision makers tend to resist 'expert systems' even though when tested the computer expert systems consistently outperform human judges. Selection of the correct sectoral

model and stage allows the applicant to see that the evaluation
is being closely matched to his particular innovation.

In the introduction we suggested that new product success was
linked to four main groups of factors: Technical Feasibility -
Business Capability - Commercial Viability and Personal
Competences. The study is based on paired comparisons of
Abandon-Success, Market failure-Success cases within firms.
This approach was selected to partly confound the variability
resulting from Personal Competence factors describing the owner
or manager of the firm.   There will be some cross correlation
between such personal factors and the 'proficiency of
activities undertaken' but as far as possible we have attempted
to base the screening model on the product and its markets, the
non-personal factors. The aim is to predict what the idea
should do in the market. A highly skilled entrepreneur may
make a success of a 'poor' idea, a bad one may fail with a
potentially good new product.

Many investors and backers pride themselves on being able to
pick the man. Their decisions, usually based on highly
subjective criteria and incomplete information, are often
correct, but they also select many failures. The use of
empirical evaluation techniques to make more objective forecasts of what should happen, which can then be used as
reference points or yardsticks for assessing performance, opens
up new dimensions in the study of entrepreneurial attitudes and
abilities. Comparison of achievement with potential allows
track records to be put into perspective. Detailed empirical
evaluation of new projects offers more information on areas
requiring specific abilities or resources to maximise the
essential match between the man, his business and the idea.
The essence is to complement backer's existing skills, to use
information more effectively to improve both initial commitment
and subsequent monitoring decisions and, to enhance their
learning process by offering clearly structured and reliable
information feedback.

From this study we have the basis of an effective and
powerful evaluation technique and which can be further improved
by additional sampling. For practical application we can
reduce the number of data input variables to the minimum
necessary to determine the discriminant factors. User
acceptability can be increased by offering sectoral models -
tailor made to his requirements, and, by offering a much more
objective and detailed feedback of strengths and weaknesses of
his idea than at present. Such detailed feedback can form a
key input into his learning process and should lead to an
improvement in levels of entrepreneurial skills.

In this research we have established a large and detailed data base which can be extended and updated by data capture during application for project evaluation. Although many individual findings challenge past ideas on the selection and management of new product ventures the main importance of this empirical approach is that it is based on making the most effective use of the information available. Thus the current single, conceptual, global, models and evaluation techniques should be replaced by one of a limited set of sectoral models. As the decision may be made at any stage of the innovation from initial screening of ideas to review of the idea in the post-market stage, models based on success/ market failure only are of limited use and should be replaced by using one of a sequence of stage models.

Such 'expert' systems will never replace the 'illogical' human hunches which can lead to breakthroughs. In the majority of cases judgements are made on a more routine and rational basis. The ability of such a system to use all the relevant information and combine it in the most effective way guarantees higher levels of decision quality and consistency than are currently made with existing techniques.

REFERENCES

Adams, A.H. and Walbank, W.M., (1981), 'The Introduction of New Products by Smaller Manufacturing Firms', SRC Final Report GR/A 71072, Management Sciences Department, UMIST.

Adams, A.H. and Walbank, W.M., (1983), 'New Products - Risks and Strategies for Smaller Firms', Int. Jnl. Operations and Production Management, vol.3-2, pp.33-36.

Albala, A., (1975), 'Stage Approach for the Evaluation and Selection of R & D Projects', IEEE Transactions on Engineering Management, vol.22-4, pp.153-164.

Augood, D.R., (1973), 'A Review of R & D Evaluation Methods', IEEE Trans., Engineering Management, vol.20-4, p.112-120.

Baker, D.G. and Udell, G.G., (1980), 'PIES II - Manual for Innovation Evaluation', University of Wisconsin Small Business Development Centre, Madison, Wisconsin.

Bruno, A.V. and Cooper, A.C., (1974), 'Predicting Performance in New High Technology Firms', American Academy of Management Conference Proceedings, pp.426-428.

Cooper, R.G., (1980), 'Project NewProd - What Makes a Product a Winner', Quebec Industrial Innovation Centre, Montreal, Quebec.

Feller, W., (1969), An Introduction to Probability Theory and its Applications, J. Wiley, New York.

Hart, A., (1966), 'A Chart for Evaluating Research and Development Projects', O.R. Quarterley, vol.17, pp.347-358.

Leyshon, A., (1982), 'The U.K. Government Small Business Model - A Review', European Small Business Journal, vol.1-1, p.58-66.

Longstaff, R., (1981), Diploma Dissertation Management Sciences Department, UMIST.

Mansfield, E. and Wagner, S., (1975), 'Organisational and Strategic Factors Associated with Probabilities of Success in Industrial R & D', Journal of Business, vol.48, p.179-198.

O'Meara, J.T., (1961), 'Selecting Profitable Products', Harvard Business Review J.F., p.83-89.

Parker, R.C., (1974), 'R & D Evaluation', Institute of Mechanical Engineers, Conference Publication, no.12, p.12-17.

Rothwell, R., (1972), 'Factors for Success in Industrial Innovation - Project Sappho', Science Policy Research Unit, University of Sussex, Brighton.

Small firms, large firms: theoretical and research strategies for the comparative analysis of small and large firms in the wider environment

JAMES CURRAN AND JOHN STANWORTH

INTRODUCTION

In the explosion of research on the small firm over the last decade or so, the tendency has been to concentrate almost exclusively on the small firm itself with little or no systematic comparison with its counterpart, the large firm. Given the previous neglect of the small firm or the tendency to treat small firms as simply large firms writ small, this narrow, inward theoretical and research focus might be seen as having been entirely explicable and even desirable. Now, however, with the emergence of a mature body of theory and findings on the small enterprise, the problem of situating the small firm in its wider environment has re-emerged.

Of course, much of the research of the recent past has made assertions about the environment of the small enterprise but rarely on any systematic, theoretical basis. The present paper is concerned with one aspect of relating the small firm to its organisations. Our central argument is that research on the small enterprise now suggests that previous approaches are fundamentally deficient and that a new, more sophisticated approach is required.

APPROACHES TO UNDERSTANDING SIZE STRUCTURE RELATIONSHIPS

Undoubtedly, the most important set of studies analysing
relationships between size and organisational structure were
those of the Industrial Administration Research Unit of the
University of Aston in the 1960s and early 1970s (Pugh and
Hickson, 1976; Pugh and Hinings, 1976). The approach and style
of these studies may be taken as paradigmatic of the great
majority of studies on the topic conducted in both Britain and
the United States. Their influence on other theorists and
researchers has been enormous and continues up to the present
(see, for recent examples, Agarwal, 1979a and b; Zey-Ferrell,
1979; Grinyer and Yasai-Ardekani, 1981).

The major stimulus for the Aston Studies was Woodward's
research (1965) on manufacturing firms which identified
technology as the major determinant of organisational structure.
The Aston Group replicated Woodward's study using a more
refined conceptualisation of organisational structure and more
sophisticated methodological strategies. They concluded that
size was a much more important dimension than Woodward had
implied, particularly in larger organisations, though
technology still had wide structural effects in smaller
organisations (Hickson et al, 1969, p.395).

An important theoretical weakness in this whole series of
studies may be seen as stemming originally from Woodward's work.
She deliberately excluded all firms employing less than 100
people on the grounds that there was no clearly defined level
of management between Board and operators, and that such firms
had few organisational problems (Woodward, 1965, p.9). Yet
small firms in this way constituted almost half of her
potential sample and, as a number of studies have clearly shown,
small firms are just as prone to organisational problems as
large firms (Collins et al, 1964; Stanworth and Curran, 1973;
Kets de Vries, 1977; Curran and Stanworth, 1979b).

The Aston Group researchers apparently followed Woodward in
constructing their samples. Their main samples were the
original 'main study' with 52 organisations ranging from 241 to
25,052 personnel (Pugh et al, 1968, p.67) a replication study
of 40 organisations ranging in size from 'over 250' to 'over
5,000' (Inkson et al, 1970, p.320), a small sample of nine
manufacturing organisations ranging from 114 to 2,454 (Hinings
and Lee, 1971, p.85) and the 'National Sample' where the 82
organisations' sizes ranged from 108 to 9,778 (Child, 1972, p.
166). Since a high proportion of the units in several of these
samples were in fact branches of larger organisations, the
above figures understate the bias towards large organisations.

It may be assumed that this exclusion of small firms was primarily motivated by methodological convenience. Small organisations are notoriously difficult to research. Their owners are often busy people with little time for, and often also little sympathy with, academic research. They are essentially practical people with a strong distrust of the abstract and theoretical (Kets de Vries, 1977). Each negotiation of entry into a firm tends to be time consuming yielding relatively little data simply because the organisation is small. The temptation, therefore, is to devote available research resources to medium and large sized organisations. In Britain, as in most other industrial societies, the size distribution of firms, as measured by the number of persons employed, is highly skewed. For instance, in manufacturing industry well over 90 per cent of firms employ less than 100 people (Report on the Census of Production 1980, 1983, p.246).

Most researchers adopting the Aston Group approach have recognised the problems arising from the highly skewed distribution of samples of organisations by using a logarithmic expression of size for most of their calculations. Otherwise the skewed size distributions would lead to 'extreme score' effects in many statistical manipulations. Logarithmic transformation techniques therefore seek to compensate for the way in which small organisations greatly outnumber large organisations in so many economic and other contexts but this does not explain why researchers have so often excluded small organisations from their samples entirely. It is also noticeable that, when an analysis has used both logarithmic and natural size values, there have sometimes been large differences in the results obtained (Robey et al, 1977; Agarwal, 1979a, pp.445-447). This renders any analysis arrived at entirely by using the logarithm of the number of organisational members somewhat suspect.

But perhaps the most serious weakness of this pre-eminent approach to the analysis of size-organisation relationships, concerns the failure successfully to incorporate or articulate non-structural aspects of size (Silverman, 1970; Benson, 1977; Salaman, 1979; Zey-Ferrell and Aiken, 1981). The Aston Group researchers virtually ignored non-structural aspects of size although in an original statement of aims they indicated an awareness of their importance (Pugh et al, 1963 pp.312-314). In the relatively few attempts to investigate non-structural aspects of size in their samples, the emphasis tended to be on elite members of the organisation, particularly managers, and the findings were only imperfectly related to size (Pugh and Payne, 1977).

INDIVIDUALS AND ORGANISATIONS

A limited number of studies have focussed on the impact of organisational size on the individual reactions to size, and on the inter-connection between size and social relations within the organisation (Porter and Lawler, 1965; Ingham, 1967; Hall, 1977, pp.113-119; Berger and Cummings, 1979). The impact of these studies has been diffuse since those involved have not formed a 'school' in the same way as the Aston Group, and their existence and results have been considered independently of the work of the latter. The overall consensus of these individual organisational analyses is that large size is linked with feelings of lack of involvement, lower morale and lower levels of intrinsic job satisfaction, the precise relationships often depending on type of organisation context - economic, political, etc., as well as on the characteristics of organisational members themselves.

As Porter and Lawler pointed out (1965, p.40) there is a good deal of vagueness in these studies. For instance, there is often doubt as to whether members' reported reactions refer to the immediate work group or to the organisation as a whole. Such reactions may also refer to other sub units or collectivities within the organisation such as a particular branch, site, geographical region or occupational grouping. Berger and Cummings, in their more recent review (1979, pp.188-89) list only six further studies on the relationship between organisational size and attitudes and/or behaviour of members, since the Porter and Lawler review. They conclude that this additional data has not substantially clarified the relationships thought to exist.

Most studies of individual organisational relations usually assume simple causal relations linking variations in individual attitudes and behaviour with differences in organisational size. But, as some studies have shown, size may be a moderating variable coupled to other more basic influences. For instance, Batstone (1975) concluded that 'the ethos of small town capitalism', a set of community based beliefs and experiences, was the most important determinant of relations within the small enterprise rather than influences directly attributable to the number of people involved.

Curran and Stanworth (1979a) reported that in small printing firms worker-supervisor relations were more conflict prone than in large printing firms because the greater opportunities for direct contact between worker and supervisor went against the industry's strong sub cultural emphasis on shop floor worker autonomy. In small electronics firms, on the other hand, they reported closer worker-supervisor relations than in large electronic firms because the industry's sub culture stressed a close, consultative relationship between worker and supervisor and this was more easily realised in the smaller firm.

A THEORETICAL FRAMEWORK FOR THE UNDERSTANDING OF SIZE RELATIONSHIPS

Reconceptualising size

As a necessary preliminary to developing an alternative, more integrated approach to the study of size-organisation relations, the conceptualisation of size employed needs to be refined. As Kimberly (1976) and Gupta (1980) have pointed out, most researchers define 'size' in terms of the number of organisational members. They have often been aware of the possible limitations of using this single criterion but have generally argued that it tends to correlate strongly with alternative measures such as assets, financial turnover or output level. However, this tends not to hold for hetero-geneous samples since organisations in different industries have widely differing ratios of organisational members to assets, turnover or output. When the sample of organisations is drawn from both economic and non-economic spheres further doubts must arise (Agarwal, 1979b).

Researchers, for example like the Aston Group, often lump together a highly heterogeneous sample of organisations and assume that consistent notions of 'small' and 'large' may be applied across the sample. For example, in the Aston Group's original 'main study' sample (Pugh et al, 1969, p.120), organisations were drawn from such diverse economic areas as vehicle and confectionery manufacture, printing, shoe repairing and insurance, as well as from local and national government.

Researchers exploring the size dimension tend to have pre-conceived notions of 'small' and 'large' whether they are conscious of their origins or not. Generally, they are derived from those generally dominant in their own society. Where the sample is cross cultural, this raises problems. For example, a researcher in Britain might see a 'large' university as one with 10,000 or more students but a researcher in the United States might adopt a substantially higher number to represent the bottom limit of 'large'.

The Aston Group researchers seem to have only recently attached increasing importance to cultural influences. For instance, a review of studies employing their approach carried out in countries other than Britain (Pugh and Hinings, 1976, pp.167-89) showed no awareness of these cross cultural issues but a more recent collection of papers (Hickson and McMillan, 1981) displays much greater caution although cultural variations in the notion of size or their implications for the approach as a whole, are not directly examined.

A reconceptualisation of size in organisational analysis requires the formal incorporation of our received notions, that is, that we make explicit and include with our quantitative elements, the interpretations of size which originate among those involved with the organisation. Non-structuralist studies of size have usually implicitly assumed that all members of the organisation perceive size in more or less the same way and that their perceptions influence their behaviour in relatively unproblematic ways. However, we might suggest that those involved with the organisation - which may include a wider grouping than those conventionally labelled 'members' such as clients, suppliers, banks, or others whose definitions of the organisation affect its structure and functioning - will have three crucial sets of meanings associated with size which are highly relevant to organisational analysis.

First, it is proposed that the concept of size adopted for organisational analysis should formally incorporate the perceptions of those directly involved in the sample(s) of organisations being researched. The production of a grounded conceptualisation of size should be an integral and necessary part of any pilot study stage. Actors in specific sectors of the economy will generally show a sufficiently coherent consensus on what may be regarded as 'small' or 'large' in their sector to enable researchers to convert their perceptions into suitable quantitative indicators.

Organisational actors' perceptions of size may centre on numbers of organisational members or may be based on other measures - output levels, turnover values etc. - culturally significant in their organisational sphere. It may be objected that actors' definitions may be so variable in relation to the notion of size that producing a grounded conceptualisation is not possible. But most sectors of industry develop a sub culture sufficiently clear on size to present few problems of this kind, and it may even be that the sub culture contains highly refined size notions relative to particular sub divisions within the industry.

In other words, a grounded conceptualisation of size may not emerge from preliminary study without positive decisions by the researcher on how best actors' perceptions may be formalised and quantified. But such an approach will be superior to the adoption of arbitrary numerical definitions of size for they will at least be anchored in social reality.

Of course, such a grounded conceptualisation of size implies that grand pan industrial or pan cultural definitions of size in organisational analysis can no longer be realistically sought. Such grand definitions belong to an earlier, cruder stage of analysis whose potential has been exhausted, but this does not preclude comparative analysis between different kinds of organisations or across cultures. Rather comparative analysis will have to take into account differences in meanings associated with size in different industries and societies in attempting to arrive at more general propositions.

A second important set of size meanings associated with organisations may be labelled Evaluation Meanings. These refer to the ideas and attitudes, positive or negative, used to evaluate size. It is widely accepted that, on the whole, most people prefer small to large organisations. Yet, clearly, there are good reasons for supposing that this will not be the case for all involved: elite members of business organisations for example may well see large size as, overall, eminently desirable since size is likely to be positively correlated with levels of personal rewards - material and non material - and their ability to influence the wider environment (Child, 1972, p.16).

Thirdly, we refer to what can be termed Salience Meanings. These concern the centrality or importance of size meanings in the overall set of attitudes and definitions attached to involvement with the organisation. For example, if asked whether they prefer to be involved with small or large organisations, many people might opt for 'small' but such a preference tells us little about the salience of their choice. In a study of occupational placement, for example, it was found that size of organisation was of only peripheral importance in shop floor workers' decisions about whether to take or leave a job when compared to other factors such as geographical location, job availability, or opportunities for overtime working (Curran and Stanworth, 1979a).

Of these three sets of meanings, the first, concerned with establishing organisational actors' notions of the upper and lower limits of 'small' and 'large', is the most obviously helpful in establishing an initial conceptualisation of size. Evaluation and Salience meanings become crucial at the analysis stage and are especially important for understanding the links between attitudes and behavioural outcomes. They provide us with indicators as to the likely significance of organisational members' notions of size in our overall interpretation of the organisation(s). In other words, our initial conceptualisation of size and the data on the evaluation and salience meanings associated with size, also serve the theoretical framework that is to be developed.

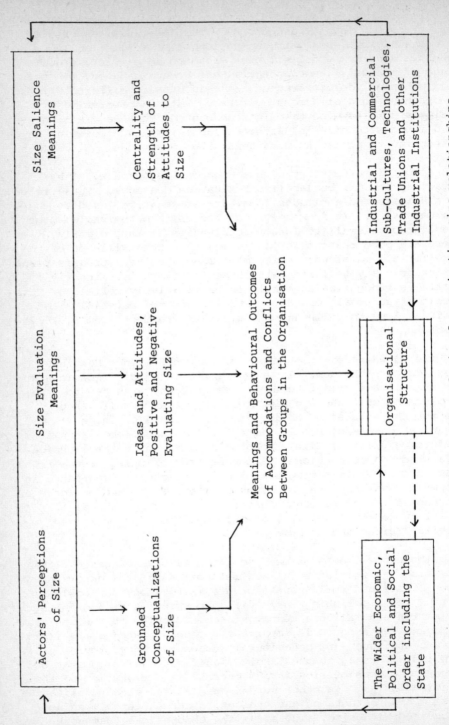

Figure 1 A structure-meaning model for the analysis of organisation-size relationships

Size, structure and meaning

To simply recognise the respective importance of structure and meanings in the analysis of organisation size relationships is not sufficient to provide an adequate theoretical framework for analysis. Such an emphasis may still promote simple correlational analysis linking individuals' reactions to structural properties including organisational size. What is needed is a full integration of these two dimensions within a single theoretical thrust. One approach might be derived from the structure meaning analysis developed by Benson (1977).

Benson's dialectical approach sees organisational structure as emerging out of conflicts and accommodations among those involved which, at the same time, reflect the wider social order in which the organisations are located. These conflicts and accommodations are closely linked to contradictions and potentials inherent in the superordinate/subordinate relations of industrial society which inspire a continuous reconstruction by those involved. In other words, we propose a three way starting point which takes into account the meanings of those involved in the organisation, the structure of the organisation and the inter connections between these and other influences in the wider society as schematically outlined in Figure 1. Naturally, organisations will show stronger links with some parts of the external social order than others, and this will contribute to the overall organisational climate, that is, the meanings, attitudes and ideological emphasis most influential on participants' relationships with each other.

In analysing the situation of the small [1] manufacturing enterprise, we may view it broadly as involving two key groups, owner manager(s) and employees. Others, who may be significantly connected with influences on its structure and functioning, such as suppliers of credit and financial services or a dominant customer may, for the moment, be left out of consideration. The influence of the meanings and world views of owner managers on the structure of the small manufacturing business has been amply demonstrated by research in Britain and the United States (Collins et al, 1964; Stanworth and Curran, 1973 and 1976; Kets de Vries, 1977; Scase and Goffee, 1980 and 1982). On the whole, they tend to favour a relatively unstructured organisation framework, with highly centralised decision making even in routine, day to day decisions. Forward planning is usually limited with organisational structure following major changes rather than anticipating them, and organisational recruitment reflects particularistic rather than universalistic criteria.

What is sometimes under emphasised, however, is the position of the small business owner in the wider society. They form an inbetween or marginal class in advanced capitalist societies who often feel both economically and politically insecure (Bechhofer and Elliott, 1978; McHugh, 1979; Scase and Goffee, 1980 and 1982). Their economic insecurity frequently stems from having only limited capital or fears about surviving in an economy increasingly dominated by large enterprises. Their political insecurity is based on a suspicion that, although all the major parties profess a strong commitment to small business, in practice other more numerous sections of the population such as organised labour or groups with more resources such as big business, will fare better under governments of whatever persuasion.

Entry into the petit bourgeoisie often represents an attempt at gaining independence from the mounting constraints of modern society. Increasing bureaucratization and credentialism means that many who, for one reason or another, fail to gain acceptable qualifications and experience, are consigned to unfulfilling social roles. Small business ownership, despite its insecurity, is a possible alternative which leads to a greater sense of self worth. Research on social mobility has shown that many find it difficult to maintain their petit bourgeoisie status and are forced back into employment only to bounce back again and again trying to attain the psychological and social rewards of owner manager status (Goldthorpe et al, 1980). In short, this dominant group in the small business organisation is drawn from a particular social context. Their world view includes a distinctive set of attitudes towards business which feed into the structure of the organisation. Their views on the desirable extent of role specification, levels of hierarchy, the most efficient forms of intra organisational communication and so on, are clearly among the more important influences on the structure of the organisation.

The structure meanings pattern of the small business organisation may be contrasted with that of the large business organisation whose executives occupy a very different universe of meanings (Winkler, 1974; Whiteley, 1974; Fidler, 1981; Useem, 1982). The rational bureaucratic organisational structure, it may be argued, is largely an outcome of their world views and their position in the wider society. Those who have adopted a solely structural analysis of the organisation, however, have usually asserted that the bureaucratic structure of the large business organisation is somehow the inevitable outcome of large size itself combined with the influence of technology.

But, as Marglin (1977) has argued, any 'inevitability' in the structure of the modern large scale business organisation is highly questionable to the extent that organisational structure is predominantly the outcome of the ideas and aims of elites. In other words, as Weber (1948) pointed out long ago, the existence of facilitating technologies do not, by themselves, provide the necessary conditions for the emergence of modern bureaucracy. It takes specific groups and individuals to make the potential of technclogy take on particular social forms which they believe will serve their interest.

The implications of these varying sets of meanings for business organisations of differing size are clear. They include principles and prescriptions for structural patterns which are a major source of actually observed structures. Each major group - owner managers and large enterprise elites - has its own organisational rationality and the 'logic' of organisational structure will reflect these differing rationalities. They are not the sole origin of organisational structure since others associated with the organisation are also influential and allowance must be made for the working out of contradictions between the groups of actors.

In small business organisations the other influential group is the employees. Over the last decade there has been considerable debate about the precise ways in which small firm employees may be distinguished from their large firm counterparts (Ingham, 1970; Curran and Stanworth, 1979a and b) but what is agreed is that there are such differences. More recently, economists and others have discussed the relationship between size of firm and primary and secondary labour markets again supporting the notion that there are differences in the types of workers likely to be recruited by differently sized firms (Bosanquet and Doeringer, 1973; Friedson, 1977; Stolzenberg, 1978).

It has been commonplace to stress the harmonious relations between owner managers and employees in small firms in contrast to the conflictual relations between management and employees in large firms. However, there is evidence that both these views represent exaggerations; small firms are less harmonious than is often imagined (Commission for Industrial Relations, 1974; Curran and Stanworth, 1979b and 1981; Scott and Rainnie 1982) while large firms appear more harmonious than popularly depicted (Smith et al, 1979).

Differences between small and large firm workers are also linked to wider differences in outlook and behaviour in, for instance, politics (Curran, 1980) and community involvement (Curran, 1981). Small firm employees, like their bosses, are located in the wider society in specific ways. Their organisational and non-organisational experiences cross fertilize to produce distinct world views and behavioural outcomes which differ sharply from those of workers in the large firm, primary labour market. Each will have an impact on the business organisation through the translation of meanings into structural outcomes and hence will be related to organisational size.

Besides owner managers and employees, a whole range of others' prevalent meanings and external institutions influence the organisation in relation to size. The budding entrepreneur, for instance, finds that there are powerful influences working towards the reproduction of existing organisational structures. In order to obtain capital and credit, in order to be deemed 'reliable' by potential customers and suppliers, he is constrained to follow modes of organisation seen by these outsiders as 'proper'. The State prescribes a range of organisational practices from employment law and contracts to accounting procedures, which again act as significant constraints on the choice of organisational form and structure. These constraints, however, do not impinge equally on organisations of all sizes. Small business organisation owner managers, for example, protest that State imposed organisational practices are more of a burden on their resources than those of the large firm (McHugh, 1979; Bannock, 1981; Scase and Goffee, 1980 and 1982).

More subtly, wider economic and social forces affect particular kinds of economic activities in differing ways to affect small and large firms to differing degrees. For example, besides forces promoting the general reproduction of existing organisational forms, there are more specific forces promoting the reproduction of particular organisational forms in specific industries. In construction, for example, the modal organisational form constrains employer employee-relations towards more casual, short term relations than in many other forms of economic activity (Stinchcombe, 1965). It is only in larger firms in the industry that bureaucratic employment relations are more evident. Similar industrial sub cultural influences have been found in other industries which affect organisational structures (Burns and Stalker, 1961; Curran and Stanworth, 1979b; Scott and Rainnie, 1982).

The impact of technological change will also differ for organisations of varying size. For instance, it is easy to assume that new technology tends to benefit larger organisations through the effects of economies of scale. But a good deal of the most recent technological innovation in, for example, plastics and electronics, reduces the scale of profitable operation significantly (Blair, 1972, Ch.6), thus favouring small organisations. Changes in the forces of production interact with social and attitudinal influences in highly complex ways and the inherent possibilities make it very unlikely that their impact on small and large organisations in different industries, will confirm to the simple linear or curvilinear relations favoured by previous researchers.

Trade unions are another important external grouping which differentially affect organisational structures. On the whole, they exert most influence on larger organisations since trade union membership is strongly correlated with size of organisation (Bullock Report, 1977). This influence is seen in the formalisation of employee-employer relations, restrictions on employers' decisions on who to employ, termination of employment and the fixing of wages and benefits.

The empirical tracing of the complex of influences on the structure-meanings patterns of organisations has hardly yet begun. Nevertheless some indications of the interpretive power of such an overall approach may be gathered from existing studies of both large business organisations (Nichols and Beynon, 1979) and smaller scale economic activities (Newby, 1979) as well as at the more general level of the industry including the differences between large and small firms over time (Friedman, 1977; Edwards, 1979).

SOME RESEARCH AND METHODOLOGICAL IMPLICATIONS

To illustrate the kinds of hypotheses and topics which our proposed approach to size analysis would be helpful in exploring, four suggestions on size effects in the small enterprise may be briefly considered. First, although owner manager influences on small business organisational structures have been studied, those of employee participants have been neglected. To what extent do non owner manager participants' attitudes and behaviour influence the structure of the small business organisation and to what extent, for example, do they affect growth patterns in the enterprise?

Second, the examination of the relations between size and technology has usually been seen in structural terms and as a relatively straightforward linear relationship. But as some recent writings have stressed, the choices of organisational decision makers may intervene heavily between technology and organisational structure (Clegg and Dunkerley, 1980, pp.339-65). The structure meanings approach suggests that there will be a size related variation in the choices made to introduce or resist technological change which arises out of the differing world-views, resources and aims of those involved in the organisation. In other words, it is hypothesised that the major influences shaping the impact of technology on organisational structure will derive from the differing types of participants recruited to organisations of differing sizes. Such analysis would also throw further light on how small firms are affected by new technology.

Third, the structure meaning approach may be used to explore the impact of external influences on the small organisation in rather different ways to previous approaches but which would add considerably to our understanding of size effects. For example, recent Government action has generated new influences on employee rights and relations in the small enterprise but their impact in practice is unclear. The structure meanings perspective suggests three avenues of analysis through which this impact might be assessed. One, through the decisions of owner managers to ignore or translate government policies into organisational structure and practice. Two, through employees' awareness and reactions to both the policies themselves and managerial responses. Three, through the influence of other external forces on the impact of these policies on the enterprise such as the activities of trade unions and small employer pressure groups. Again such analysis could be easily extended to large business organisations to provide a fuller analysis of size variations.

Fourth, the structure meanings approach offers a new view of what might be considered the most basic issue in the study of organisation-size relationships, that is, to what extent is organisational structure the outcome of a necessary 'logic' of administration as opposed to being the residual of the values, behaviour and social relations of those associated with the organisation? Traditionally, structural approaches have argued that there is a necessary logic of administration which constrains actors to adopt particular structural arrangements as the size of the organisation increases. The structure-meanings approach suggests the opposite hypothesis, that is, that any logic of administration, if it exists, is secondary to the world views and aims of those involved and that differences in organisational structure simply reflect the typically different kinds of people associated with variously sized organisations.

This shift in emphasis to a qualitative approach means that the organisation can no longer be observed at a distance through examining external quantitative indicators such as published figures on output, profit levels and assets or through interviews with a single organisational representative such as the chief executive. Rather the researcher must enter the organisation, sampling meanings and interaction patterns across the spectrum of organisational involvements. The organisation, in short, is interpreted in social terms and organisation size phenomena are seen as socially produced: the notion of 'size' as some unexplained, sourceless 'cause' of structural interactional patterns in the organisation is firmly rejected.

CONCLUSION

This paper has offered a critique of the existing dominant approach to the study of size aspects of the organisation. This was shown to be primarily structuralist, mainly offering correlations of structural phenomena in relation to size but ignoring the actors' involvement in the organisation. The approach outlined and developed in this paper, derived from the dialectical perspective offered by Benson (1977), suggests how interpretations of the 'size effect' in organisational analysis can be accomplished through a systematic integration of findings concerning structural dimensions and the meanings and behaviour of those involved with the organisation.

The structure-meanings approach brings people firmly back into a fully explicit structural analysis of the organisation in relation to size. In addition, it adds something that neither structuralists nor other researchers (with the rare exception) have given much attention to - an explicit linking of organisational size phenomena to environmental influences arising out of the wider social, political and economic domains. For small business researchers it offers a theoretical framework for exploring the small firms' comparative position in relation to the large firm - an avenue of analysis which requires more effort than it has received in the recent past. For the policy maker, the structure-meanings approach provides an alternative framework for assessing the likely impact of various policy initiatives. Such frameworks urgently need developing if policy making is to be realistic rather than blindly optimistic.

NOTE

[1] In the following discussion the terms 'small' and 'large' will, of necessity, follow the usage of the authors of the secondary studies cited. The latter have been carefully selected to be representative of studies of economic organisations which would be regarded uncontenteniously as 'small' and 'large' by most observers whether researchers or participants. In other words, had the alternative approach to size proposed in the present paper been employed there is a high probability that the organisations studied would have received similar size designations.

REFERENCES

Agarwal, N.C., (1979a), 'Nature of Size-Structure Relationship:
Some Further Evidence', Human Relations, vol.32, no.6, pp.
441-50.

Agarwal, N.C., (1979b), 'On the Interchangeability of Size
Measures', Academy of Management Journal, vol.22, no.2, pp.
404-09.

Bannock, G., (1981), The Economics of Small Firms: Return from
the Wilderness, Blackwell, Oxford.

Batstone, E.V., (1975), 'Deference and the Ethos of Small Town
Capitalism', in Bulmer, M., (ed.), Working-Class Images of
Society, Routledge and Kegan Paul, London.

Bechhofer, F., Elliott, B. and McCrone, D., (1978), 'Structure,
Consciousness and Action: A Sociological Profile of the
British Middle Class', British Journal of Sociology, vol.29,
no.4, pp.410-33.

Benson, J.K., (1977), 'Organisations: A Dialectical View',
Administrative Science Quarterly, vol.22, no.1, pp.1-21.

Berger, C.L. and Cummings, L.L., (1979), 'Organisational
Structure, Attitudes and Behaviour', in Staw, B. and
Cummings, L.L., (eds.), Research in Organisational Behaviour,
vol.1, pp.169-208, JAl Press, Greenwich, Connecticut.

Blair, J.M., (1972), Economic Concentration, Structure
Behaviour and Public Policy, Harcourt Brace Jovanovich,
New York.

Bosanquet, N. and Doeringer, P.B., (1973), 'Is There a Dual
Labour Market in Great Britain?', The Economic Journal, vol.
83, pp.421-35.

Burns, T. and Stalker, G.M., (1961), The Management of
Innovation, Tavistock, London.

Child, J., (1972), 'Organisation Structure and Strategies of
Control: Replication of the Aston Study', Administrative
Science Quarterly, vol.17, no.2, pp.163-77.

Clegg, S. and Dunkerley, D., (1980), Organisation, Class and
Control, Routledge and Kegan Paul, London.

Collins, O.F., Moore, D.G., with Unwalla, D.B., (1964), The
Enterprising Man, Michigan State University Press, East
Lancing.

Commission for Industrial Relations, (1974), Small Firms and
the Code of Industrial Relations Practice (Report No.69),
H.M.S.O., London.

Curran, J., (1980), 'The Political World of the Small Firm
Worker', Sociological Review, vol.28, no.1, pp.75-103.

Curran, J., (1981), 'Class Imagery, Work Environment and
Community: Some Further Findings and a Brief Comment',
British Journal of Sociology, XXXII, vol.1, pp.111-26.

Curran, J. and Stanworth, J., (1979a), 'Self-selection and the
Small Firm Worker - a Critique and an Alternative View',
Sociology, vol.13, no.3, pp.427-44.

Curran, J. and Stanworth, J., (1979b), 'Worker Involvement and
  Social Relations in the Small Firm', Sociological Review,
  vol.28, no.2, pp.317-42.
Edwards, R., (1979), Contested Terrain, the Transformation of
  the Workplace in the Twentieth Century, Heinemann, London.
Fidler, J., (1981), The British Business Elite, its Attitudes
  to Class Status and Power, Routledge and Kegan Paul, London.
Friedson, A.L., (1977), Industry and Labour, Class Struggle at
  Work and Monopoly Capitalism, Macmillan, London.
Goldthorpe, J., Llewellyn, C. and Payne, C., (1980), Social
  Mobility and Class Structure in Modern Britain, Clarendon
  Press, Oxford.
Grinyer, P.H. and Yasai-Ardekani, M., (1981), 'Strategy
  Structure, Size and Bureaucracy', Academy of Management
  Journal, vol.24, no.3, pp.471-86.
Gupta, N., (1980), 'Some Alternative Definitions of Size',
  Academy of Management Journal, vol.23, no.4, pp.759-66.
Hall, R.H., (1977), Organisations Structure and Process,
  Prentice-Hall, Englewood Cliffs, New Jersey.
Hickson, D.J., Pugh, D.S. and Phesey, D.C., (1969), 'Operations
  Technology and Organisation Structure: An Empirical
  Reappraisal', Administrative Science Quarterly, vol.14, no.3,
  pp.378-97.
Hickson, D.J. and McMillan, C.J., (eds.), (1981), Organisation
  and Nation, the Aston Programme IV, Gower Press, Westmead.
Hinings, C.R. and Lee, G.L., (1971), 'Dimensions of
  Organisation Structure and Their Context: A Replication',
  Sociology, vol.5, no.2, pp.83-93.
Ingham, G.K., (1967), 'Organisational Size, Orientation to Work
  and Industrial Behaviour', Sociology, vol.1, no.3, pp.239-58.
Ingham, G.K., (1970), Size of Industrial Organisation and
  Worker Behaviour, Cambridge University Press.
Inkson, J.H.K., Pugh, D.S. and Hickson, D., (1970),
  'Organisation Context and Structure: An Abbreviated
  Replication', Administrative Science Quarterly, vol.15, no.3,
  pp.318-29.
Kimberly, J.R., (1976), 'Organisational Size and the
  Structuralist Perspective: A Review, Critique and Proposal',
  Administrative Science Quarterly, vol.21, no.4, pp.571-97.
Kets de Vries, M.F.R., (1977), 'The Entrepreneurial Personality:
  A Person at the Crossroads', Journal of Management Studies,
  vol.14 no.1, pp.34-57.
Marglin, S.A., (1971), 'What Do Bosses Do?', Review of Radical
  Political Economics, vol.6, pp.60-112.
McHugh, J., (1979), 'The Self-Employed and the Small
  Independent Entrepreneur', in King, R. and Nugent, N., (eds.),
  Respectable Rebels, Middle Class Campaigns in Britain in the
  1970s, Hodder and Stoughton, London.
Newby, H., (1979), The Deferential Worker, a Study of Farm
  Workers in East Anglia, Penguin Books, Harmondsworth,
  (originally published 1977).

Nichols, T. and Beynon, H., (1977), Living with Capitalism, Class Relations and the Modern Factory, Routledge and Kegan Paul, London.

Porter, L.W. and Lawler, E.E., III,(1965), 'Properties of Organisation Structure in Relation to Job Attitudes and Behaviour', Psychological Bulletin, vol.64, no.1, pp.23-51.

Pugh, D.S., Hickson, D.J., Hinings, C.R., Macdonald, K.M., Turner, C. and Lupton, T., (1963), 'A Conceptual Scheme for Organisational Analysis', Administrative Science Quarterly, vol.8, no.2, pp.289-315.

Pugh, D.S., Hickson, D.J., Hinings, C.R. and Turner, C., (1968), 'Dimensions of Organisation Structure', Administrative Science Quarterly, vol.13, no.1, pp.65-105.

Pugh, D.S., Hickson, D.J. and Hinings, C.R., (1969), 'An Empirical Taxonomy of Structures of Work Organisations', Administrative Science Quarterly, vol.14, no.1, pp.115-25.

Pugh, D.S. and Hickson, D.J., (1976), Organisational Structure in its Context: the Aston Programme I, Saxon House, London.

Pugh, D.S. and Hinings, C.R., (eds.), (1976), Organisation Structure, Extensions and Replications: the Aston Programme II, Saxon House, Farnborough.

Pugh, D.S. and Payne, R.L., (1977), Organisational Behaviour in its Context: the Aston Programme III, Saxon House, Westmead.

Robey, D., Bakr, M.M. and Miller, T.S., (1977), 'Organisational Size and Management Autonomy: Some Structural Discontinuities', Academy of Management Journal, vol.20, no.3, pp.376-97.

Report on the Census of Production, 1980, (1983), H.M.S.O., London.

Report of the Committee of Inquiry on Industrial Democracy, (Cmnd. 6706), (1977), H.M.S.O., London, (The Bullock Report).

Salaman, G., (1979), Work Organisations, Resistance and Control, Longman, London.

Scase, R. and Goffee, R., (1980), The Real World of the Small Business Owner, Croom Helm, London.

Scase, R. and Goffee, R., (1982), The Entrepreneurial Middle Class, Croom Helm, London.

Scott, M.G. and Rainnie, A., (1982), 'Beyond Bolton: Industrial Relations in the Small Firm', in Stanworth, J., Westrip, A., Watkins, D. and Lewis, J., (eds.), Perspectivies on a Decade of Small Business Research, Gower Press, Aldershot.

Silverman, D., (1970), The Theory of Organisations, a Sociological Framework, Heinemann, London.

Smith, C.T.B., Clifton, R., Makeham, P., Cleigh, S.W. and Burn, R.V., (1978), Strikes in Britain, A Research Study of Industrial Stoppages in the United Kingdom, (Manpower Paper No.15), H.M.S.O., London.

Stanworth, M.J.K. and Curran, J., (1973), Management Motivation in the Small Business, Gower Press, Epping.

Stanworth, J. and Curran, J., (1976), 'Growth and the Small
    Firm - an Alternative View', Journal of Management Studies,
    vol.13, no.2, pp.95-110.
Stinchcombe, A.L., (1965), 'Social Structure and Organisations',
    in March, J.G., (ed.), Handbook of Organisations, Rand
    McNally, Chicago.
Stolzenberg, R.M., (1978), 'Bringing the Boss Back In: Employer
    Size, Employee Schooling and Socioeconomic Achievement',
    American Sociological Review, vol.43, pp.813-28.
Useem, M., (1982), 'Classwide Rationality in the Politics of
    Managers and Directors of Large Corporations in the United
    States and Britain', Administrative Science Quarterly, vol.27,
    no.2, pp.199-226.
Weber, M., (1948), 'Bureaucracy' in Gerth, H.H. and Wright
    Mills, C., (eds.), From Max Weber, Essays in Sociology,
    Routledge and Kegan Paul, London.
Whitley, R., (1974), 'The City and Industry: the Directors of
    Large Companies, Their Characteristics and Connections', in
    Stanworth, P. and Giddens, A., (eds.), Elites and Power in
    British Society, Cambridge University Press, London.
Winkler, J.T., (1974), 'The Ghost at the Bargaining Table',
    British Journal of Industrial Relations, vol.12, no.2, pp.
    191-212.
Woodward, J., (1965), Industrial Organisation: Theory and
    Practice, Oxford University Press, London.
Zey-Ferrell, M., (1979), Dimensions of Organisations, Goodyear
    Publishing Co., Santa Monica.
Zey-Ferrell, M. and Aiken, M., (eds.), (1981), Complex
    Organisations: Critical Perspectives. Scott, Foresman and
    Co., Glenview.

Predictable casualties: the sacrificial role of the older small firm

JOHN RITCHIE

INTRODUCTION

Newcomers to the study of small business may well wonder whatever happened to older small firms. So would any time
traveller from the 1960's. Then they were made to look like
all too predictable casualties of decidedly modern capitalist
industrial progress. Only the exceptional were deemed likely
to survive let alone grow. Their very occasional rescue and
revival would largely depend upon concessionary mergers and
takeovers. Those that were left were simply doomed.

There would have been real concern had any larger scale
organisation been consigned to this particular fate. But once
regarded as so very predictable casualties most older small
firms were hardly thought worth the effort. So much so that
neither the frequency nor the actual process of their decline
were every really measured.

This same conventional wisdom has too long gone frankly
unquestioned. Younger growing firms frequently dominate even
the 'new politics' of small business. They have become the
torch bearers for Britain's 'coming entrepreneurial revolution'.
Many older small firms established over twenty years and no
longer under founder entrepreneur control appear almost counter-
revolutionary in comparison.

Not shrouded with the same forward looking optimism they
appear to be more difficult to represent, defend, and also to
advise and support through current small business promotion
networks. Inheritor management rarely enjoys the same prestige
as original founder entrepreneurship, nor does it inspire the
same thoughts of an entirely new and thriving generation of
small business person that so enthuses both education and the
media. In the end many such firms seem likely decidedly
limited longer term investments. Everyday folk stories make
their eventual decline and demise seem almost tragically
predictable and familiar. Lost founders, weak successors,
encrusted organisations, backward technology, sterilised
investment, and being trapped among failing 'traditional'
industries all loom large in these unscripted corporate mini-
dramas. So much so that their business epitaphs might almost
be written in advance.

Such is the background for this short enquiry. It is not the
whole story. Such easily dramatised tragedies rarely are. Not
just one but several further lines of enquiry are now urgently
needed. This one will begin by considering how these firms
have been made to appear amongst the most weak and vulnerable
of all contemporary capitalist enterprises. Following a case
illustration of the implications of this 'weakling' role in
practice it then reviews the problems of whether and how that
role could or should change in future.

PERSISTENCE, SURVIVAL, AND THE OLDER FIRM IN THE CHANGING
POLITICS OF SMALL BUSINESS

Whether these firms are seen and regarded as particularly
problematic very often depends upon the politics of their
relationship with their surrounding society. These politics
are here seen and described as falling into three successive
over-arching patterns. These patterns begin - and to some
extent now end - by making the new and growing entrepreneurial
firm the archetype for all small business. That dominance only
faded during the intervening 'modern' period when comparatively
older small family firms were made to look much more central.
Unfortunately they only achieved that position because they
above all were thought to exemplify the problems of persistence
and survival that faced so many small businesses at that
particular time.

The classical politics of the new and growing entrepreneurial
firm

Small scale industry dates back well into antiquity. But new
entrepreneurial enterprise was only made to look like the vital

148

spark of 'industrial revolution' with the rise of early
competitive capitalism. In Adam Smith's world they were
assumed to be in a state of more-or-less continuous readiness
to enter the economic contest. Not until Mill and Marx did
their subsequent persistence and survival seem particularly
problematic. Then came Alfred Marshall. Deploring the growth
of large joint stock companies the Marshallians constructed a
picture of enterprise growth that was almost entirely dependent
upon founder entrepreneur initiative. Whenever these founder
figures aged and/or faded stagnation and decline were almost
automatically expected. This Marshall illustrated with his
famed 'trees of the forest' analogy thus:

> One tree will last longer in full vigour and attain a
> greater size than another: but sooner or later age
> tells on them all ... And as with the growth of trees,
> so it was with the growth of businesses before the
> recent great development of vast joint stock companies,
> which often stagnate, but do not readily die. Now that
> rule is far from universal, but it still holds in many
> industries and trades. Nature still presses in on the
> private business by limiting the length of life of its
> original founders, and by limiting even more narrowly
> that part of their lives in which their faculties
> retain full vigour. (Marshall, 1920, p.315)

By deploying the metaphors of 'nature' and the 'life cycle' -
and making enterprise growth highly dependent upon founder
entrepreneur inspiration alone - the Marshallians made longer
term stagnation and decline look almost natural and inevitable.
Founder entrepreneur succession and replacement has been
problematic for like thinking classicists ever since. To be
classically 'beautiful' it was necessary to be young and
growing as well as small. On seeming to lose these particular
characteristics the whole status and prestige of small business
declined dramatically during the subsequent 'modern' era.

The modern politics of small firm persistence and survival

Especially during the 1950's and 1960's the whole politics of
small business was closely interrelated with the then ongoing
debate over whether capitalism would itself either survive or
change out of all former recognition. Much modern 'progressive'
opinion saw the very persistence and survival of these firms as
largely symptomatic of the increasingly 'stagnant society' all
around. According to Harris (1972, p.207) there were shades of
such opinion in both Conservative and Labour Party approaches
during the immediate post World War years, provided one
distinguishes the former's rhetoric from their actual practices
where nominally they:

were pledged generally to assist small business, but
little specific was done ... Stability and efficiency
suggested the need for large firms was greater than for
small, a case made more urgent by international
competition between very large firms, and the need for
large scale investment and research in the new technologically intensive industries ... an attitude was
suggested that small business was not the key element
in the neo-Liberal economy, but rather a tolerated
luxury which should not be permitted to infringe the
interests of the major element in the corporate
society, large firms.

Faced with parliamentary opposition party duties the
Conservative leadership talked more about the previously rarely
specifically debated fate of small business. While debating
certain provisions of the 1965 Finance Bill leader Edward Heath
therefore expressed particular concern that they would be
'damaging and lead up to the break-up of family companies on
death'. In a revealingly rapid response Austen Albu, then
Minister of State at the Department of Economic Affairs,
sharply retorted 'and about time'.

That celebrated comment indicated just how deeply the
hereditary transmission of ownership and control (coupled with
organisational and social position) was then disdained. And
not merely because of possible economic inefficiencies. Small
family businesses were also very potent symbols of non-merito-
cratic succession into management. So with the further 'rise
of the meritocracy' (Young, 1961) much more challenging
organisational and managerial ideals were being promoted.
These determined that selection and development should proceed
according to 'technical' qualifications and merit rather than
traditional seniority factors. Measured against these up-and-
coming new ideals many small firms apparently lacked much more
than so-called 'economies of scale'. They were also rather
nepotistic, tradition bound organisations that would quite
probably fade and disappear as the organisational revolution
proceeded further.

Others equated this possible disappearance with the changing
nature of capitalism itself. Since Schumpeter (1939) this was
seen as classically dependent upon the periodic 'stock of the
new'. This both overturned the established order while helping
maintain the socially vital sense of momentum and continuing
progress. It therefore drove relentlessly forward toward
specifically new markets, products, technologies, and related
corporate forms and transactions. Now under 'mature
industrialism' this turmoil was disdained. Change was to
become much better planned and controlled with greater

stability in mind. And small family businesses were
particularly difficult to fit into the required corporate
pattern. The doubtful contended that their survival only
really depended upon deliberately self protective price fixing,
cartels, and similar 'gentleman's agreements'. Such common
assumptions were then well encapsulated in the 'failing older
small firm syndrome' of the time.

The 'failing older small firm syndrome'

Despite looking decidedly vague and shadowy through hindsight
the several major themes of this syndrome together implied that
the survival chances of these particular firms were limited
indeed. To begin with the 'fading entrepreneur' theme supposed
that meritocraticly appointed management would increasingly
champion modern innovation and change. Where their accession
was denied the 'weakening succession' theme then implied that
most family inheritors could never really match the original
founder's business purpose and drive. Concerning the rest of
the enterprise the 'lost organisational momentum' theme saw
advancing corporate years and experience resulting in
considerable slowing down and routinization. More widely
'corporate industrial ageism' saw whole industries being
afflicted with this phenomenon. Mere individual firms were
thus cast as relatively hapless victims of larger structural
forces lying well beyond their control. Much weakened they
sometimes became easy prey for exploitative 'liquidators'.
According to this theme they were then 'asset stripped' for
their dubious financial advantage alone.

   Certain themes were then referenced against associated
research. Classic works like Christensen (1953) clearly highlighted the problems of founder withdrawal and succession.
From within the United Nations two years later came the bold
pronouncement that:

> When the family does play an important part in business
> it is often a reflection of the economic immaturity of
> the population, the absence of a tradition of impersonal
> service in industry and the unreliability of employees
> who have no kinship ties. Industrial development cannot
> but be handicapped by inappropriate standards of
> economic morality.

Again looking at family businesses of varied size - small,
medium and otherwise - Miller and Rice (1967) later concluded
that only the most exceptional would survive. The particular
psychodynamic 'conflicts that plague the family business' were
further elaborated by Levinson (1971). Other organisational
and larger structural themes were much less directly addressed
except where these touched upon owner manager interests.

So long as they were so dismissively cast as 'predictable casualties' - if not outright corporate sacrifices - there were precious few attempts to observe and record just how these firms did actually disintegrate in practice. Even contemporary concern about so-called 'business failures' often turns out to be largely preoccupied with so-called 'infant mortalities'. Otherwise relatively few have really been concerned about how the corporate casualty ward actually works in practice. And that disinterest owes much to the late modern splitting of newer from older small firms.

The late modern splitting of newer from older small firms

The Bolton Committee is now widely regarded as the main institutional turning point in the contemporary politics of the small firm. But they found many problems working with the restricted data then available. Some of their positive pronouncements now seem more like acts of faith. Such declarations were forerunners of the revival of the 'classical' political picture of the new and growing small firm in particular. Bolton's findings and conclusions were therefore prefaced (Bolton, 1971, p.xix) with the normative statement that:

> We believe the small firm is in fact an essential medium through which dynamic change in the form of new entrants to business, new industries, and new challengers to established market leaders, can permeate the economy. We therefore believe that in the absence of an active and vital small firm sector the economy would slowly ossify and decay. To ask whether there is a future for the small firm in the new age of giant companies, international combine and universal intervention by governments, is therefore tantamount to asking whether the future of private enterprise capitalism as we have known it in this country is threatened.

In this way the Committee were able to situate their view within the long standing cultural tradition that associated the new firm with dynamic capitalism, even though that tradition had faded somewhat during the preceding period. But in terms of small firms in general their submissions were remarkably contradictory. They initially drew upon the findings from the Merrett Cyriax survey, which covered 604 firms trading in 1963 and another 96 that had subsequently ceased trading by 1970 (Merrett Cyriax, 1971). This actually showed that many such firms were hardly classifiable as new any longer. The median age varied from 26 years in retailing, 29 in manufacturing, and 36 in wholesale. The oldest 25 per cent in manufacturing were aged over 80 years and 54 years or more in retailing. In all

sectors, between 25-50 per cent of firms were controlled by a
second or subsequent generation of the founding family.
Merrett Cyriax also reported detecting some 'primary
correlation' between growth and management characteristics
depending upon whether firms were founded by their present
managements and determined that:

> The small firm is still overwhelmingly proprietorially
> and family managed with 76 per cent of chief executives
> having a significant stake in the business but
> recruited from extremely narrow bounds and typically
> without formal qualifications. The sector is in
> relative decline, with high mortality and very marked
> variability in growth rates. (Merrett Cyriax, 1971, p.4)

From the evidence they had themselves commissioned the Bolton
Committee were therefore informed that a substantial part of
this small business sector was neither new nor growing nor
indeed anything like dynamic generally. And it is difficult to
see how this was reconciled with their own original idealised
picture of its role and functions. They later expressed some
concern that Britain had proportionately more older small firms
than the USA, especially after Merrett Cyriax had offered
'tentative evidence' from their own limited data base that
firms under twenty years old were the most dynamic and growth
conscious. But by estimating age according to existing rather
than original ownership, they changed the Merrett Cyriax data
to make the overall age distribution seem much younger than the
original survey findings, and left themselves even more open to
criticism because 'the enormous contrast between this and the
original survey is not explained' (Boswell, 1973, p.41).

Boswell's own work which by his definition covered both small
and medium sized British manufacturing firms then affirmed this
splitting of the small business sector into new and older
segments: 'on the one hand a source of vitality and renewal, on
the other a spectacle of inefficiency and decay'(Boswell, 1973,
p.4) which typified the late modern view. 'Age' here becomes
the most important single predictor of corporate and organisational character and performance thus:

> There are major divisions within the small firm sector,
> divisions which are clear and pronounced. Moreover,
> the most important of these divisions do not follow the
> size of firm or the nature of industries and markets.
> Instead, they appear to depend mainly on the age of
> firms - and then, linked with this factor, on the
> changing pattern of the industry, the descent from
> founders to inheritors and the sociological evolution
> of the business. (Boswell, 1973, p.179)

Boswell's key hypothesis was thus explicitly ageist. It asserted that 'the older the firm, the greater the incidence of decline' (Boswell, 1973, p.121). In their first twenty years firms were not expected to be especially problematic once adequately founded. Succession and 'congealment' problems could then constrain the 'transitional' firms during the following twenty years. But once 'elderly' (founded between 40 and 70 years) and then really 'old' (founded over 70 years), deterioration and decline were seemingly endemic. Since between 20-25 per cent of all such sized firms were estimated to be 'transitionals' and 50-55 per cent were then 'elderly' and really 'old', very serious problems were apparently developing. From the evidence derived from an admittedly small sized sample of manufacturing firm managements, Boswell was generally very doubtful about their potential resolution. A few select 'revivals' apart, most would apparently fade and disintegrate unless his proposed Small Firms Transitions Trust could possibly intervene. His doubts were expressed as follows:

> The concept of reform via self-cure and education, of permeation by new attitudes and professional managers, is useful in a minority of cases, but only a minority. This optimistic view is largely nullified by the constraints of psychology, history and inheritance, of structure and scale ... Age, smallness, owner management, inheritor characteristics and sociological trends all produce a deep resistance, both psychological and structural, to the fluidities of management and labour, ownwership and capital, of business marriage and death. (Boswell, 1973, p.162)

Interpretations built into everyday culture also saw such 'decline and fall' as both predictable yet also tragic and lamentable. In both novels and television such sagas have proved particularly popular. 'Clogs to clogs in three generations' aptly summarised associated conventional wisdom. And still the Bolton Committee did not favour deliberate discrimination in favour of 'small firms', partly because of the image constructed around their younger variety. Not until the mid 1970's did definite resistance appear. At that time assorted 'respectable rebels' tried to mobilise self employed, small business, ratepayer, and other explicity 'middle class' associations to secure more 'personal' influence over related policy. These counter movements arose in several European societies as well as Britain. Very soon the political rehabilitation of the newer small firm was well under way.

The 'new politics' of the young and growing small firm

In the emergent 'postmodern' pattern the politics of small business has become much less concerned with survival and persistence alone. It has rather elevated and praised one particular type of small firm beyond all other - the young and growing firm. Political parties even compete to court their welfare, and none more so than during the original 'Thatcherite Experiment'. But their comeback considerably predates even that. The critical lead was provided by the Bolton Committee's own approach to the whole problem of small business sector renewal, thus:

> We believe the sector as it now stands to be capable of performing the regenerative function which is its special contribution to the health of the economy. We base this belief mainly on the quality of new formations ... Furthermore, in spite of the falling number of small firms, we have seen no evidence of an abnormal rate of business failure, or other symptoms of wide-spread distress.

Through both the specialist deliberations of the Wilson Committee and the much misquoted Birch Report the young and growing small firm has been made to look like the pioneering corporate crusader. Even today the number of new trading company registrations is treated with great significance as the one best measure of small business sector health and welfare. All this has furthermore been glossed with the 'false naturalism' of the so-called corporate life cycle. As recently as March 1980 Governmental Under Secretary of State with particular responsibility for Small Firms, David Mitchell was reported in Hansard as informing the House of Commons that:

> Small firms are the seed corn from which larger firms of the future will come. When one looks at the national economy, one sees that businesses have a life cycle. Like human beings, they get old, tired, out of date and die. Their places are taken by the young, the thrusting and the vigorous with new ideas, new products, new technology and new ways. We are in a phase of contraction in which many of our older industries must concede the take off of younger, newer businesses.

In many other ways corporate rise and decline has been dramatized to look remarkably human and lifelike. Protected with such 'corporate ageism' there is much less probability that its true nature and frequency will be suitably recognised. Rare studies of how older small firms do actually fade and disintegrate - like that of Adamsez Ltd which follows - raise serious questions about their fate in this brave new small business world.

ADAMSEZ LIMITED: AN OLDER SMALL FIRM DISINTEGRATES

The disturbing realities of the disintegration process are
particularly well illustrated by the case compiled from the
special Benwell Project Report (1980) and associated archive
material. Adamsez was formerly one of the longest surviving
small British fireclay sanitaryware manufacturers. From its
Tyneside production base it worked right through from the early
1900's into the mid 1970's having originally been inspired by
its Quaker founders' inventive product designs. Using many
local resources its often hand craft based workforce produced
well priced products that were commonly regarded as the 'Rolls
Royce' of their particular trade. Their special niche within
that trade made them particularly dependent upon public sector
contracts and schemes and its founders and their first
successors kept strictly to the motto of 'keep it small'. By
the mid 1960's their joint strategy was beginning to bring
about further organisational strains. Established customers
were becoming more price and utility rather than craft and
quality conscious. The sector was increasingly dominated by
four multinational corporations apparently much more adept at
exploiting these changes than the many small firms that were
disappearing at this time. While Adamsez initially survived
there were management succession and other developmental
problems calling its future into question, not least because
its family owner-controllers had not appreciated the radical
import of many of the changes then taking place. Their initial
resort to price cutting to maintain the former status quo
merely undermined their longer term economic viability. So
when losses duly mounted they finally went outside their
established family circle to appoint a Managing Director who
would 'streamline' the remaining concern with such stringency
that any potential buyer of their stake would soon be impressed.
A 40 per cent reduction in workforce size was one of the first
steps in that direction.

Some such efforts apparently did impress certain distant
'businessmen' enough to pay £160,000 for that stake while using
a £100 company specifically floated for their purposes. Among
them were some acknowledged speculative buyers and sellers of
troubled companies not unacquainted with 'asset stripping'
practices of the time. However they soon appointed thirty two
year old Harvard Business Graduate James Lee to front a revival
operation which the local press reported with considerable
admiration. Annual turnover was to be doubled to exceed
£1,000,000 from a product range reduced from over 300 down to
around 70 individual items, with consultative management and
other such promises built into well forwarded plans. So well
forwarded that both banks and government disregarded more
critical independent evaluations and continued their support
for an apparently 'entrepreneurial' turnaround.

But those plans and promises soon ran into much more
formidably real production problems. Whole production runs
were mismatched and lost with the consequence that customer
complaints and dissatisfaction grew once again. Poor premises,
dated technology, and lack of genuine trade and organisational
skill and knowledge had created major constraints which massive
cash discounts once again never dispelled. By March 1975 -
nearly twenty seven months after the original takeover -
outside stakeholders were seeking the appointment of a Receiver
for Adamsez affairs. The magical entrepreneurial turnaround
had not materialised. Adamsez total debts came to £683,691.
The £345,627 owed to the unsecured creditors was never repaid.
After deduction of Receivership expenses both bank depositors
and taxpayers also lost considerably. But not the same loss
that its last remaining workforce experienced. One third of
them were not even entitled to claim redundancy payments. As
an essentially older aged, locally tied, lower paid, poorly
represented male group they hardly understood what 'fringe
benefits' actually implied. And they found precious few jobs
they could easily transfer over into. Even when they
eventually did, the more skilled men - Adamsez had few
recognised apprenticeships - often lamented the 'quality of
working life' they had formerly created, enjoyed and now lost.
None attempted to start their own business. A small number
nevertheless finally found employment with the very much
smaller company specifically set up to exploit a few select
Adamsez lines. That company is all that remains from the
Adamsez complex although by current standards it may be counted
relatively 'young' with even some possible 'growth' potential.

On the surface Adamsez was another likely 'predictable
casualty', not least according to the 'failing older small firm
syndrome' of the 1960's. But merely cosmetic corporate changes
carried out in the name - if not actual substance - of so-
called 'entrepreneurship' offered too little too late at
considerable further cost. Genuine skill and knowledge rather
than symbol manipulation were urgently required. Once given
over to the rites and rituals of Receivership as then practised
their absence made it seem there was no real choice of future.
And it is to the recovery of such choices of future that the
rest of this chapter is devoted.

A CHOICE OF FUTURES?

It is still surprisingly easy to doubt whether there is any
real choice of future for the older small firm. As social
symbols they have become too closely associated with likely
stagnation and decay. Both fading entrepreneurs and weak
successors are acknowledged lead players in the associated

corporate mini-dramas. The stage is completed with certain organisational and industrial scenic effects. Only sometime 'asset stripping' speculators whose true entrepreneurial identity remains doubtful occasionally disturb the cast by dashing across the stage as dubious villians of the piece. Meanwhile others watch this play being acted out with such an indifferent outlook that they hardly take account of the true sacrifices involved.

Many such firms are sadly miscast as the Thatcher Experiment's true new corporate crusaders. That role is definitely monopolised by their young and growing counterparts who are being preferentially subsidised to that effect. This has already created some ill feeling among certain real small business associations. Yet some of their fears are not always what they seem. For example, Chesterman (1982) argued strongly that recent taxation and other exempting legislation was actually making hereditary transmission of ownership, control and wealth very much easier, irrespective of the desirability of that objective. Otherwise those immersed in the 'new politics' of small business would do well to recognise just how many real small firms are neither young nor growing. Elsewhere writers like Alcorn (1980) have called for another renaissance for the 'family firm'. Some such firms are decidedly well valued among certain European societies too. Unfortunately the harbingers of renaissance make their calls in the name of growth and expansion potential, little realising how many such firms may do well to survive at all.

Meanwhile 'corporate ageism' extends beyond individual firms into whole industries, regions, and even nations. These are discriminated against on the grounds of their allegedly greater age in particular. A new vocabulary has developed around 'sunrise' against 'sunset' industries. Even their seemingly middle aged counterparts are said to require progressive 'dematuring'. For that reason cosmetic corporate facelifts are very much in vogue.

Older small firms do not come well out of this changed appearance game. That is very well illustrated by the Adamsez case. But much of the discrimination they encounter still depends upon rather weak and superficial overgeneralisations backed with little or no real evidence. Fortunately critical corporate strategists like Harrigan (1980, p.2) have also pointed out the case against 'proposed strategies which treat all declining industries as if they behaved homogeneously'. Porter (1980, p.255) also adds that:

> in-depth study of declining industries suggests that the
> nature of competition during decline as well as the

strategic alternatives available to firms for coping
with decline are a great deal more complex. Industries
differ markedly in the way competition responds to
decline; some industries age gracefully, whereas others
are characterised by bitter warfare, prolonged excess
capacity, and heavy operating losses. Successful
strategies vary just as widely.

Although they are not necessarily tied to declining industries
as such this still contains an important message for older
small firms, for it suggests that there is some choice of
future. What is now urgently required is an optimum selection
of strategies that recognises that they are not all of one
uniform type. These prospective strategic choices are now
outlined.

The strategic choices of framework

Figure 1 shows the four over-arching strategies that have been
constructed for this purpose. They are each theoretically
'pure' ideal types. Reality in its fullest sense is not so
clear, concise, and free from contradiction and overlap. For
example, tactics and methods from different strategies may be
combined together, and others missed out altogether. Moreover
more than one strategy may be adopted as circumstances change
over longer periods of time. But these particular intellectual
constructs should help identify the broad range of strategic
choices available in the first instance.

  Individually they have been termed Traditionalist, Liberalist,
Reformist and Radicalist respectively. Because there are
internal differences of emphasis in each, two particular sub-
types have been further identified. Each particular subtype
moreover employs its own distinctive 'change metaphor'
describing how they would ideally change older small firms'
situation as the future unfolds. These 'change metaphors' have
been adapted from Mintzberg's conceptions of the power to
change organisations generally (Mintzberg, 1983). Specific
methodologies for effecting desired changes then follow from
each particular metaphor.

Traditionalist strategies are constructed according to their
highly selective version of the practices that allegedly made
the past appear more successful. Continuity and respect for
family, property, and capital accumulation and retention are
often important for their vision of the better future. Older
small firms can still fit into their idealised world picture
because they resemble those traditional values. Ideally
capitalist Traditionalists would either like to better induce
them to survive or fully restore them to their alleged former

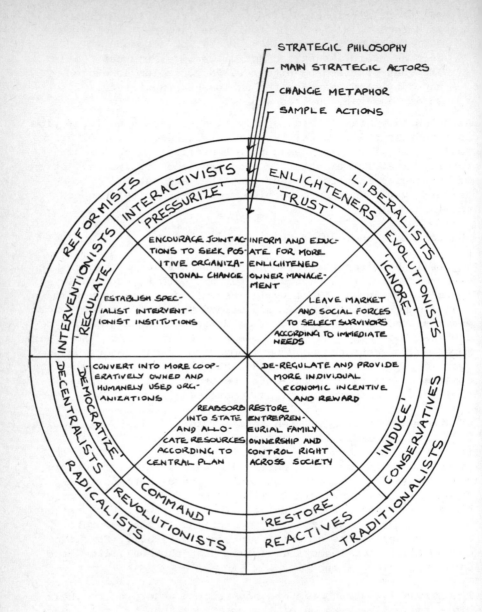

STRATEGIC PHILOSOPHY

MAIN STRATEGIC ACTORS

CHANGE METAPHOR

SAMPLE ACTIONS

REFORMISTS

INTERACTIVISTS

'PRESSURIZE'

ENLIGHTENERS

LIBERALISTS

'TRUST'

EVOLUTIONISTS

'IGNORE'

INTERVENTIONISTS

'REGULATE'

ENCOURAGE JOINT ACTIONS TO SEEK POSITIVE ORGANIZATIONAL CHANGE

INFORM AND EDUCATE FOR MORE ENLIGHTENED OWNER MANAGEMENT

ESTABLISH SPECIALIST INTERVENTIONIST INSTITUTIONS

LEAVE MARKET AND SOCIAL FORCES TO SELECT SURVIVORS ACCORDING TO IMMEDIATE NEEDS

DECENTRALISTS

DEMOCRATIZE

CONVERT INTO MORE COOPERATIVELY OWNED AND HUMANELY USED ORGANIZATIONS

DE-REGULATE AND PROVIDE MORE INDIVIDUAL ECONOMIC INCENTIVE AND REWARD

REABSORB INTO STATE AND ALLOCATE RESOURCES ACCORDING TO CENTRAL PLAN

RESTORE ENTREPRENEURIAL FAMILY OWNERSHIP AND CONTROL RIGHT ACROSS SOCIETY

'INDUCE'

CONSERVATIVES

TRADITIONALISTS

RADICALISTS

REVOLUTIONISTS

'COMMAND'

'RESTORE'

REACTIVES

Figure 1   The strategic choices framework

ascendance. Conservative Traditionalists are most attracted
toward the 'induce' tactic. This makes them turn to individual
economic incentives and rewards for these firms' owners and
controllers in the first instance. Reactive Traditionalists
envisage much wider ranging changes generally. Claiming
justification from older historical tradition they believe
entrepreneurial family ownership and control is a 'natural' and
time honoured desire for even the novitiate entrepreneur as
well as his successors to eventually aspire to. They see the
modern state and corporation as straying too far from that
traditional ideal. So they would ideally reverse that entire
trend and restore such ownership and control right across
contemporary society. For they believe there are relatively few
intrinsic reasons why these firms should become so problematic
compared with the long run effects of recent state, welfare and
other liberal organisational reforms.

Liberalist strategies take no such inspiration from the alleged
past. Rather than enter the future facing the past they seek
more choice about whether and how to deal with these firms.
Ideally this should not entail any dramatic intervention in the
current 'normal' processes of selecting which will persist or
deteriorate and then exit. Firms should merit continuity by
matching or outperforming their other organisational counterparts for the work they actually do. Market and social forces
are naturally influential here. This is the essence of
Evolutionary Liberalism which in its most positive sense has
lately been equated with the 'population ecology' approach
toward organisational selection and deselection from the
environment. Any imperfections and failures of these market
and social forces to become fully effective derive less from
the actual nature and structure of the surrounding society and
its economy than false and inadequate knowledge and information.
To the Enlightened Liberalist better education and training
concerning these firms and their management could well
compensate for such shortcomings.

Reformist strategies are much more positively convinced that
these firms face problems that can be productively acted upon
within the prevailing context. The object would be either to
make them more useful and effective, or else ease and effect
the progressive discontinuation of the ineffectual
organisations some might well have become. Reformists therefore basically favour more direct intervention to produce these
desired results. Some select the Interactivist (or pluralistic)
approach which encourages the other organisations concerned to
pressure for these changes. Banks, financial institutions,
professional advisers and consultants, customers, suppliers and
government itself might have influencing roles here. But that
very plurality of 'influencers' makes the change process itself

relatively diffuse and the results more difficult to measure
compared with the specialist agencies their Interventionist
Reformer counterparts would ideally establish. Boswell's Small
Firms Transition Trust would have exemplified this approach.
They would retain the option to radically reorganise such firms
along cooperative and similar lines, but this would not be so
obligatory as it would be for the Radicalists.

Radicalist strategies are similar to their Traditionalist
rivals in that they would ideally change the whole system in
which these particular firms are situated, rather than work
within that system like Reformists and Liberalists.
Decentralist Radicalists would ideally fully democratize both
these firms and the way their inputs and outputs are owned,
distributed and used. Their 'alternative technology' approach
would supersede capitalist purpose, ownership and control once
it progressed from its initial utopian and experimental stage
of development. More orthodox Revolutionist Radicalists assume
that these firms can be converted into quite different
organisational forms and uses. But they would effect this
change less by choice than central command according to some
predetermined plan for production and distribution generally.

Interpreting Adamsez' late demise: the strategic choice
framework applied

Used to interpret this late demise each strategic frame
generates its own particular perspective. Reactive
Traditionalists would see this only as an isolated symptom of
the deeper malaise instituted by the corporatist bureaucratic
state. Conservative Traditionalists might search for
explanations based around the long run effects of over
regulation and insufficient individual economic incentives and
rewards for Adamsez' original owner managers in particular
despite acknowledging certain other market factors. These
would be especially important to the Evolutionary Liberalist
who might trace Adamsez deterioration back to the changing
nature and structure of the sanitaryware industry which had
made it an increasingly peripheral organisation some time before
its abortive revival. The inability of the academically well
qualified James Lee to effect that revival would nevertheless
concern the more Enlightened Liberalist. And the Reformist
would interpret that 'failure' as further proof of the need for
more purposive direct interventions by suitably qualified
agencies (central and/or local) in the ownership and management
of these companies. Otherwise Radicalists (including the
Benwell Community Project Team) would interpret this demise as
another outgrowth of the 'dual economy' emerging within late
monopoly capitalism whose considerable costs are passed on to
employees and other less powerful groups. Many would not be

content with the institutional and educational solutions proposed by Reformists and certain Liberalists. They would rather stress the need for much more fundamental change in the purposes and nature of late capitalism itself.

Clarifying and informing strategic choices

If there is to be more choice of future for these firms - whether that choice involves selecting between developing, persisting, or even exiting from their present situations - it is vital to understand the range of strategic choices available. Overlap and conflict between certain strategies and tactics have hitherto made their real situation and potential rather confused. Thatcherite rhetoric nevertheless suggests that Conservative Traditionalism has an important role. But this is glossed over by reference to the alleged growth potential of all small firms seemingly irrespective of their age and type. Elsewhere the more apparently indifferent 'ignore it' and 'trust it' tactics of the Liberalists have continuing impact. In the event it is possible that many older small firms have been, and will continue to be, as likely 'predictable casualties' as before.

Greater selectivity would require fresh consideration of further possible Reformist strategies in particular, although this would be difficult to reconcile with the present 'new politics' of small firms and the accompanying party political prestige. Critics like Boswell and Chesterman have made valuable contributions that merit wider consideration in this respect. Meanwhile many Decentralist Radicalists remain on the periphery although their cooperative experiments might still provide useful alternatives. Other Radicalists desire quite different structures and cultures to those that presently shape contemporary Britain. And certainly more cross-cultural awareness of the situation of older small firms might further inform the debate now required.

Research could help promote and facilitate that debate. But it remains much constrained by the continuing lack of appropriately qualified basic statistical and related data. So far rather more attention and resources have been devoted toward the incoming entrepreneur and new small firm. Soon this may have to be counter-balanced with equal commitment and concern about the very many small firms that are neither new, nor growing, nor likely ever to be so in the immediate future unless there are important changes in their nature and situation. Those enquiries promise to reveal much more about the small business sector than has hitherto been realised.

REFERENCES

Alcorn, P.B., (1980), Success and Survival in the Family Owned Business, McGraw-Hill, New York.

Benwell Community Development Project Team, (1980), Adamsez: The Story of a Factory Closure, Final Report, no.8, Benwell CDP, Newcastle.

Bolton, J., (1971), Report of the Committee of Inquiry on Small Firms, HMSO, London.

Boswell, J., (1973), The Rise and Decline of Small Firms, Allen and Unwin, London.

Chesterman, M., (1982), Small Businesses, Sweet and Maxwell, London.

Christensen, R., (1953), Management Succession in Small and Growing Enterprises, Division of Research, Graduate School of Business Administration, Harvard University, Boston.

Harrigan, K., (1980), Strategies for Declining Businesses, Lexington, Heath, Mass.

Harris, N., (1972), Competition and the Corporate Society, Methuen, London.

Levinson, H., (1971), 'Conflicts that Plague Family Businesses', Harvard Business Review, vol. 9, no.2, pp.90-98.

Marshall, A., (1920), Principles of Economics, Macmillan, London, 8th Edition.

Merrett Cyriax Associates, (1971), 'The Dynamics of Small Firms', Research Report No. 12, for the Bolton Committee, HMSO, London.

Miller, E. and Rice, A.K., (1967), Systems of Organisation, Tavistock, London.

Mintzberg, H., (1983), Power In and Around Organisations, Prentice Hall, Englewood Cliffs, N.J.

Porter, M.P., (1980), Competitive Strategy, The Free Press, New York.

Schumpeter, J., (1939), Business Cycles, McGraw-Hill, New York.

Young, M., (1961), The Rise of the Meritocracy, Penguin, Harmondsworth.

SECTION II
THE NEEDS OF
SMALL FIRMS

How can action learning be used effectively in small business programmes?

DAVID BODDY AND JOHN LEWIS

INTRODUCTION

This chapter attempts a critical evaluation of a small business
development activity which was based on the ideas of action
learning. Since it was first elaborated by Revans (1965),
action learning has been used as the basis for a variety of
management development programmes, mainly in large
organisations. Particularly following an initiative by the
Manpower Services Commission in 1981, several institutions and
groups now offer programmes for small companies based on the
concept. In view of the time and money now going into these
activities, it seems appropriate to begin to ask whether these
efforts are worthwhile, and to identify realistic criteria for
evaluation.

Such a process is in any case consistent with the philosophy
of learning from the results of action. Staff and institutions
offering such programmes can only benefit from going through a
critical evaluation of the overall impact of a programme, and
from trying to identify which bits worked, and for whom, and
which bits are best forgotten. In addition, such programmes
are in competition with other uses of resources. In the case
of the present activity, the alternatives include, for example,
additional counselling and advice services, or more conventional short courses for small companies. Those with an
interest in small business action learning programmes need to

take a hard look at what they are doing, and what they have to show for it.

This does not deny the difficulties of evaluation in this area, where useful outcomes are often intangible, and where many external factors influence the outcomes. However, more is likely to be learned from engaging the difficulties than from avoiding them.

The chapter begins with a brief review of the basic ideas of action learning, and of how these ideas were made operational in the particular programme under review. Section 2 considers each main element of the programme, examining in turn our initial expectations and what appeared to happen in practice. Section 3 assesses the results of the programme so far against several criteria, and considers the general problems of evaluating this kind of activity. The concluding Section 4 draws out the main implications for those designing or funding this kind of programme for small businesses.

1. ACTION LEARNING AND ITS APPLICATION

A business environment increasingly characterised by change and uncertainty has fundamental implications for those concerned with management education and business development. In particular, it raises the question of how to help managers and entrepreneurs to learn to deal with change - not only to respond to change initiated by others but how they themselves can bring it about. It is unlikely that satisfactory education for change, for dealing with 'what will be', can be achieved by methods designed to educate people to deal with 'what is'. Pedler has emphasised that "To help people cope with new situations and new problems which have not yet arisen, objectives cannot be set in the usual way. What we can do is to try and prepare the individuals themselves for the diffi- culties involved" (Pedler, 1974).

Although it is by no means clear how this preparation can best be carried out, one starting point is to consider the kind of learning most likely to be useful. What is it that will help people develop the skills of proactivity, of asking new questions, of creativity and so on, which are most likely to help them work successfully in a changing environment? Professor Revans distinguishes between two kinds of learning, P and Q. P refers to the acquisition of existing, programmed knowledge, while Q refers to the acquisition of the ability to ask fresh questions - of learning how to cope with new problems and new situations. Both types of learning are necessary for the owner of a small business - who needs to keep up to date in

168

the technical aspects of his work, and to be aware of routine
business procedures; but who must also develop the skill to
cope with the ambiguities and uncertainties of innovation and
policy making if the business is to grow successfully.
Conventional institutions and courses have developed to trans-
mit established knowledge - but the problem remains of how to
develop the ability to pose useful questions in conditions of
change.

The specific model of the learning process which Revans put
forward was a particular application of the classic Western
model of scientific inquiry. Faced with a problem, the manager
uses his existing stock of understanding in general and of the
situation in particular to decide a strategy and how he will go
about implementing it. He then goes into an action phase, when
he tries to put his ideas into practice. This is followed by a
stage of reflection in which the results expected are compared
with what has occurred. This comparison, between what was
expected to happen and what actually happened, often leads to
some critical insight into earlier assumptions about, for
example, market growth or the reaction of employees. This,
probably different, understanding can then be used by the
manager as the next problem is faced, and so on through an
unending cycle of

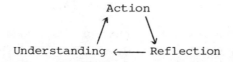

A final point is that great stress is placed on learning as a
social process. That is, the insights a manager gains from
working on a significant problem are likely to be enhanced if
he undertakes the learning experience in the company of several
others who are doing likewise. Not only can such groups
provide new ideas or approaches to each other's problems but
the group meetings themselves can become vehicles for significant learning.

In some degree, a manager will be going through this cycle in
the course of his everyday work. The problem seems to be that
of how to confront the manager with new situations which
require a more intense activity at each stage of the cycle. In
particular, that he is obliged to ask new questions, or look at
things in a different way in order to make progress on the
analysis of the problem; that he goes beyond the comparative
safety of diagnosis, and into the riskier stage of action: and
that there is a deliberate review of the results of action
against what was expected.

The way of doing this suggested by Revans, which is central to action learning, is to give the manager a real project to work on, either in his own, or in another organisation. He implied that managers, being essentially practical people, are more likely to undertake and benefit from this learning process if it is geared to a current organisational situation, in all its realistic complexity. He also viewed learning as a form of social process - "managers learn best with and from each other". Therefore although each manager is responsible for his own project, or activity, he meets regularly with others who are engaged on similar exercises, to give and seek assistance (Revans, 1966; 1971).

Some Basic Propositions of Action Learning (from Boddy, 1981)

(1) Managers are, above all, men and women of <u>action</u> exercising a range of practical skills and emphasis should be given to the development of those skills.

(2) Reading books and listening to lectures, even analysing cases, are <u>not</u> the most effective ways for experienced managers to develop these skills, though these methods do make a contribution. Rather, these skills can best be learned by taking action in a real managerial situation with a period of reflection on what has been done.

(3) More will be learned by this process when it takes place in the company of others who are taking part in a similar exercise.

(4) The best opportunities for learning take place in a manager's everyday job. This is viewed formally as embodying three broad activities - the formulation or development of strategy, acting to implement strategy, and finally reviewing the outcome - in particular comparing what was expected to happen with what did happen. This comparison is seen as the beginning of a learning experience.

Stated like this, it will be immediately clear that many quite common practices in organisations embody some or all of the ideas of action learning. For example, planned job rotation could be very similar to the provision of a project; setting up a project team to work on a particular assignment could be used for learning as well as for task purposes; while a well conducted appraisal system can be a basis for learning from the actions of the previous period.

All of these clearly have much to contribute to management

development; but the discussion in this paper is concerned with what might be called 'explicit' action learning programmes in the sense that someone (either in a company or a training institution) deliberately sets about putting together projects, participants, group meetings and so on.

Early examples of such explicit action learning programmes were those developed by Revans himself, notably the Hospital Internal Communications project and the Belgian Inter-University project, and a review of some more recent activities has been published by Pedler (1983). All of these programmes are based on the idea of action learning; yet closer examination reveals that each one is unique in its design. Clearly the basic concepts have been put into operation in a variety of different ways, suggesting that, as with organisations themselves, there is no universally appropriate way of designing an action learning programme. The strength of this is the adaptability of the approach to meeting the needs of particular managers and organisations. The question with which this chapter is concerned is whether, and how, the approach can usefully be used in the development of small businesses.

The Glasgow programme

The basic ideas outlined were used to guide the detailed design of a series of five courses which made up the Small Business Growth Programme at Glasgow University. This was funded by the Manpower Services Commission, and, in its early stages, was carried out in association with EMAS Consultants. The programme consisted of five courses, each of which was intended for about eight owners or directors of companies with between 5 and 50 employees. Each course lasted about 6 months, consisting of a weekend and 9 full day group meetings.

The main criteria for entry to the programme were that participants were effectively running the business concerned (as distinct from being a junior partner, or an equal member of a management team), and that they were able to express some vision that they wanted the business to be significantly different in 2-3 years time. Care was also taken to stress that they would be expected to help other businesses on the programme, as well as receiving help.

Each participant was asked to specify a 'project', which would be the focus of the group discussion and analysis. We took the view that some such focus was required to provide at least a starting point for the exchange of ideas, and to give some sense of continuity to their participation. It was pointed out that the project definition could be wide - to quote the programme outlines, the project "could concern a new product, some new technology, or perhaps a new system: any reasonably significant development upon which they would welcome practical ideas and advice from other people running small businesses, and from course staff".

   Group meetings were to be held at regular intervals, to perform two functions. First an opportunity to review project work and other developments in each business, and to exchange ideas, information and advice. This was the 'conventional' action learning element, of people "learning with and from each other". In addition, we decided to use about half of the time available at the group meetings for 'staff inputs'. This reflected our belief that there are certain ideas and techniques which can help small businesses to make sense of their experience, and to clarify the most fruitful areas for development. This seemed particularly appropriate if we assumed that few if any of the participants would have had any formal management training. Obvious broad 'areas' for staff input were expected to be marketing, particularly segmentation and positioning; finance, particularly estaimating and budgeting; operations management; personnel selection and job specification.

   The first course began with a weekend meeting in May 1982, and was completed in December 1982. The other four courses commenced at four-monthly intervals and the programme was completed by May 1984.

2.   THE PROGRAMME IN OPERATION

In order to highlight the significant things we have learned from the programme, each element is examined in turn, on the basis of a comparison of our initial expectations with what happened.

The participants

We initially expected that those running small businesses, and who are attracted to relatively 'open' development programmes such as ours, would have the following characteristics. They:

   (1) have personally decided to commit the time to attend
   (2) are relatively open to new ideas
   (3) have the authority to try out new ideas if they are felt likely to be useful
   (4) are looking for new ideas that they can apply easily (they will not have staff or time to experiment or adapt complicated techniques)
   (5) are chronically short of time, will be impatient of

172

       unstructured discussion, and will manage time in
       group meetings firmly
 (6)   will be familiar with the array of information on
       grants and support agencies available for small
       businesses.

   Expectations 1, 2 and 4 were broadly confirmed by experience.
Item 3 was true in most cases, but in a minority of cases was
not. For example, one person admitted to the programme was the
son of the still active founder of the business: our
anxieties about this situation were allayed at the selection
stage by assurances that he would be directly responsible for a
new autonomous division being created, and his project would be
related to that. In the event, the bulk of his time continued
to be spent working in the main business, where his independent
authority was severely limited. This has implications for
selection. Item 6 was generally true of the common agencies
and grants (e.g. Scottish Development Agency, Regional
Employment Grants); but some of the more specialised sources of
funds such as the Department of Industries Microprocessor
Application Project were not common knowledge. A useful
function was served within the groups of exchanging information
of this sort among participants so that some participants now
claim grants where they had not previously done so. Short
notes are being prepared for distribution to future programmes
about those sources which emerge in this way.

   Item 5 is particularly significant to programme management.
Although chronically short of time, participants often appeared
particularly bad at managing it. Meetings rarely started on
time with everyone there, and group discussions frequently
digressed or avoided the main issues. Members either did not
feel strongly about wasted time, or did not feel skilled enough
to make proposals to improve it. They clearly enjoyed the
exchange of views, but this did place a responsibility on
course staff to intervene and provide prompts from time to time
to help ensure constructive and action oriented discussion.

The projects

A central feature of action learning is that participants work
on a real project - some significant problem or situation which
is hurting, and which they are committed to doing something
about. This becomes the focus of the group meetings, and of
the action ➔ reflection ➔ learning cycle.

   This was reflected in the publicity and stressed during
selection discussion, and most were able to articulate a
project of some sort, e.g. 'to expand the customer base', 'to
develop production, sales and service organisation capable of

                               173

handling four times present level of sales','to market new
system to the travel trade'. Even at this stage, we detected
unease amongst some participants, and a sense that some
'projects' were being articulated because they were asked for.

   In the event, some participants continued to focus on clearly
defined projects, which in varying degrees they pushed through
towards a conclusion. A significant number of participants,
however, found difficulty in this; either their 'project'
changed several times, or their discussions at group meetings
related to developments in their business generally. The
significant point is that this did not necessarily detract from
their learning or their benefit from the programme.

   The lession we draw is that the notion of a 'project' as
something distinct from, though clearly related to, the
business as a whole is often a difficult idea for the owner of
a small business. His effort and interests are instinctively
directed at current issues. Over concentration on these would
defeat the point of the programme; but over emphasis on a
'project' could appear unreal, and again defeat the point. In
other words the project for a small business is much more
likely to be an integral part of the total operation of the
company.

   The danger is that unless some specific development concern
is articulated, discussion will centre on currently topical
issues, of little long term significance. The skill for those
running such a programme seems to be to stress the need for
some such articulation, but accept that the emphasis may change
over time.

Group meetings

Group meetings are expected to serve various purposes within an
action learning programme, and each can be evaluated from this
programme.

Task help. They served substantially their purpose of
providing a sounding board to try out new ideas and to enable
members to get the benefit of the experience of the other group
members. This covered general advice and ideas on projects, to
very specific things like helping one member to work out a
major capital reconstruction. Also by providing a chance to
make and receive comments on each others' business
developments, they may have contributed substantially to the
much greater awareness of their business as a whole, which most
participants felt they gained. Finally, as already mentioned,
they enabled information on grant and support agencies to be
exchanged very productively.

<u>External pressure</u>. Other reports of action learning programmes
have drawn attention to the value of a group of colleagues in
being able, by not letting the matter drop, to oblige a member
to undertake disagreeable but necessary tasks. It became clear
in the programme that entrepreneurs live comparatively isolated
lives, and can always find a reason for putting such tasks off.
In several instances here, once the group had become convinced
of the necessity of an action - such as the dismissal of an
ineffective production manager, or the dissolution of a
partnership arrangement - they regularly nagged the 'evader',
until action was taken.

<u>Plan and review</u>. Since the course design is based on the
notion of learning from deliberate action, it was important
that members left each meeting with a specific plan of action
to undertake before next time. As a control against inaction
the practice was developed of asking each member at the
conclusion of a meeting to note down the main things they
planned to do before the next meeting, and leave this behind.
That was then the starting point of the group's discussion at
the next meeting.

<u>Reflection and learning</u>. It proved very hard to build in a
substantial reflection element into the group meetings, at
which members could review the particular activities they had
undertaken, and then draw out the wider implications. Learning
and insight undoubtedly occurred, but it was predominantly in
terms of specifically practical tasks and techniques, rather
than under 'self development'.

   As we shall see in the evaluation, the group work was felt to
have significant value; task help and external pressure seem to
have been the element within the group work which contributed
most, rather than the more 'process' directed activities.

Formal inputs

When designing the programme, we took the view that while it
should above all be an opportunity for the mutual exploration
of business problems, there would also be value in consciously
including some relatively structured inputs by appropriate
members of staff. The reasoning was that there are now some
relatively clear areas of knowledge and techniques which can be
helpful to someone running a small business; half of the time
at each group meeting was given to this.

   In the first programme, the topics covered in this way
included marketing, finance, job specification and personnel
selection, production planning, company organisation and so on.
These were quite well received, but it was observed by course

members that while clearly relevant they were not sufficiently
closely related to the project work and developments in the
business. Once the 'formal sessions' were completed, the
groups got on with their own business analysis.

To cope with this, a rather different arrangement was adopted
in the second programme. Potential topics for staff inputs
were identified during project discussions, and confirmed at
the end of a meeting, with as much precision as possible.
Staff inputs were, as far as possible, based on the analysis
and interpretation of a particular situation in the group, from
which general principles were drawn. For example, contributions on budgeting or partnership structures were based on two
such issues in the group. The presentation ended with a series
of key questions, and these were used as an initial framework
for the group discussions. For example, after a session on
market segmentation, the ensuing business analysis session
concentrated on helping each member to clarify and define his
own market segment, and his position within that segment.

Discussion then moved on to other aspects of the project or
business development that concerned members, but it was noticeable that the conscious reinforcement of the staff inputs
seemed to result in much more frequent reference back to them
in subsequent meetings.

The topics which have emerged and been dealt with in this way
may also be of interest:

  Market orientation and segmentation -
    seeing problems from the viewpoint of user needs and
    benefits, and developing an ability to identify
    market opportunities

  Costing, estimating, budgeting and forecasting -
    the key element of linking the past to the future,
    and developing an information system to give guide-
    lines on performance

  Specifying jobs and selecting personnel, and broadly
  creating an appropriate organisation structure -
    particularly for management staff, where mistakes
    can be disasterous in a small team: developing
    appropriate financial and management structures

  Control and delegation; including also ownership and
  partnership structures -
    a key problem as a business grows from a size where
    the owner can personally supervise, to one where
    control is inevitably less direct. Both cognitive
    and psychological aspects

Time management –
  a desperately scarce resource, preventing small
  businesses taking a longer view of strategy.

Though the broad headings are fairly predictable, the group
was able to be fairly precise, if staff pressed for
clarification, in what areas were most likely to be 'triggers'
of effective action. We concluded that the ability of staff to
enable and help groups to articulate precise learning needs to
these or other areas will be a significant factor in a
programme's success.

What this implies is that the design can benefit substantially from careful identification and effective delivery of
relevant staff contributions. These must be presented in a way
that relates directly to a perceived problem in the group, and
which enables subsequent group analysis to be based on the
framework. Done in this way, it represents a substantial
additional resource to the experience already present in the
group.

4.   EVALUATING THE PROGRAMME

Since a principle reason for MSC funds being used to finance
the programme was the hope that successful small businesses
would provide employment, any evaluation must begin by trying
to assess whether the programme has had any effect on this
employment. The basic information is shown in Table 1.

Table 1
Employment change in participating companies
May 1982–June 1983

| | Company | | | | | | | | | |
	1	2	3	4	5	6	7	8	9	Total
May '82 (start)	25	12	30	5	2	5	3	35	12	129
Dec. '82 (finish)	37	10	3	9	2	6	5	35	8	115
July '83 (6 months later)	37	14	3	12	3	8	8	35	19	146

The total movement clearly reflects some significant shifts
in individual companies. At one extreme, Company 3 experienced
severe financial difficulties and the original firm was wound
up in the course of the programme. At the other, and not
evident from the table, is the development of Company 8.

Although the number of employees is the same, there were substantial shifts within this, including the creation of a new management structure. Company 8 also grew by acquisition but these figures have been excluded.

The commonest pattern, in 6, and possibly 7, of the nine companies is of a small, but proportionately significant, growth in employment. Clearly, however, these figures can be interpreted in many ways; and in particular, we do not know what would have happened without the course, or how much, if any, of the change can reasonably be attributed to the course. It is also quite possible that employment gains in these companies are offset by losses in competitor companies - so that the public gain would be nil.

Some light can be thrown on at least the first two points by taking account some of the more qualitative judgements of members. Some examples of these, most related to employment generation, are shown in Table 2.

Table 2
Examples of qualitative comments, by company

Company 1   Some trade from other group members

       2   Was an engineer, now a manager - would be out of business but for the course; aware of need for financial controls

       3   Now more commercial, realise cash and accounts the key

       4   Frame of mind for sorting out company, and greater interest in growth

       5   -

       6   Developments encouraged, and timing brought forward

       7   Attitudes picked up from colleagues - a real company now

       8   -

       9   Better organisation to realise opportunities

(Note: 1, 5 and 8 probably most qualified/sophisticated of course members, and this does have some implications for selection.)

Apart from employment gain, what other significant business developments, did members report, and to what 'extent' did they attribute this to the programme? It was stressed during the evaluation discussions that we were not seeking justification of the programme, but a critical evaluation, and replies appeared to be given in that spirit. The replies are summarised in Table 3.

Table 3
Judgement by participants on significant developments
since programme started

Company	Significant Developments	How far due to Programme? %
1	Four, independently of programme	0
2	3 year agreement negotiated with licensing company	50
	Likely SDA funding	50
	Non-executive director appointed	100
	Business plan prepared	50
	Cash flow project done	100
	Financial controls introduced	100
	Plus 1 independently of programme	
3	Introduced new financial controls	75
	Plus 4 independently of programme	
4	Marketing of new product	50
	Suing former partner	50
	Plus 6 independently of programme	
5	Six independent of programme	0
6	Positive advertising	25
	Promotional conferences managed more vigorously	25
	Plus 3 independently of programme	
7	New production manager	25
	Business plan produced	25
	Plus 4 independently of programme	
8	Five, independently of programme	0
9	Four, independently of programme	0

(Note: This assessment of benefit seemed to refer more to the academic inputs than the group discussion. Notes of the programme indicate that further developments were influenced by the group.)

Finally, it is worth recording some of the benefit which members made during the evaluation discussion, both for what was learned, and of which elements of the programme were seen as most useful.

Table 4
Further benefits and comments on course by participants

Company	Other benefits	Comment on course
1	Understanding other businesses with which I deal	Project groups most useful
2	More commercial and professional	Lectures important, but groups also very important
3	Now more commercial	Group discussions supportive, weekend excellent
4	Watching how others do things: how to deal with crisis	Weekend most useful
5	Group as a sounding board: thoughts and ideas from group	Project groups most use Different style for formal inputs needed
6	Developments encouraged	Preferred formal inputs
7	Need to look ahead. Attitudes picked up from colleagues	Group meetings most useful
8	Longer term look at business	Group discussions excellent Group pressure very effective Weekend had impact
9	Aware of things that need doing	Lectures important

An overview

The general idea of action learning is that by working with others to tackle a real business problem, people are able to develop individually, the group becomes relatively self supporting, and observable progress is made on tackling business issues. In this particular application, designed for small businesses, the problem upon which attention was focussed was usually nothing less than the future strategy of the businesses represented.

Against these criteria of company development, individual development and self support, the programme has been a mixed success; the first group is still meeting six months after the final formal session, all but one of the companies have grown, and most of the participants acknowledge some ongoing benefit or change of attitude. Against this must be the question of how much of the development would have taken place without the programme. When comparing the results with the normal course criteria of acceptability to the participants, and meeting the objectives of an action learning based programme, the course has been successful with good feedback. Participants have recommended the course to colleagues and made several minor suggestions for improvement, which were incorporated on the later courses. This chapter is based mainly on information from the first group with some input from the second and third, but despite the small sample, it is possible to draw some tentative lessions for future programmes.

The participants

Two groups of participant can be clearly identified, the more sophisticated, who had some previous business knowledge especially of accountancy and marketing; and those who were looking for inputs in these basic areas. The more experienced had received some professional training, either through previous business development courses or from their professional background for example, in accountancy. The other group could fairly clearly be defined as craftsmen using the Norman Smith model (Smith, 1967). These groups had much to learn from each other and it is important that the working groups should cut across this natural divide if all are to benefit.

While the working groups were self selecting it was important that each should contain at least two members, able and willing to analyse business problems in depth and willing to probe the bland statements of fellow participants. The second course which was more biased towards the less sophisticated owner revealed a need for more academic control and participation. The third course reverted to the previous balance and was able to follow the earlier pattern of allowing self support. In the early part of the programme, the more sophisticated participants gained most from the group interaction being generally more open and willing to discuss their strategic problems. As the programme developed along with mutual confidence, all felt able to take part.

A major factor in the development of mutual confidence was the initial weekend programme, and within that, an exercise especially designed to facilitate mutual understanding alongside skills in problem analysis. This exercise developed by EMAS Consultants (1981) involves the use of two groups with each interviewing every member of the other group. During analysis and discussion, all become involved and this exercise

181

was probably the key to the success of the weekend, and led directly into the group meetings. While initial discussions were inevitably fairly general, involving a relatively high element of information transfer, the later meetings were able to analyse specific issues of immediate concern to the participants. For example, one participant was able to rehearse some critical negotiations upon which the company's future strategy depended and was eventually far better prepared than the initial practice indicated. In another, the real benefit only came after confidence had been established, but the group assisted and an analysis of the company's customers helped development of alternative strategies. The company which collapsed caused some surprise to all in the group, but real assistance with the restructuring was offered, once the situation was apparent.

The benefits

Since the programme is sponsored by the Manpower Services Commission, the measure of its success must be the increase in employment within the companies. Even allowing for the initial reduction, the six months figures would indicate that most companies were stronger after the programme than before it. The programme was funded by MSC and marketed specifically to companies with an identified interest in growth, both by letter and referral by other agencies. The fact that employment was reduced initially in many of the companies is a sign of the programme's strength, since it forced a deeper analysis of problems and the creation of a stronger base from which future developments could come. The total cost, including the initial residential weekend and all tuition, was about £1,000 per participant for eleven days of teaching spread over six months. Although difficult to directly quantify, the benefits would appear to justify the costs and to compare favourably with alternative programmes.

Selling of these benefits is however, not necessarily easy. The companies were originally identified by the main support agencies such as the Scottish Development Agency, Regional Council and development corporation, but even so, it was not easy to sell. It is apparently easier to attract companies without the initial weekend as the fourth course has shown, but there is as yet, no evidence of the strength of the group within that course. Without public funds, it is unlikely that companies would have attended, though some have made a contribution to the costs at the end of the course.

Academic input

Two issues remain very open - the value of the academic input and the extent of academic guidance during the group discussions. For the less sophisticated, the inputs were of considerable value and the later idea of linkage to the discussion has been very successful. For the others, these sessions were something of a waste of time. Academic guidance was, however, essential in the group meeting, regardless of knowledge and background of the participants. This can be compared to other courses where a detailed analysis of the transfer of knowledge from the classroom to the organisation showed that learning and application is directly related to the support which the participants gained from their organisation (Huczynski and Lewis, 1979). For owner/manager, this support can be provided by the group and its constructive management, which can give a formal institutional support as well as relating the teaching to the problems and encouraging in-depth analysis of the issues presented. Without this management, the groups avoided the required depths of analysis, wasted time and so became less motivated.

Overall implications

In summary, this programme appears to be both of benefit to the companies involved, and cost effective. The balance of the group is important but the action learning approach is of more relevance to a group containing several more professional owners. For these participants, the critical ingredient is the management of the group, in order to ensure that discussion is of sufficient depth and relevance, and that the knowledge and lessons are applied within the company. Action learning is therefore not an easy option, but involves skills of group management, and the ability to pick up issues as they arise. While specialist teachers in marketing, accounting and production made major contributions to the programme, the leader who bridges the organisational and small business management divide, would appear best able to manage this type of course.

REFERENCES

Boddy, D., (1981), 'Putting Action Learning into Action', Journal of European Industrial Training, vol.5, 5th November.
EMAS Consultants Ltd., Organisers Formation Manual, Ref. 1018.
Huczynski, A.A. and Lewis, J.W., (1979), 'The Influence of Organisational Variables on Management Training Transfer', Journal of Enterprise Management, vol.2 no.1.
Huczynski, A.A. and Lewis, J.W., (1979), 'Response to Cooper and Burgoyne: Organisational and Individualistic Approaches to Learning Transfer', Journal of Enterprise Management, vol.2, no.1,.

Revans, R.W., (1971), Developing Effective Managers, Praeger.
Pedler, M., (1974), 'Learning in Management Education', Journal of European Training, vol.3, no.3.
Pedler, M., (ed.), (1983), Action Learning in Practice, Gower.
Smith, Norman R., (1967), The Entrepreneur and his Firm, Michigan State University.

The female entrepreneur in Britain: some results of a pilot survey with special emphasis on educational needs

DAVID WATKINS AND JEAN WATKINS

INTRODUCTION

The supply of women to the labour market in western developed
economies shows little sign of abating, despite recession and
the highest recorded levels of unemployment. The reasons were
summarised well if somewhat emotively by the US Interagency
Committee on Women's Business Enterprise:

"....There is no sign that women's entry into the work
force will diminish. In fact, the Department of
Labour predictions of the number of women who enter
the labour pool have consistently underestimated the
actual numbers in the last decade. With so many more
women in the work force, the need for job creation is
critical. Many lives depend on these jobs being
created. As women marry later and the divorce rate
remains high, more and more households are headed by
women. Women are the sole bread-winners in four and a
half million families. In millions of other families,
the woman's paycheck is the difference between poverty
and a decent standard of living." (SBA, 1980)

The 1981 estimate of the UK labour force was 26.3 million
(15.9 million men and 10.4 million women), an overall growth of
some 5 per cent on the decade. However, between 1971 and 1981
male economic activity reates had actually <u>declined</u> somewhat

whereas those of women continued a long-standing upward trend
(see Table 1).

Table 1
Economic activity rates of married women 1911-1981

	1911 %	1921 %	1931 %	1951 %	1961 %	1971 %	1981 %
All ages above school leaving age	9.6	8.7	10.0	21.7	29.7	42.3	49.5

Source: Adapted from E.O.C. 7th Annual Report (1982). Date
          based on those periodically reported by Employment
          Gazette.

These figures for economic activity rates include those men
and women who are self-employed or are proprietors of small
companies. Unfortunately no information is available from
official sources on the proportion of UK small firms which are
owned and controlled by women. 1975 figures are available,
however, for the breakdown by sex of those registered as self-
employed: around 9 per cent of economically active males and
4 per cent of females (Royal Commission on Wealth, 1979). This
lack of data is particularly annoying, since US evidence shows
that the recent emergence of women into the workforce in not
just greater numbers but in a wider range of employment
categories than hitherto has greatly increased the observed
rate of female entrepreneurship. Thus between 1970 and 1979
the overall number of self-employed women increased by 52.8 per
cent (reversing a historical decline) and the number of women-
owned businesses increased by 30 per cent between 1972 and 1977
(SBA, 1980). It would not be surprising to find this sort of
increase happening now in the UK and there is some evidence
from unofficial sources that the proportion of businesses owned
and controlled by women is now around 6 per cent of the total
(Forum of Private Business, 1982).

In the UK the distribution of female self-employment across
different sectors is highly variable, with a strong bias to
services of all kinds and to (retail) distribution in
particular (Table 2). This merely reflects the present nature
of much of women's economic work in general. As the EOC
commented recently:

  "All the available information about women's position in
  the labour force points to their being concentrated in
  industries and occupations which are very largely
  female. In manual employment this concentration is
  increasing; 60% of all female manual workers are employed
  in catering, cleaning, hairdressing or other personal
  services compared with 46.7% in 1975." (EOC, 1982).

Table 2

Distribution by industry of UK

Male and female self-employment (1975)

	Men %	Women %
Manufacturing	6.9	5.2
Agriculture, forestry and fishing	13.9	8.4
Miscellaneous services	14.5	33.6
Professional and scientific services	11.5	10.0
Insurance, banking and financial services	2.6	3.8
Distributive trades	19.6	38.0
Transport and communications	5.2	0.5
Construction	25.8	0.5

Source: Adapted by authors from Department of Employment
Gazette, June 1975.

Almost automatically, the non-manual occupations entered by
women tend to centre on these same industries. However, the
five years to 1982 saw a drop in the proportion of women in the
occupational labour force classified as 'general managers'
(Department of Employment 1975, 1982).

This picture of the employment prospects for women as yet
takes no account of two further changes.

The first is the gradual levelling up of educational
opportunity for women. For example, the percentage of GCE 'A'
level passes accounted for by girls had risen from 40.4 per
cent in 1970 to 45.0 per cent in 1980 and during the decade
there was some shift towards those subjects traditionally
regarded as masculine (e.g. maths and physics). Numerous other
examples could be cited (DES, 1980).

The second factor, largely unquantifiable as yet, is the
impact of microprocessor technology on what have come to be
seen as growth points for women's work over the past two
decades. We are thus likely to see the increasing substitution
of word processing methods for general typing, the electronic
management of routine office functions and the substitution of
cash or 'credit' dispensers for the cashiering function.

We are therefore likely in the next decade to see large
numbers of women who are unemployed, underemployed or
frustrated in their career aspirations turning to the option of
creating their own business in much the same way that redundant
managerial males have sought to do in the past five years.

THE ORIGINS, EDUCATION AND WORK EXPERIENCE OF FEMALE
ENTREPRENEURS

Given the employment dilemmas above which suggest increasing
numbers of women may wish to consider entrepreneurship or self-
employment as a career option it is appropriate to ask, 'What
is known about the origins, backgrounds, characteristics,
problems and successes of the current generation of women
owner-managers?'

The authors have recently reviewed the existing (exclusively
American) literature on this topic (Watkins, J.M., 1982) and
presented some preliminary findings which relate to a sample of
58 women running between them some 49 independent businesses
(Watkins and Watkins, 1983). In some cases it was also possible
to identify a male control group and make direct female/male
comparisons of entrepreneurial background. A brief resumé of
certain of the latter work is appropriate here in so far as it
relates to training needs.

Parental background

The general entrepreneurial literature suggests that a high
percentage of (male) entrepreneurs had fathers who were also
entrepreneurs or otherwise self-employed (e.g. Collins and
Moore, 1970; Shapero, 1971). It has come to be accepted that
this paternal link provides the most credible role model for
filial entrepreneurial endeavour in later life. To what
extent, then, does an entrepreneurial father perform a similar
role for the future female entrepreneur? And what maternal
roles might also influence the entrepreneurial decision
positively?

Thirty seven per cent of the female entrepreneurs had fathers
who had run a business of their own or were otherwise self-
employed. (A further 10 per cent had fathers whose occupations
were directly related to business activity but were probably
not self-employed). This is an extremely high figure when
compared to the general incidence of self-employment in the
male labour force (relatively stable at around 9 per cent).

Sixteen per cent of the mothers of the women in our sample
also had direct own business experience either on a completely
independent basis or as a partner in a wider family-run firm.
This compares with an average rate of female self-employment of
around 4 per cent (Royal Commission on Wealth, 1979).

Thus a female entrepreneur is some four times more likely to
have been subject to the influence of an entrepreneurial parent
(father and/or mother) than a member of the general population.

These figures certainly support the view that an entrepreneurial father is as critical an element in the socialising influences on the female entrepreneur as on her male counterpart. The small numbers involved do not permit us to form a view on the relative importance of a male versus a female entrepreneurial role model. However, the figures do demonstrate that a maternal role model can have at least as great an influence as a paternal one.

Age at start of business

Previous American work has suggested that the age of (male) entrepreneurs at the point of business formation lies in the range 25 to 40 (e.g. Cooper, 1973). Thus Liles (1974) describes this as the 'free choice period' in that experience, self confidence and a financial base have been developed, but social and business prestige and family and business responsibilities have not developed to the point where they are significant constraints to entrepreneurial risk. In a European context, where advancement may be as much dependent on age as ability and the accumulation of capital from income is more difficult, this analysis has always appeared suspect. Thus the average age of our male control group (Median 39 years; Mean 39.2) was no surprise. However, the distribution of the women entrepreneurs' ages was quite different. First, it was bimodal. Second, the average age of the prime mode (Median 32 years; Mean 32.07) was significantly lower than the more evenly distributed male sample.

Educational background

Nineteen per cent of the women were educated to 'O' level (16 years), 10 per cent to 'A' level (18 years) and 26 per cent to first degree level or equivalent. In addition, 19 per cent had qualifications in commercial subjects at a sub-degree level (secretarial courses or the equivalent) and 26 per cent had professional qualifications.

Almost nothing that had been studies in the education system per se was perceived as relevant to the choice of eventual businesses as founded and operated (as listed in Table 3). In only two cases was the 'highest level' (viz. degree course) educational content relevant to the business eventually pursued. It emerged clearly in interviewing that this was a result of pressure to pursue non-practical ('liberal arts') subjects while at school (and hence at university) because 'nice' girls did not indulge in practicalities.

In complete contrast, 80% of the professional qualifications obtained has been of some direct relevance to the business

Table 3
Business operation areas:
Female versus male entrepreneurs

Business Area	Women's Businesses (%) N = 49	Men's Businesses (%) N = 43
Distribution	12	2
Catering	6	0
Other consumer services	14	2
Industrial/commercial services	29	21
(All services)	(61)	(25)
Manufacturing/remanufacturing	31	67
Construction	0	2
Transportation	2	2
Primary extraction	0	2
Agribusiness	6	2
	100	100

career pursued, as had some 55 per cent of the commercial qualifications. However, despite the high frequencies the perceived impact - except in a handful of cases - was very low. This raises interesting questions for the professionalisation of entrepreneurship through training for women as a whole.

It is interesting to compare this with the number of men for whom educational/professional experience was directly relevant. The overall educational level of the male control group was very similar to that of the women (see Table 4). However, as one might expect, almost no men had taken so-called 'commercial' subjects on leaving school. Instead, exactly twice as many (52 per cent against 26 per cent) had taken recognised professional qualifications. Moreover, in 88 per cent of cases the educational or professional qualification was also of relevance to either the specific business venture undertaken or to business in general.

Thus the process of education and professionalisation can for many members of the male sample be seen as a steady progression culminating eventually in the formation of a specific business venture well suited to that individual's interests and skills. (albeit the entrepreneurial event may well have been triggered by some other displacement.)

In contrast, the female entrepreneurs were basing their businesses on a more restricted experience base acquired after the cessation of a largely irrelevant educational process

(which had in many cases also disbarred them from the higher
level professional qualifications related to business).

Table 4
Educational level of female and male entrepreneurs

Level	Women (%)	Men (%)
'O' level or below	19	23
'A' level or below	10	2
Degree or equivalent	26	22
'Secretarial' type qualifications (sub-degree commercial)	19	2
Recognised professional qualifications	26	52

Work experience

It has been recognised that prior attempts to create a business
constitute good learning which increases the chance of future
success and that patterns of repeated entrepreneurship may
themselves form a distinct career path or paths (Ronstadt,
1982). However, it is surprising to note that only 60 per cent
of our sample were on their first business. One woman was on
her fourth (successful) business and several others had had the
experience of running more than one successful venture (often
in parallel). No case of previous outright failure was
reported, although there had been a number of conscious
decisions made to discontinue marginal or unproftable
businesses. Interestingly, although the creation of
successively complex ventures did not appear to be a conscious
strategy of the women interviewed, the subsequent ventures were
normally both larger and more sophisticated businesses than the
earlier ones. (Usually a progression from simple retailing to
more complex services or to manufacturing as well as trading.)

Among the male sample there had been somewhat fewer prior
attempts to initiate a business (48 per cent reported such
attempts). This difference was not significant taken in
isolation but it should be remembered that the male sample was
significantly older than the female one.

For those women not entering their current venture as part of
an already established pattern of entrepreneurial activity, the
nature of their immediate prior employment can be seen as
crucial. There is considerable evidence that different kinds
of employment situation 'incubate' new ventures at different
rates (Cooper, 1971). Do women's patterns of employment then
lead them to work in more or less productive incubators?

Even when one includes women who moved directly from a previous own-venture to a current one managerial responsibility was rare. Only 24 per cent of the group could previously be termed 'managers' (male sample: 72 per cent). Moreover, the previous work experience was related to the venture formed in only 40 per cent of the cases studied (male sample 84 per cent).

When one considers both direct experience of a related business and managerial responsibility together, the picture is even more sharply defined. Only 5 per cent of men entered a venture of which they had no direct prior experience without any managerial experience in a different business context. Fully 50 per cent of the women did so. For the male sample, the modal route into entrepreneurship was to replicate a business of which the man had good prior knowledge in both technical and managerial terms as an employee of someone else; for the female sample this was almost unknown.

Table 5

Prior venture-specific and managerial experience by gender

	Women % (N = 58)	Men % (N = 43)
Management role	24	72
Non management role	76	28
Specific, prior knowledge of venture type	40	84
No such knowledge	60	16
Neither specific knowledge nor managerial experience	50	5

CAREER PATH AND ENTRY INTO ENTREPRENEURIAL TRAINING

It seems clear from the survey data summarised above that the background and experience of women entrepreneurs prior to the entrepreneurial event differs substantially from that of male entrepreneurs. This severely constrains the business-choice decision and may force women into stereo-typically 'female' businesses where the prior existence of successful female-led businesses reassures potential financiers, customers and suppliers.

On the other hand, our control group of male entrepreneurs acquired technical and business-related educational and professional qualifications and moved on steadily through an employment-based career structure which gave them the experience of managing a business or business-unit which they could comprehend technically. Redundancy, policy differences or changed personal circumstances then precipitated these men into an essentially similar occupation on an independent basis. The occupational change, and hence the motivation required, was quite small.

For the women studied the situation was quite different. Little or nothing in their educational and professional back- grounds had prepared the women interviewed for running an independent business. (Moreover, women in general require a much greater stimulus even to push for self-advancement, let along push themselves into an independent business venture, Hofstede, 1978.) Thus whereas the occupational choice for the men was logical and, in its context, the pursuit of that activity on an independent basis not an illogical decision, for many of the women the decision to enter entrepreneurship was determined not by logic but because of a strong motivation to autonomy and achievement - which had been frustrated by the individual's prior training and background. In many cases, too, the choice of business appears illogical simply because no logical alternative existed which would fulfil the women's over-riding motivational requirements. This may force female entrepreneurs to seek out business areas where technical and financial entry barriers are low and where the managerial requirements are not immediately central to success or failure. Thus the choice of business can be seen in terms of high motivation to immediate independence tempered by economic rationality, rather than a conscious desire to operate 'female- type' businesses.

It is at this point that the entrepreneurial woman may come into contact with the training system. What is the likely result?

Most entrepreneurship training in the UK is undertaken by educational institutions and/or consultants financed by the Manpower Services Commission under part of the TOPs scheme. The higher level courses conform to a greater or lesser degree to the design of the original courses at MBS dating back to 1976/7 (Morris and Watkins, 1982), in which a short but intensive residential business skills course is followed by a supervised project-learning period in which learning is focussed on the development of the business plan for the individual's venture.

As the concept has been developed and expanded to an increasingly wide range of education providers, the entry criteria to such programmes have become much more clearly defined. They include, ideally, (1) a business idea which is

only months from the market place (2) proven experience in a
central role in a similar business (3) some prior management
experience (4) a substantial proportion of the necessary
initial capital available from personal resources (5) evidence
of commitment to starting a business.

It should be immediately apparent that most of the women
interviewed as having successfully started and operated a
business would have difficulty meeting criteria (2) and (3)
simply because of the typical career patterns followed by women.
As will become apparent below, there are additional barriers
which face women seeking entrepreneurship training which
operate at least as effectively to exclude them.

First, however, it is important to demonstrate that even this
defined group of successful women owner-managers would have
perceived and responded to an appropriate training opportunity
had it existed when they began their businesses.

PERCEIVED BUSINESS PROBLEMS OF FEMALE ENTREPRENEURS

Each woman interviewed was asked - inter alia - to indicate on
a five point scale the seriousness or otherwise of a series of
thirteen problem areas which a pilot study had shown to be of
potential importance. Responses were combined using simple
numerical weighting to give the rank order shown in Table 6.
This also lists the frequency with which any item was perceived
to be the most important problem of all.

To the researchers' great amazement a perceived 'lack of
business training' was both the most frequently cited problem
and the first ranked problem on a weighting basis, taking
precedence in the minds of the respondents over the problems of
raising finance, obtaining property or other 'expected' replies.
This perceived need emerged also in more open-ended discussion
where it centred on training in the finance/accountancy area as
being the major (but by no means only) area of concern. This
reinforces our belief that the result is considerably more than
an artifact of statistics or interviewer bias.

NEW STRUCTURES FOR FEMALE ENTREPRENEURSHIP TRAINING

Having demonstrated that successful female entrepreneurs
believe a basic lack of business training is the most
significant problem they have to face in running their
companies it is now possible to identify the barriers which
prevent such women and an unknown number of other potential
female entrepreneurs from entering the established system of

194

Table 6
Areas highlighted as problems in running the business

Rank order	Problem Area	Frequency as most important problem
1	Lack of business training	11
2=	Obtaining finance	9
2=	Poor security for loans/special conditions	6
4	Obtaining property	9
5	Demands of business affecting personal relationships	5
6	Society's beliefs about women in general	6
7	Lack of technical expertise	7
8	Problems with the tax treatment of women	5
9	Lack of management expertise	3
10	Potential suppliers not taking women seriously	2
11	Lack of business colleagues to talk to	2
12	Problems obtaining business insurance	-
13	Potential customers not taking women seriously	2

New Enterprise Programmes and Small Business Courses. For the most part the discussion is based on the interviews conducted with the reference group of successful female entrepreneurs.

These barriers fall into four broad categories: psychological, criteria-based, content-based, and structure-based.

Psychological barriers

The women interviewed clearly felt existing programmes of entrepreneurship training were (a) aimed at men and (b) would be almost exclusively male as regards both participants and staff. Despite attempts to make the adverts not just gender-free in phraseology but positively encouraging towards women, they were still regarded as male-oriented and as being placed in male-oriented media. The expectation that women would be in a tiny minority not just on entrepreneurship training programmes but on management development activities in general was widespread among respondents and was exemplified by the experience of one woman who was accepted onto an MSC sponsored programme at an educational institution in the North East.

"I never want to be the only woman on a course again.

The course was good but the whole thing nearly cracked
me up. <u>All</u> the lecturers were males. All the outside
lecturers always made a comment about me being the
only woman. I sat through the lectures quietly and
wouldn't say a word. I felt an outsider."

Criteria-based barriers

The typical (and often sensible) entry criteria for training
courses - developed idea, some evidence of technical and
managerial skill, some personal finance, evidence of commitment
- obviously do not sit comfortably with our research-based
picture of the successful female owner-manager. Yet there is
some evidence - based on the looser criteria adopted in Mid-
Wales where entrepreneurship training has always been seen as
much in the context of long-term rural development as short-
term business development (Jackson, 1982) - that it is possible
to take strongly motivated women with <u>no</u> business training,
experience <u>or</u> business idea and help them become successfully
functioning owner-managers in highly competitive market
conditions. However, it is important to note that eliminating
criteria-based barriers almost certainly involves structural
and content changes, too.

Content-based barriers

The corollary of an educational and experiential background
which is likely to be less rich than that of a man of the same
age and intelligence is that the level of initial teaching
required (in finance and accounting particularly) will be lower
for a woman. In terms of MSC's market segmentation this may
mean that women with the quality of ideas and high level of
motivation which would normally fit them for an NEP require
initial training at the SBC equivalent level prior to NEP
entry. Thus 'content-barriers' do not necessarily imply
additional women-oriented content, but rather a restructuring
of existing materials to meet different needs.

Structure-based barriers

A full-time residential training programme lasting as little as
two weeks may well make greater demands on a woman's home and
family life than does the <u>business</u> when she finally starts it!
The full-time residential management course is a prime example
of the 'masculine culture' evidenced by most management
training until very recently. Moreover, a structure which
demands full-time application to analysis of a specific
business idea from day one does not fit the needs of many

potential female (and, one supposes, some male) entrepreneurs who (a) need more time to assimilate new knowledge as they are beginning from a lower base point and (b) may well be identifying the business idea in parallel to acquiring the skills with which to analyse it. Here a cascade recruitment to an eventual NEP-level course as developed by MBS in Mid-Wales and elsewhere promises to be a fruitful model for female entrepreneurship training courses.

Over the past few years there has been a substantial growth in the number of management programmes aimed exclusively at women. These have been intended to overcome the additional obstacles facing women who want to move into managerial positions. Such programmes are now widely accepted as conferring specific benefits on participants which could not be achieved through mixed sex training (e.g. Langrish, 1980).

The evidence presented in this chapter seems to indicate that one problem facing the female entrepreneur wanting training assistance to establish and succeed in her own business are at least as great as those which face her counterpart climbing the corporate ladder. How long will it be before specific training for female owner-managers becomes the accepted norm here that it is in the USA? Or will British society continue to turn its back on the job and wealth creating potential of fully one half of the population?

ACKNOWLEDGEMENT

This chapter forms part of a wider study of female entrepreneurship sponsored by SHELL U.K. under its SMALL BUSINESS INITIATIVE. Shell's generous sponsorship is warmly acknowledged.

REFERENCES

Collins, I. and Moore, D., (1970), The Organisation Makers, Meredith, New York.
Cooper, A., (1971), The Founding of Technologically-Based Firms, Centre for Venture Management, Milwaukee, Wn.
Cooper, A., (1973), 'Technological Entrepreneurship: What do we know?', R & D Management, vol.3, February.
Department of Employment Gazette, (1975), London, June.
Department of Employment, (1975), New Earnings Survey, Part E, Table 135.
Department of Employment, (1982), New Earnings Survey, Part E, Table 135.

Department of Education and Science, Statistics of Education 2: School Leavers. Annual Figures.

Equal Opportunities Commission, (1983), 7th Annual Report, HMSO.

Forum of Private Business, Personal communication from S.A. Mendham Esq.

Hofstede, G., (1978), 'Cultural Determinants of Individualism and Masculinity in Organisations', working paper 78-4, EIASM, Brussels.

Langrish, S., (1980), 'Single Sex Management Training', Women and Training News 1.

Lamont, L., (1972), 'What Entrepreneurs Learn from Experience', Journal of Small Business Management, July.

Jackson, G., (1982), 'The Identification and Development of Entrepreneurs: The Experience from New Enterprise Promotion in Rural Wales' in Webb, T. et al (eds.) q.v.

Liles, P., (1974), New Business Ventures and the Entrepreneur, R.D. Irwin, Homewood, Ill.

Morris, J. and Watkins, D., (1982), 'U.K. Government Support for Entrepreneurship Training and Development' in Webb, T. et al (eds.), Small Business Research: The Development of Entrepreneurs, Gower Publishing Company, Aldershot.

Ronstadt, R., (1982), 'Does Entrepreneurial Career Path Really Matter?' in Vesper, K. (ed.), Frontiers of Entrepreneurship Research, Babson College, Wellesley, Mass.

Royal Commission on the Distribution of Income and Wealth, Report No. 8, (1979), (Fifth Report of the standing Reference), Cmnd. 7679, HMSO, London, Table 2.11.

Shapero, A., (1971), An Action Program for Entrepreneurship, Multi-Disciplinary Research, Austin, Texas.

Small Business Administration, (1980), Annual Report to the President - Interagency Committee on Women's Business Enterprise, U.S., Washington D.C.

Stanworth, J., Westrip, A., Watkins, D. and Lewis, J., (1982), Perspectives on a Decade of Small Firms Research: Bolton 10 Years On, Gower Publishing Company, Aldershot.

Vesper, K., (1982), (ed.), Frontiers of Entrepreneurship Research, Babson College, Boston, Mass.

Watkins, J., (1982), 'The Female Entrepreneur - American Experience and its Implications for the U.K.' in Stanworth, J. et al (eds.), Perspectives on a Decade of Small Firms Research, Gower Publishing Company, Aldershot.

Watkins, J. and Watkins, D., (1983), 'The Female Entrepreneur: Her Background and Derterminants of Business Choice - Some British Data', 3rd Annual Entrepreneurship Research Conference, Babson College, Mass.

Webb, T., Quince, T. and Watkins, D., (1982), (eds.), Small Business Research: The Development of Entrepreneurs, Gower Publishing Company, Aldershot.

Small business requests for bank finance: reasons for decline

MALCOLM ROBBIE

INTRODUCTION

Bank managers are often criticised for being too conservative
and too anxious to look for security for their loans and
overdrafts. But the business of banking is as much dependent
on lending money as it is on attracting deposits and there is
evidence to suggest that two thirds of manufacturing businesses
and one half of non-manufacturing businesses are borrowing from
their bankers over any twelve month period (Bolton, 1971;
Wilson, 1979). The clearing banks conducted a survey of
applications for new or increased borrowing facilities for the
six months period October 1981 to April 1982 which indicated
that a quarter of a million new facilities (including increases
to existing facilities) were extended to small firms during the
period, amounting in total to £2.8 billion (CLCB, 1983). It is
therefore apparent that bankers do lend money and a lot of
businesses do borrow from the banks.

Having made this point, few people would contend that bankers
ought to lend to every business that wished to borrow money
irrespective of the commercial merit in the proposal or the
risks associated with it. A pertinent question is then to ask
whether the banks are allocating money to the most commercially
deserving cases in terms of the economic and social goals of
the UK. It is, of course, a huge question that is impossible
to answer objectively because highly subjective judgements of

risk and commercial potential have to be made. Although it is not possible to assess whether banks are lending money to the 'right' businesses, it is certainly possible to look at some of the businesses that are refused bank finance and consider why they were refused: this is the purpose of this chapter.

THE SURVEY

In May 1980 a questionnaire was sent to 68 bank managers in one region of a major clearing bank requesting details on the last five small business requests for loan or overdraft facilities they had sanctioned and the last five they had declined. They all responded that they had sanctioned five requests during the preious twelve month period details of which are outside the scope of this chapter. Thirty five bank managers stated that they declined three or more requests during the period totalling 184 declined requests which form the subject of this report. [1] Many interesting facts pertaining to the applicants, the applications themselves and reasons for refusal given by bank managers are presented in this chapter, but it should be pointed out that the lending decisions were made between fifteen months and twenty seven months before the introduction of the Small Business Loan Guarantee Scheme (hereafter referred to as 'LGS'). [2]

As the LGS has been closely monitored by the Economics Division of the Department of Industry some of their observations, along with the observations of Robson Rhodes, who were appointed as consultants to review certain aspects of the Scheme's operation and impact, have also been included in this chapter. In this way it is hoped to illustrate how the LGS has encouraged bank managers to alter their lending practises for some of those applications falling under the scope of the Scheme.

BASIC CHARACTERISTICS OF THE DECLINED REQUESTS

It is useful to briefly mention a few basic characteristics of the businesses comprising the declined sample. Table 1 shows the industries to which the businesses belonged and it is interesting to note that only 13 per cent of the sample were classified as 'manufacturing businesses' which is in fact probably slightly greater than in UK industry as a whole. [3] National statistics are notoriously meagre but from those that are available the industry distribution of the sample are not markedly out of line with the whole population of UK small firms.

Table 1
Characteristics of declined applicants
- industrial classification -

	No.	%
Manufacturing	24	13.0
Agriculture	16	8.7
Construction	20	10.9
Transport	15	8.2
Retail	73	39.6
Services	27	14.7
Other manufacturing and service industries	9	4.9
	184	100.0

This contrasts with the industrial activity of LGS borrowers
where manufacturing businesses figure much more prominently:
the Department of Industry report that 45 per cent of borrowers
up to September 1982 were manufacturing businesses (Robson
Rhodes, 1983a, p.7).

It may also be seen from table 2 that the majority of
declined applications were for £20,000 or less which was again
a similar distribution to the sanctioned loans in the survey.
At the upper end there were fourteen requests apparently
declined for amounts between £50,000 and £100,000 but there was
evidence to suggest that a few of these larger requests were
not strictly declined, but requests were withdrawn after
discussion on terms. The LGS average loan is about £33,000
(Robson Rhodes, 1983a, p.4).

Table 2
Characteristics of declined requests
- amount requested -

	No.	%
Unclassified	5	2.7
£1,001 - £10,000	97	52.7
£10,001 - £20,000	35	19.0
£20,001 - £30,000	22	12.0
£30,001 - £40,000	4	2.2
£40,001 - £50,000	7	3.8
£50,001 - £100,00	14	7.6
	184	100.0

Next it is interesting to note the purposes for which requests were made. Whilst the largest single purpose was for 'trading finance' about one third of businesses required finance for a fixed asset purchase and in addition there were over one fifth of businesses requiring start-up finance (table 3). It should be noted however that several businesses requiring finance for fixed assets also required trading finance. The majority of LGS loans are also granted for 'trading finance' or 'working capital' although in many cases this is synonomous with start-up costs as 50 per cent of 'Scheme' borrowers are start-ups (Robson Rhodes, 1983a, p.11).

Table 3
Characteristics of declined requests
- purpose -

	No.	%
Initial start-up finance	42	22.8
Land and buildings purchase	37	20.1
Machinery/other fixed assets	21	11.4
Trading finance	71	38.6
Finance to assist firm adversely affected by inflation, falling sales or strikes	4	2.2
Other purpose(s)	4	2.2
Not classified	5	2.7
	184	100.0

Table 4 shows the age spread of the businesses making declined applications in the survey. Whilst the majority of requests came from established businesses, a substantial proportion of declined requests were from people wishing to start a new business or from very young businesses. This was a surprising feature at the time of the survey but the LGS seems to have flushed out many new businesses and it seems likely that some of those previously declined would now be sanctioned under the scheme. This is a particularly high risk area in which bank managers have lent very warily and usually required some security (Dyer, 1980, p.68-86). It is therefore of little surprise that an analysis of the first fifty failures under the scheme reveals that one third were either start-ups or buy-outs and a further third were less than one year old (Robson Rhodes, 1983b, p.36).

Table 4
Characteristics of declined applicants
- age of business -

	No.	%
1 year or less	53	28.8
More than 1 year but less than 3 years	22	12.0
3 years or more	109	59.2
	184	100.0

FEATURES OF THE REQUESTS

Having noted a few of the characteristics of the sample the first feature about the requests themselves which deserves attention is the quality of loan requests. Of the total number of declined requests no balance sheets were available in 43 per cent of cases and in another 32.6 per cent of cases they were over one year old (table 5). In other words, in three quarters of cases bank managers were asked to make a decision on a proposition where balance sheets were either dated or non existent. Of course it was not possible for new and very young businesses to produce balance sheets (unless they only represented a few months trading) but this does not explain why eleven businesses over three years old were unable to produce balance sheets and why the delay was so long in many other cases. There is much debate in the literature about the usefulness of balance sheets as a lending tool for bankers, but there is little doubt that for many bank managers it still provides a useful starting point in almost any business lending decision. [4]

Table 5
Relationship between quality of declined requests and age and availability of balance sheets

AGE AND AVAILABILITY OF BALANCE SHEET(S)

	Under 1 Year	Over 1 Year	None Available	Not Specified	Total
Well prepared	7	2	5	0	14
Reasonably prepared	17	14	13	0	44
Poorly prepared	4	4	2	0	10
Verbal	12	40	59	5	116
Totals	40 (21.7%)	60 (32.6%)	79 (43%)	5 (2.7%)	184

Having noted that recent balance sheets were not available in
the majority of cases it is therefore not surprising that
bankers classified few requests as being 'well prepared'.
Table 6 shows the relationship between the quality of the loan
request and the amount requested. It is apparent from table 6
that the quality of requests appeared to improve with the
amount requested. Although it is not shown in table 6, it is
also interesting to point out that one half of the well
prepared requests were from manufacturing businesses.

Table 6
Relationship between amount and quality of declined requests

AMOUNT REQUESTED (£)

	1,001- 10,000		10,001- 20,000		20,001- 50,000		50,000- 100,000		TOTAL	
	No.	%	No.	%	No.	%	No.	%	No.	%
Well prepared	1	1.0	1	2.6	7	20.0	5	38.4	14	7.6
Reasonably prepared	16	16.5	16	41.0	9	25.7	4	30.8	44	23.9
Poorly prepared	3	3.1	1	2.6	5	14.3	1	7.7	10	5.4
Verbal	77	79.4	21	53.8	14	40.0	3	23.1	116	63.1
	97	100.0	39	100.0	35	100.0	13	100.0	184	100.0

Experience with the LGS suggests that most LGS borrowers
presented fairly elaborate written requests, which included
cash forecasts as stipulated on the LGS application form
(Robson Rhodes, 1983a, p.30). However Robson Rhodes were more
circumspect about the quality of presentations in their
analysis of the first fifty failures. They criticised the help
given by many accountants and small firms' advisers who
assisted in about half the presentations. It appeared that the
forecasts bore little resemblance to reality and there was
little evidence that cash forecasts or statements of monthly
income and expenditure were being used to monitor and control
the businesses in their early days (Robson Rhodes, 1983b, p.73).

Another feature of the declined loan survey that merits
attention was concerned with the applicants' past relationship
with their bankers. As shown in table 7 no less than a third
of unsuccessful applicants had already exceeded their overdraft
limit without prior consultation with the bank and an
additional 14.7 per cent had suffered the indignation of having
their cheques returned unpaid. In fact thirty customers had

Table 7
Declined applicants' relationship with the bank
- conduct of bank account -

	No.	%
Overdraft limit exceeded without consultation	62*	33.6
Cheques returned unpaid	27	14.7
Overdraft limit exceeded with consultation	15	8.2
Account maintained satisfactorily	41	22.3
Not answered	39	21.2
	184	100.0

* Includes thirty customers where cheques also returned unpaid for lack of funds.

the doubtful distinction of both exceeding their limit without authority and having had cheques returned unpaid. These figures also do not take into account that this question was not answered in about a fifth of cases, usually where the bank account was maintained elsewhere than at the respondent's bank. There were also several request from new businesses. It therefore seems likely that the majority of established businesses who had their request declined had not enjoyed a harmonious relationship with their bank. This aspect was not covered in the LGS surveys although it is interesting to note that a larger proportion of non customers of the bank than might be expected were present in the first fifty failures i.e. 37.5 per cent of failures were non customers before their LGS relationship (Robson Rhodes, 1983b, p.42).

BANK MANAGERS COMMENTS ON REFUSED REQUESTS FOR FINANCE

Turning to the reasons for decline a blank sheet was attached to the questionnaire on which respondents were asked to add any comments which they felt would be useful in determining why particular applications for finance were declined. Most respondents did not make use of this facility, but sixteen branch managers added brief comment on forty six declined applications (25 per cent of the sample). The cases on which comments were made were collated and tabulated under eight broad headings, which appeared to encompass the reasons for decline. The headings were:

Inadequate capital resources or excessive level of outside finance

Twelve of the forty six cases in the declined sample were classified under the first heading. Four of these cases were new businesses with little or no capital resources being provided or the net worth figure comprised a high proportion of goodwill.

In two other cases in the declined sample companies were trying to expand too quickly with inadequate capital resources – both were manufacturing companies. There was one retail sole proprietorship with a deficit on the balance sheet and two other businesses where losses had eroded the capital base, although one of these (a service industry company) was not becoming profitable and it appeared that the main reason for decline was that the bank was being asked to put up too much to buy some property. There were also two other cases where managers noted that level of outside debt was excessive.

Inadequate capital resources usually means an unduly heavy reliance on outside debt. The high capital gearing ratios of LGS borrowers is one of the striking features of the commentories on the scheme. It appears that about one third of LGS borrowers had initial capital gearing ratios of over 5:1 (Robson Rhodes, 1983a, p.63). In addition gearing ratios of the first fifty failures were horrendous; over two thirds of borrowers had gearing ratios in excess of 5:1 with many in excess of 20:1 (Robson Rhodes, 1983b, p.62).

Scheme viewed as unviable

Only four businesses were classified under the heading of 'scheme viewed as unviable'. All four of these applications were in fact for start-up finance. These comprised two retailers where managers obviously thought the customers were making poor decisions and two transport businesses.

Insufficient information

Under the third heading of 'insufficient information' were classified six businesses, although there were several other cases where this was stated as a secondary reason. Perhaps surprisingly none of these applicants was a new business, although one was a new company which had previously been a partnership and two other businesses were less than three years old. In none of these six cases were balance sheets available and in two cases there appeared to be some reluctance on the part of the applicants to provide information.

In fact, only one retail business fell strictly into that category, but there were two other cases where the liquidation of sister companies caused the bank manager to withdraw the facility owing to possible complications.

Trading difficulties

Under the six heading of 'trading difficulties' there were only two companies. One was a specialist retailing company which had experienced problems in collecting debtors, and the other was a manufacturing company, where the unusually high level of stock was causing the creditors to press and the company was unable to service the bank overdraft. In the two LGS telephone surveys 16.2 per cent of borrowers required finance for urgent working capital (Robson Rhodes, 1983a, p.22).

Security unacceptable

Under the sixth heading of 'security unacceptable' there was only five businesses. However, there were a further eight cases where security problems were mentioned as an additional reason for decline. Of these five cases there were two cases where the applicants appeared to withdraw their request in consequence of the bank's security conditions.

This was probably the main reason why the LGS was instituted i.e. to allow viable propositions to obtain finance even though security was unavailable. However it is clear that about 20 per cent of LGS borrowers could have obtained finance from other sources if they had been willing to deposit personal security (Robson Rhodes, 1983a, App.9).

Miscellaneous reasons for decline

The last heading in the declined survey was very much a residual category for seven applicants not otherwise classified. In two of these cases the proposition appeared to be too speculative for the bank to consider: one case was a speculative property purchase by a new construction company and the other a new micro-electronics company which was already being financed by the National Research and Development Corporation. There was also another case of a very small construction company where the product was still at a research stage. The reasons for the remaining four cases were diverse. One case involved complications under Section 190 of the Companies Act 1948 and the application was withdrawn. Another application was withdrawn owing to the death of the applicant. A third case was a young construction company requiring finance for the purchase of fixed assets where the bank manager thought that hire purchase would be more appropriate. And lastly, an application from a non customer retailing company, where there was evidence that the account had not been conducted satisfactorily with their previous bankers, there was also pressure from creditors and a matrimonial dispute had weakened the security. One is tempted to comment that the whole spectrum of human activity is somehow reflected in the diversity of these reasons for decline.

CONCLUSIONS

Over a period of time bank managers observe the progress of a great many business customers. To some they have lent money: in other cases they have refused to lend. As time passes they will alter their behaviour to reflect their experiences. Their observations are therefore useful and should be respected not-withstanding that we may feel that the line drawn between sanction and decline may be towards the low risk margin. If government money is to be used to raise the margin for the banks and underpin the major portion of the loan, as in the Small Business Loan Guarantee Scheme, bank managers may be encouraged to alter their lending practices and we should be aware of these alterations.

The commentaries on the LGS suggest that capital and income gearing ratios are frequently in excess of that traditionally accepted as prudent and there is some evidence of a change in style of lending (Robson Rhodes, 1983a, p.6). In the analysis of the first fifty failures the writers go even further:

"Banks lending has been carried beyond the bounds of conventionally understood lending against security. In many cases banks are handling what are effectively requests for venture capital as if they were normal banking propositions." (Robson Rhodes, 1982b, p.7)

Robson Rhodes formed the opinion that the eventual failure rate within the scheme is likely to be much higher than that experienced in normal bank lending and closer to that experienced by venture capitalists (1983b, p.7). Further they state that amounts recovered on failures are likely to be very small (1983b, p.7).

The majority of the first fifty failures were certainly very fragile businesses and it is worrying that little or no monitoring and control mechanisms were instituted in most cases.

In our Loan Survey, the main reasons were 'inadequate capital

resources' and 'lack of profitability'. Under the LGS these
elements appear to have become less important to the banker.
If the banker then no longer needs to be satisfied as to the
adequacy of the proprietor's capital stake and/or a record of
successful trading, perhaps more attention needs to be directed
to the other facets of the proposition, notably the future
viability of the business, which again featured as an important
reason for decline in the survey. The banker's assessment of
viability is very much dependent on the quality of information
presented to him by the businessman and this in many cases is
very questionable according to the loan survey and the comments
made by Robson Rhodes on the conduct of the LGS (1983a, p.30-1).
Robson Rhodes were particularly concerned about the use of
financial information for monitoring a loan after drawdown
(1983a, p.6). It is also evident from the analysis of the
first fifty failures under the LGS that there are many 'fragile'
businesses seeking loans and the case for a deeper analysis of
these cases seems overwhelming.

Government money has been and is continuing to be used to
encourage more liberal lending practices, particularly to new
businesses. The LGS has stimulated 'lending at the margin' as
envisaged by the Wilson Committee, but one is left wondering
where the new margin has been set. Perhaps this can only be
ascertained by a detailed study of the applications accepted
and rejected under the scheme and a closer investigation of why
LGS successful applications were not sanctioned by bank
managers using their normal lending criteria.

NOTES

[1] For the purpose of clarification the requests were for new
    or increased loan or overdraft facilities between £1,000
    and £100,000 and the businesses were only to include
    independent businesses having a net worth (including
    directors' loans) of less than £1 million and employing
    less than 200 people.
[2] The bankers were asked to classify businesses according to
    the Bank of England's Industrial Classifications (with
    which bankers are familiar).
[3] The Small Business Loan Guarantee Scheme was launched in
    June 1981. Under the Scheme a business may borrow up to
    £75,000 with a repayment period between 2 and 7 years at a
    cost of 4-5 per cent above the banks' base rate. Part of
    this cost is a 3 per cent premium on the 80 per cent
    portion of the loan which is guaranteed by the Department
    of Industry. In the first 20 months of the Scheme 8,861
    Government guarantees had been issued amounting in the
    aggregate to £295 million.

[4] For a debate on the usefulness or otherwise of historical
    financial statements in lending decisions see Bankers'
    Magazine, March-September 1979.

REFERENCES

Committee of Inquiry on Small Firms (the 'Bolton Committee'),
  (1972), Research Report No. 16, HMSO.
Committee of London Clearing Bankers, (1983), 'The Banks and
  Small Firms', Banking Information Service. 1983
Committee to Review the Functioning of Financial Institutions
  (the Wilson Committee'), (1979), Research Report No. 3, HSMO.
Department of Industry, (1982), 'Interim Assessment of the
  Small Business Loan Guarantee Scheme', Department of Industry.
Dyer, L.S., (1980), 'A Practical Approach to Bank Lending',
  Institute of Bankers.
Robson Rhodes, (1983a), 'Small Business Loan Guarantee Scheme -
  Commentary on a telephone survey of borrowers', Department of
  Industry.
Robson Rhodes, (1983b), 'An Analysis of some Early Claims under
  the Small Business Loan Guarantee Scheme', Department of
  Industry.

210

The provision of small industrial units: a study of local authority provision in three partnership areas

PAT RICHARDSON

INTRODUCTION

The lack of suitable factories and workshops has traditionally
been identified as a major problem for the small business
sector, particularly for those firms operating within the inner
cities. Perhaps as a result of this there has been a large
increase in the supply of small industrial premises, both by
public and private sector agencies, in the last five years. In
the North of England, for example, Dabinett (1982) found that
units under 500 sq.m. (5,500 sq.ft.) represented only 7.5 per
cent of industrial floor space in 1974/75 yet 26 per cent in
1979/80. [1] Local authorities have been among the most active
agencies in the provision of small industrial units,
especially those in conurbations (Department of Industry, 1980,
and Falk, 1979). To date there has been very little analysis
of such activity and the evidence that exists tends to be
rather sketchy. This chapter takes a more detailed look at the
provision by local authorities of small industrial units [2] in
the three Inner City Partnership areas [3] of Manchester/
Salford, Newcastle/Gateshead and Birmingham over the period
1975-1982. It focuses in particular on some of the results
from a questionnaire survey of small unit occupants carried out
in 1982.

THE SURVEY

In the years prior to the survey, local authorities in all three Partnerships were extensively involved in the development of small industrial premises in their inner areas. Table 1 shows the percentage of Urban Programme expenditure allocated for this purpose between 1979 and 1982.

A total of 558 units had been developed in the three areas by the end of 1981 and 398 business were in occupation. In the present survey approximately 50 businesses were interviewed in each area, which gave a total of 159 interviews in all.

The aims of the questionnaire were to determine the impact of small unit provision on:

- employment creation;
- stimulating new enterprise creation;
- assisting business expansion;
- the supply of property; and
- the working environment of small businesses.

CHARACTERISTICS OF RESPONDENTS

Table 2 shows the main characteristics of the businesses inter-viewed in each area. Respondents in all three areas had very similar characteristics in terms of status. In each case the majority were small independent firms, [4], although both Manchester/Salford and Newcastle/Gateshead Partnerhsips had a substantial number of branch plants. The bulk of the branches were non local (i.e. their headquarters were outside of the region) and they served as regional offices for their parent organisation.

Manufacturing establishments, particularly those in engineering, were dominant in each area. In the Birmingham Partnership 40 per cent of respondents were within the metal goods category (SIC XII) reflecting the importance of the jewellery and associated trades in the area. The predominance of manufacturing in all areas is not surprising given that most local authorities have a strong preference for letting their units to this sector. Nevertheless, both Manchester/Salford and Newcastle/Gateshead Partnership had a large number of tenants in the service sector, particularly in the distributive trades.

Most businesses were very young. Over half had been in existence for five years or less, although all three areas contained a few well established businesses (i.e. over twenty

Table 1

Expenditure on different economic initiatives as a % of total urban programme expenditure on the economy[1]

	1979/80			1980/81			1981/82			1982/83		
	N/G*	M/S*	B*	N/G	M/S	B	N/G	M/S	B	N/G	M/S	B
Factory units	22	45	44	28	38	47	11	20	21	9	20	21
Industrial sites	22	9	1	23	17	3	1	30	6	5	9	9
Infrastructure	32	.5	-	28	-	22	23	25	16	31	25	8
Environmental improvements	6	10	20	5	34	16	43	6	24	33	21	17
Financial assistance	13	14	29	9	9	5	4	14	8	3	16	9
Promotion	2	.5	3	1	-	1	.5	-	1	1	-	1
Training	1	10	3	1	1	5	.5	1	12	6	6	15
Other	2	11	-	5	1	1	17	4	12	12	3	20
Total%	100	100	100	100	100	100	100	100	100	100	100	100

(1) Total approved expenditure not actual expenditure.

*   N/G = Newcastle/Gateshead Partnership
    M/S = Manchester/Salford Partnership
    B   = Birmingham Partnership

Source: Partnership Programmes

Table 2

Characteristics of the businesses in the survey

	NEWCASTLE/ GATESHEAD %	MANCHESTER/ SALFORD %	BIRMINGHAM %	TOTAL %
STATUS				
Independent firm	70	71	81	74
Branch plant	20	19	7.5	16
Subsidiary	5	8	7.5	7
Headquarters	5	2	4	3
Total	100	100	100	100
INDUSTRIAL SECTOR[a]				
Engineering	20	25	23	23
Other manufacturing	40	29	56	41
Construction	4	6	-	3
Service	36	40	21	33
Total	100	100	100	100
AGE OF BUSINESS				
< 1 year	4	4	-	3
1-5 years	58	54	48	54
> 5-15 years	24	19	36	26
> 15-20 years	3	10	6	6
> 20-100 years	11	13	10	11
Total	100	100	100	100
TYPE OF BUSINESS				
Start up	35	35	21	30
Mover	65	63	71	67
In situ change[b]	-	2	8	3
Total	100	100	100	100
TOTAL IN SAMPLE	55	52	52	159

(a) Engineering = SIC VII-IX; Other manufacturing VI, XI-IX; Construction XX and Service XXII-XXVI.

(b) In situ change = Businesses which have moved into the unit from elsewhere but continue to operate in all or part of the original premises.

Source: Small Premises Survey

years old). The oldest business interviewed was in Newcastle
and had been operating for 94 years.

In all areas over 60 per cent of respondents had moved into
the premises from a previous location. Variations from this
occurred within each Partnership. For example, 82 per cent of
respondents in Gateshead Borough Council's units had relocated
as opposed to only 42 per cent in Tyne and Wear Council units.
This difference did not appear to reflect the size of premises
built nor any deliberate policy on behalf of the authorities
concerned.

IMPACT OF UNIT PROVISION

Employment creation

Unemployment has for some time been recognised as a major
problem in the inner cities. Not surprisingly, therefore, job
creation or job preservation was regarded by all authorities as
an important objective behind small premises provision. Table
3 shows that the bulk of businesses were very small, employing
five or less persons. A total of 1,344 jobs were provided in

Table 3

Size of businesses in the survey

NUMBERS EMPLOYED	NEWCASTLE/ GATESHEAD %	MANCHESTER/ SALFORD %	BIRMINGHAM %	TOTAL %
0 Persons	–	2	2	1
1-5 "	53	35	58	49
6-10 "	27	31	17	25
11-20 "	15	22	17	18
21-50 "	5	6	6	6
> 50 "	–	4	–	1
Total	100	100	100	100
Total Establish- ments in sample	55	52	52	159

Source: Small Premises Survey

the three areas: 417 in Newcastle/Gateshead; 567 in Manchester/
Salford and 360 in Birmingham. However, this does not
represent jobs actually created because many of the jobs were
already in existence before the policy assistance. [5] In fact,

215

a total of 553 jobs were created and in all three areas new businesses created the bulk of them. (See Table 4.)

Table 4

Total numbers of jobs created by businesses in the survey

	PREVIOUS TOTAL*	PRESENT TOTAL	JOBS CREATED
NEWCASTLE/ GATESHEAD			
Start up	–	128	128
Mover	195	289	·94
Total	195	417	222
MANCHESTER/ SALFORD			
Start up	–	154	154
Mover	328	386	58
In situ change	27	27	–
Total	355	567	212
BIRMINGHAM			
Start up	–	88	88
Mover	223	259	36
In situ change	18	13	–5
Total	241	360	119
TOTAL	791	1,344	553

* Previous = Total employment before the business moved into its present premises.

Source: Small Premises Survey

There was no identifiable pattern to the job losses or gains in terms of establishment status, type or industry. For example, in the Manchester/Salford Partnerhsip the largest job gain (+24) and loss (-28) both occurred within the construction sector. The type of jobs created were essentially male, full time and skilled. As such they were not necessarily catering for those groups in the inner city generally regarded as most vulnerable to unemployment, namely the unskilled (Thrift, 1979).

Given that the provision of small units was part of a programme for inner city regeneration it was important to see whether the jobs provided had actually gone to inner city residents. The businesses were therefore asked where the majority of their workforce lived.

Table 5 shows that a large percentage of respondents said
that the bulk of their workforce lived within the city,
although few (13 per cent) said from the local district (i.e.
within one mile).

Table 5
Location of employees place of residence
with respect to the unit

	NEWCASTLE/ GATESHEAD %	MANCHESTER/ SALFORD %	BIRMINGHAM %	TOTAL %
Local district	16	4	18	13
City	51	41	47	46
Conurbation	26	41	25	31
Region	7	14	10	10
Total	100	100	100	100
Total Establishments in sample	55	51*	51*	157

* In each case units with no employees have been
  excluded.

Source: Small Premises Survey

Taking into account the preliminary nature of the above
assessment of job creation, it would appear that the occupants
of the small premises surveyed did not create large numbers of
jobs for those living in the inner city especially in relation
to the number of jobs which have been lost in such areas.

The local economy

Stimulating new enterprise. The inner areas of the large conurbations have long been regarded as incubators or seedbeds for
new enterprises. It is not surprising therefore that several
local authorities saw the provision of small units as a means
of enhancing the seedbed environment and assisting the
formation of new businesses in their area.

Forty eight of the businesses interviewed were new enterprises, although only 27 were new small businesses, the
remainder being new branches or subsiduaries of larger
organisations. Hence local authority premises appear to have
met a demand for premises by those new establishments which
require a better standard of accommodation than is offered by
the older industrial stock of the inner city.

Only three of the 48 start ups were new in the sense of making a new product or using a new process and all three were located in the Manchester/Salford Partnership. Given this the premises appear to have played a limited role, if any, in assisting innovation in their areas.

Having said this, it is important to note that the survey examined only the standard small units provided. Local authorities in all three areas have also provided specialised premises aimed specifically at new enterprises. For instance, at the time of the survey a small science park (8 units) near Salford University housed two new businesses, one developing a completely new method of screen printing. In Birmingham and Newcastle a total of 53 enterprise workshops had been developed (35 in Birmingham and 18 in Newcastle) ranging in size from 115-530 sq.ft. These are available on a short term licence, allowing business ideas to be tested and developed with the minimum risk and cost to the entrepreneur. [6]

Assisting Business expansion. Not only do local authority premises enable some new businesses to start, they also encourage, or at least facilitate, the expansion of existing businesses. A substantial group of movers (over 50 per cent) had relocated as part of a plan for the expansion of their business. Eighty per cent of those who had moved to expand had previously been located within the same city, and of these 50 per cent had been within the same district. In addition, their search for new premises was confined to these areas. It would appear, therefore, that local authority units have met some of the demand for small business expansion within the inner city. This is important given the lack of starter premises (Department of the Environment, 1982a, and Fothergill, Kitson et.al., 1982).

The units may also have helped firms to start up or expand given that many businesses had vacated property to come into the local authority units. Such a filtering mechanism had been identified in Lambeth by Valente and Leigh (1983). In the present survey only twelve occupants had relocated because of a compulsory purchase order (in which case such premises are usually demolished or not available for re-use). Thus it is quite possible that such a process has taken place in the three study areas. Indeed, the survey identified three cases of the filtering process operating within the local authority units themselves.

Having said that the units have assisted expansion, there could be difficulties as regards any further expansion. For example, three quarters of the businesses said they envisaged some expansion in the near future. However, four in five of these foresaw difficulty in expanding within their present premises. Most of the units have been built in a terraced form on small sites, so there is no possibility of expanding on site. Some authorities have allowed multiple letting but this is a limited solution to the problem and tends to defeat the purpose of building small units in the first place.

Those affected by compulsory purchase orders. One quite specific role some units played was to rehouse those affected by compulsory purchase orders. During the 1960s local authority clearance and redevelopment activities were allegedly a major reason for the destruction of small factories and work-shops in inner areas (Thomas, 1975; Chalkley, 1978). However, today such activity has substantially decreased and local authorities have become more aware of the needs of small businesses. One response has been to provide suitable accommo-dation and space locally for those affected by redevelopment. In the present survey twelve businesses had moved because of compulsory purchase orders. Nine of these had relocated within a mile of their previous premises, the remaining three within two miles.

Whilst the local authority units have obviously helped to rehouse several business affected by redevelopment they are unsuitable for certain others. The survival of many small businesses depends upon them paying the very low rents characteristic of older obsolete industrial buildings. These firms cannot afford the rents of modern premises and when affected by redevelopment they must either find alternative older premises elsewhere or cease trading altogether. Hence, ideally, a wide range of industrial accommodation would be available to cater for the whole spectrum of small business requirements which exist in the inner areas.

Supply of property. Local authority construction of small premises has helped to improve the stock of new and refurbished property for small businesses in the inner city. From the first developments in 1977 until the end of 1981, 558 units of varying sizes were provided in the three areas. (See Table 6.)

The major reasons given by the local authorities for their initial intervention were a high demand for small premises, what appeared to be a gap in the market and the reluctance of the private sector to fill it. However, it is very difficult to assess the scale and nature of a gap in the market for small premises and the extent to which local authority premises have filled it. It is important to note, for instance, that there is no single small premises market. Small premises vary in size and condition from disused railway arches to new 5,000 sq. ft. purpose built factories. Moreover, the type of

219

Table 6
Total number of units built by local authorities within the inner areas (sq.ft.)[a]

Sq.ft.	0-500	501-1000	1001-2000	2001-3000	3001-5000	>5000	TOTAL	
LOCAL AUTHORITY								
G.M.C.	-	3	-	7	-	-	10	
Manchester	-	11	45	6	-	-	62	
Salford	-	30	45	29	5	-	109	
Tyne & Wear	2	9	18	19	4	-	52	
Newcastle	5	10	10	13	5	4	47	(13)[b]
Gateshead	-	-	18	10	2	-	30	
W. Midlands	-	7	30	21	16	2	76	(61)
Birmingham	49	75	35	11	2	-	172	(37)
TOTAL	56	145	201	116	34	6	558	

(a) Excludes the enterprise workshops which at the time of survey included: 35 units @ 150-530 sq.ft. in Birmingham and 18 units @ 115-550 sq.ft. in Newcastle.

(b) Figures in brackets denote the number of refurbished units.

accommodation required varies according to the type of activity undertaken by the business (Falk, 1982). This study considers the section of the market for new or newly refurbished units of less than 5,000 sq.ft.

There appears to be a wide range of evidence, albeit much of it circumstantial, to suggest that there was a gap in the market for small modern premises. Throughout the 1970s various private sector reviews of the property market consistently reported a high demand for premises less than 5,000 sq.ft. [7] In 1970 the Estates Gazette noted:

> There is a growing demand for nursery factory estates where units from 1,000 sq.ft. to 5,000 sq.ft. only are erected and not enough provision is being made for this type of smaller user. (Estates Gazette, 1970, p.261; also see Bozeat, 1979)

In the three study areas, the estates officers interviewed all said they had received a high ratio of enquiries to the number of small units available, although this was not quantified in any way. This has also been experienced elsewhere. Coopers and Lybrand, for example, noted an inner London Borough had received a ratio of 34:1 enquiries for units less than 2,500 sq.ft. in comparison to 7:1 for larger units (Department of Industry, 1980). The high letting rates and low incidence of voids for local authority small units in all three areas was another indication that demand exceeded the supply of premises in this market. In January 1982 the average occupancy rate in the three areas was 86 per cent (77 per cent, 83 per cent and 92 per cent in Newcastle/Gateshead, Manchester/Salford and Birmingham respectively).

Given the above evidence it was perhaps surprising to find that the majority (57 per cent) of businesses interviewed claimed to have had little trouble in finding suitable premises. Thirty six per cent of respondents had found their present unit in less than a month and another 42 per cent within six months. From this it might appear that there was no great gap in the stock of small premises in these areas. However, it is important to remember that the respondents were those who had successfully found premises. It was not possible to identify those who had not. Moreover all of the occupants interviewed had been in their premises for less than five years and were therefore looking for accommodation during a period of increased small unit provision. It is not surprising that few of them experienced major difficulties in this respect.

Accepting a degree of disparity existed between the levels of supply and demand for modern small premises, to what extent might the local authority provision of units have filled the gap? Unfortunately, no detailed systematic data on the stock of premises in the three study areas has been kept. Nevertheless there have been a number of studies which lend support to the idea that local authorities have filled a gap in the small premises market. For example, the Coopers and Lybrand study of small premises noted that:

> Provision has been undertaken almost exclusively by
> public bodies, notably local authorities, New Town
> Development Corporations, the Development Corporation
> ... and most recently also the EIEC. (Department of
> Industry, 1980, p.10)

With respect to the Newcastle area, Smith felt "when the local authorities in Tyne and Wear started to build factories late in 1975 they were filling a definite gap in the market - a lack of provision of small units up to 3,000 sq.ft. in floorspace" (Smith, 1978, p.35; also see Department of Environment, 1982b, p.69). The Estates Gazette reported that during 1977 local authorities were playing an increasing role in inner city industrial development, "particularly in the provision of nursery units which are traditionally less popular with private developers" (Estates Gazette, 1978, p.212). Only in 1979 was it observed that "developers and institutions at last began to cater for the small industrialists' demand for units under 3,000 sq.ft." (Estates Gazette, 1980, p.241).

The extent to which local authority premises have filled a market gap is clearly difficult to resolve. However, the evidence presented above does show that the role of local authorities in the supply of industrial property has been a useful one. Having said this, was it important that the units were developed in the inner city areas? Did an inner city location correspond with any special requirements of the businesses studied? In the survey a substantial group of respondents said they had looked for premises within the city as a whole. However, of these, a significant number of businesses wanted accommodation within a particular district of the city. (See Table 7.) These districts were largely within the inner city areas.

Table 7
Areas considered by respondents in their
search for accommodation

	NEWCASTLE/ GATESHEAD %	MANCHESTER/ SALFORD %	BIRMINGHAM/ %	TOTAL %
Local area*	16	29	65	37
City	73	56	31	53
Region	9	15	4	9
Elsewhere	2	–	–	1
Total	100	100	100	100
Total Establish-ments in sample	55	52	52	159

* Local area = Districts within the city such as:
   Small Heath (Birmingham) or Moss Side (Manchester)

Source: Small Premises Survey

Market considerations were the main reasons given for this localised demand, coupled with the fact that the business was well established and widely known in the area. When asked about their location, the businesses interviewed expressed a high level of satisfaction. Indeed, 92 per cent of all businesses felt their location was very good in terms of access to markets and 89 per cent felt the same as regards

accessibility to supplies. Thus it would appear that local
authority units sited in the inner city have been useful in
accommodating a significant localised demand for premises
within these areas.

   To conclude, the provision of small units by local
authorities has made a useful contribution to the supply of
industrial property in the three study areas. It also appears
to have stimulated the involvement of other agencies in the
building of factory units. By demonstrating that there is a
demand for small units, local authorities have encouraged both
private sector developers and public bodies such as EIE (EIE,
1982) to get involved in this sphere.

Improving the working environment. Local authorities in all
three Partnership areas recognise that many inner city
businesses operate in obsolete, cramped and often dangerous
premises. Consequently improving the working environment of
such businesses was an important aim behind the provision of
small units. (See Birmingham Inner City Partnership, 1979, for
example)

   In the survey bad conditions were second only to expansion as
the main reason for moving, especially in the Birmingham and
Manchester/Salford Partnerships. Poor physical conditions were
mentioned by 20 per cent of respondents, poor access to and
within the buildings by 18 per cent and sharing premises by 12
per cent as reasons for moving. Thus it is clear that a significant number of those who had relocated had done so in order
to improve their working environment. The majority of occupants (over 65 per cent) considered their new premises to be
good or very good in terms of their suitability and physical
condition. Only two problems emerged. Poor roofing and
subsequent dampness was a problem on specific sites in all
three areas, even though all of the units were new or newly
refurbished. Poor design also proved a problem. The majority
of the units had been built with high ceiling space, with the
manufacturing sector in mind. For many service sector
businesses and some manufacturers such space is considered
superfluous and a burden because it is very costly to heat
(also see Ogden, 1979). In addition, many of the units were
only bare shells and occupants had to invest heavily in fitting
them out for use. Such changes are an expensive undertaking
especially when, as in some cases, the units have to be
returned to their original state if the business ever moves out.
Most authorities acknowledge such problems and steps have been
taken to solve some of them. For example, rent free periods are
frequently given as the unit is being fitted out. In terms of
the basic design of the units, however, the local authorities
all felt some problems were inevitable because fairly

standardised units were being provided for a group of
businesses with very varied requirements.

On the whole most businesses were satisfied with the terms on
which they occupied their new premises. Only 4 per cent of
firms expressed dissatisfaction with the level of rent charged
and 58 per cent felt it was very good or good. It must be
noted, though, that seventeen of the respondents were receiving
some form of rent concession at the time of the survey. Three
quarters of those interviewed were similarly satisfied with the
terms of their lease on the unit. The only complaints made
concerned the long leases (25 years) given by some authorities,
notably Tyne and Wear, Newcastle and Salford Councils.
Subsequently these authorities have relaxed their lease terms
somewhat, indeed Tyne and Wear County Council have offered a
tenancy agreement with a one month break clause on their latest
developments.

Little mention, so far, has been made of the different circumstances pertaining in each of the three study areas. Yet the
local context within which the policy measure was pursued was
an important determinant of its impact.

For instance, in the Birmingham Partnership the units built
by Birmingham City Council (BCC) fulfilled a special role as
regards one particular group of customers, the jewellery sector.
This sector is dominated by very small firms with specific
requirements as regards accommodation and location. They
require small, light, airy premises with good access. In
addition, each jewellery business depends upon being very close
to its suppliers and rivals, hence the existence of a jewellery
quarter! BCC have built the bulk of their small premises in
this area, aimed specifically at updating the old premises and
layout of the quarter. Of the 172 units built within the study
period 103 were in this quarter and another 49 within half a
mile.

West Midlands County Council were unique among the authorities studied in that the bulk (80 per cent) of their units were
refurbished as opposed to new build. By focusing on refurbished premises the local authority have been able to utilise
several of the old vacant buildings which are commonly found in
inner city areas. These old buildings are otherwise rather a
problem as there are few alternative uses to which they can be
put.

In Salford the first units built were specifically aimed at
assisting those businesses affected by compulsory purchase orders.
The provision of units in this way played an important part in
the redevelopment of the Lower Broughton area of Salford where

nearly a third of the Council's units were built. This re-accommodation function has now largely been completed and the local authority is now concentrating on assisting new enter-prise creation.

What is unique to the Newcastle/Gateshead study area is the very large area over which the units have been provided. The area as a whole is split by the River Tyne and the units have been built to the north and south alongside the river banks. This division has always had repercussions in terms of employ-ment in the area and this was reflected in the survey. Over 70 per cent of respondents north of the river employed people who lived in the north and the situation was similar for those to the south.

Conclusion. Assessing the impact of local authority provision of small premises is by no means a simple task. Nevertheless, a number of important observations can be made. The number of jobs created by the unit occupants had only a marginal impact on unemployment in the three areas. Yet the provision of premises did encourage, or at least facilitate, the development of small businesses in several ways. Hence this chapter argues that the construction of small premises has been a useful form of local authority activity in the inner areas studied.

However, to what extent should such action continue? In answering this, two considerations must be taken into account: the level of private sector activity in such areas and the extent to which demand for small premises has been satisfied. Both questions are difficult to answer in view of the lack of comprehensive information.

As early as 1979 local authorities were criticised for pre-cluding private sector activity in small unit development. For example:

> Local authorities should resist the temptation to
> continue with a measure once their innovation has
> called the attention of the private sector. (Hookway,
> 1979, p.3)

Falk endorses this view:

> Many authorities are in danger of using up public
> funds at their disposal doing things the private
> sector could be induced to do. (Falk, 1979, p.6.)

The government's industrial building allowance scheme for small units has certainly increased the general level of private sector provision (Department of Industry, 1982; Grant, 1981). Yet the extent of such activity is unclear,

particularly in the three areas studied here. There was
certainly some evidence of private development: Slough Estates
have built twenty units between 800-1,600 sq.ft. in Salford and
more recently an elaborate craft arcade with workshops has been
completed in Birmingham's jewellery quarter. However, estates
officers in all three areas, whilst agreeing that private
development had taken place, claimed it was limited in three
ways: to the prime locations within the city (usually adjacent
to main transport routes); undertaken by local developers with
little evidence of the major financial institutions from the
south getting involved; and to units over 1,000 sq.ft. Hence
there may be complementary roles for the private sector and
local authorities with the latter building where the rates of
return are at present insufficient for the private sector. One
example is enterprise workshops. Such developments require a
great deal of management responsibility which tends to preclude
private sector investment. [8] Gateshead Borough Council are
at present considering such a scheme in South Tyneside and Tyne
and Wear County Council are providing small unit accommodation
for those using their innovation centre. A second example is
the refurbishment of old buildings for small units, which is
often not feasible for the private sector. Birmingham City
Estates department are at present refurbishing several old
buildings in the jewellery quarter. Most of these buildings
are very dilapidated, but cannot be demolished because they are
listed. This makes refurbishment very expensive.

In addition local authorities are in a position to improve
the provision of small premises in other ways. For instance,
they could provide subsidised premises. Coopers and Lybrand
(Department of Industry, 1980) were very much against rent and
rate concessions in their study of small premises provision.
Yet the present survey revealed that such concessions could be
very useful if applied selectively. They might, for example,
assist those tenants affected by redevelopment schemes to
adjust to the higher levels of rent which are bound to occur in
new developments.

Partnership arrangements between the public and private
sectors are also possible. Several such ventures have already
been undertaken quite successfully especially in the Newcastle/
Gateshead study area. However, some authorities interviewed
were not in favour of partnership arrangements which they felt
merely subsidised the private property developers.

More generally, though, there does appear to be a part for
both the public and private sector in small unit provision. Of
course, this assumes and depends upon a demand for such units.
In follow-up interviews undertaken in the Spring of 1983, the
majority of local authority estates officers felt that demand,

at least at the present level, had been satisfied. Any further factory development beyond their commitments at that time would depend on the successful letting of their existing stock. Some local authorities have adopted alternative measures to the direct provision of premises. For example, several have facilitated 'self help' schemes in the small business sector. As Howick and Key (1980) showed in Tower Hamlets many firms in old premises do not wish to move out to new ones. Local authorities can assist such firms by giving them grants to refurbish or extend their premises as desired. A scheme of this sort with 90 per cent grants was undertaken very success-fully in the City of Newcastle (see Tyrrell, 1983).

NOTES

[1] Such figures because they are for total floorspace will tend to understate the nature of this trend as the number of smaller industrial units being built must have been considerable in comparison to the number of larger units.
[2] Taken as units below 10,00 sq.ft. in order to include a wide range of smaller premises into the survey population. However only 4 respondents in the survey occupied units in excess of 5,000 sq.ft.
[3] There were originally 7 Partnerships designated in 1977: i.e. Birmingham; Docklands; Hackney/Islington; Lambeth; Liverpool; Manchester/Salford and Newcastle/Gateshead. There are still 7 in that Docklands is no longer a Partnership and Hackney and Islington operate separately.
[4] Taken as under 50 employees. Two establishments in Manchester/Salford had recently increased their workforce to 54 and 56 persons.
[5] It is interesting to note that when occupants were asked what forms of local authority assistance for small businesses they were aware of, very few of them mentioned small premises.
[6] N. Lindsey is undertaking an evaluation of the workshops in Birmingham as part of a collaborative research programme on local economic planning with JURUE at University of Aston, Birmingham. (See Lindsey, 1982)
[7] A distillation of the various reviews of the property market can be found in the January issues of the Estates Gazette.
[8] It should be noted that BAT Industries have recently developed a group of managed workshops in Liverpool and plan further schemes in London.

REFERENCES

Birmingham Inner City Partnership, (1979), Inner City Partnership Programme 1980/83, Birmingham Inner City Partnership, Birmingham.

Bozeat, N., (1979), The Industrial Property Market: The Opinions of Estate Agents in Birmingham, Research Note 5, Joint Unit for Research on the Urban Environment, University of Aston, Birmingham.

Chalkley, B., (1978), The Relocation Decisions of Small Displaced Firms, PhD Thesis, Department of Geography, University of Southampton.

Dabinett, G., (1982), The Supply of New Industrial Premises in the Northern Region: 1974-1980, Working Paper, Centre for Urban and Regional Development Studies, University of Newcastle-upon-Tyne.

Department of the Environment, (1982a), Industrial Change: Local Manufacturing Firms in Manchester and Merseyside, Inner Cities Research Report 6, HMSO, London.

Department of the Environment. (1982b), Local Authority Aid to Industry: An Evaluation of Tyne & Wear, Inner Cities Research Report 7, HMSO, London.

Department of Industry, (1980), Provision of Small Industrial Premises, Small Firms Division, DoI, London.

Department of Industry, (1982), Small Workshops Scheme, Survey of the effect of the 100% Industrial Buildings Allowance, DoI, London.

English Industrial Estates, (1982), Annual Report and Accounts for the year ending March 31st, 1982, EIE.

Estates Gazette, (1970), The Property Market in 1969, vol.213, 3rd January.

Estates Gazette, (1978), Factories and Warehouses in 1977, vol. 245, 21st January.

Estates Gazette, (1980), Property Market Review, Factories and Warehouses in 1979, vol.253, 19th January.

Falk, N., (1979), Local Authorities and Industrial Development, Urbed Research Trust. Paper given at the PTRC Summer Annual Meeting, proceedings, P172, pp.11-24.

Falk, N., (1982), 'Premises and the Development of Small Firms' in Watkins, D.S., Stanworth, M.J.K. and Westrip, A., (eds), Stimulating Small Firms, Gower, Aldershot.

Fothergill, S., Kitson, M. and Monk, S., (1982), The Role of Capital Investment in the Urban-Rural shift in Manufacturing Industry, Department of Land Economy, University of Cambridge, Cambridge.

Grant, A.P., (1981), Industrial Building Allowance and Small Manufacturing Businesses: An urgent case for legislation, Grant and Partners, London.

Hookway, E., (1979), Local Authorities Influence on Employment and Economic Development: An assessment of some measures

228

used to promote employment. Paper given at the PTRC Summer
Annual Meeting, proceedings P172, pp.25-30.

Howick, C. and Key, T., (1980), Inner City Industry and Inner
City Policy, a survey of manufacturing firms in Tower Hamlets,
Centre for Environmental Studies, London.

Lindsey, N., (1982), Encouraging New Business Enterprises: A
reflection. Paper given at the PTRC Summer Annual Meeting,
proceeding, P217, pp.53-67.

Ogden, C., (1979), Buildings for Industry, CALUS Research
Report, Centre for Advanced Land Use Studies, College of
Estate Management, University of Reading.

Smith, C., (1978), Local Authority Economic Development
Policies and Activities, in Bovaird, A.G. (ed.), Economic
Analysis in Local Government, Joint Unit for Research on the
Urban Environment, University of Aston, Birmingham.

Thomas, K.R., (1975), The Effects of Urban Redevelopment and
Renewal on Small Manufacturing Firms in Birmingham, PhD
Thesis, City of Birmingham Polytechnic, Birmingham.

Thrift, N., (1979), Unemployment in the Inner City: Urban
Problem or Structural Imperative? A Review of the British
Experience, in Herbert, D.T., and Johnston, R.J. (eds),
Geography and the Urban Environment, vol.2, pp.125-225.

Tyrrell, R., (1983), Newcastle Grant Plan Draws Crowds,
Planning, 515, pp.8-9.

Valente, J. and Leigh, R., (1982), Local Authority Advanced
Factory Units: A framework for evaluation, Planning Outlook,
vol.24, no.2, pp.67-69, University of Newcastle-upon-Tyne.

University science parks and small firms

CHARLES MONCK AND NICK SEGAL

INTRODUCTION

Concern about the interaction, or rather the lack of it, between universities and industry has a long and not very productive history in Britain as indeed in most other countries in the developed world. But the current strong resurgence of interest, based as it is on real financial and other pressures on both sides, promises to yield far more fruitful results than before. One has only to read the recent ACARD (1983) report on improving the links between universities and polytechnics (collectively called higher educational institutions or HEIs) and industry, as well as to talk to senior administrators and academic personnel especially in the applied sciences (in some but not yet all such institutions), to appreciate the greater realism, practicality and urgency of the present concern.

This concern stems from three main causes. First, the severe financial restrictions being imposed by government on the higher educational sector are forcing the latter to seek to generate new revenues from other sources.

Second, it is generally held that high technology small and medium enterprises (SMEs) are likely to yield greater benefits by way of exports, value added and perhaps even job creation than would 'conventional' SMEs. Consequently increasing attention is being paid by central and local government as well

231

as their development agencies to the question of how to harness the resources of HEIs to promotion of SMEs in advanced technologies. (It may be noted that the general presumption is that large firms typically already have links with HEIs and that they do not need further assistance to identify the right research or individual researcher to solve specialised problems. While basically true, this does not mean that large firms are aware of everything potentially of relevance to them in an individual HEI. Nor does it mean that large firms, notably those that conduct their own R&D, are not themselves potential sources of technology for SMEs. Nevertheless, it is justified that the emphasis of policy in the present context is on HEI-SME links.)

Third, there is much evidence, even if sometimes anecdotal, that many potentially profitable ideas and inventions originating in UK academic institutions have failed to be commercialised here and instead have been exploited by the country's competitors.

Many initiatives of different kinds are now being planned or taken to address these problems at both national and local levels. Prominent and to some extent fashionable among these schemes are the establishment of science parks based at or near a higher educational institution.

It is the purpose of this chapter to examine the role and effectiveness of such science parks (or high technology development schemes or research parks or technology incubator projects, as they are variously called) in the promotion of high technology SMEs. The chapter thus deals with a particular category of science park, leaving out of account other categories such as those that are essentially high quality real estates in an excellent business location and having no connections with academic or research institutions.

In addition to our general activity and interest in national/local economic development planning, there are three specific sources for this paper [1]:

(a) a wide perspective gained from a 1981 review of science parks and related schemes in the USA and the UK under- taken on behalf of the Department of Industry and Shell UK Limited (1982), from continuing discussion since then with UK science park operators based on or associated with universities, as well as from explora- tion with several universities in the UK and on the Continent of their strategic options for development of their whole relationship with industry;

(b) practical experience gained in setting up and operating

the first phase 'non property' marketing and management functions of English Estates' high technology
developments at Bradford and Leeds Universities,
plus a continuing role in this respect at the former
university;

(c) preparation of a feasibility study for English
Estates into establishment of a technology centre in
Newcastle upon Tyne aimed principally at transferring
technology to local SMEs drawing on the resources of
the HEIs in the region and prospectively also local
large companies with R&D capabilities; and similarly
an examination of the prospects for a high technology
development at the University of York.

The chapter has two principal purposes. The first is to
discuss the nature of the demand for space on university
science parks in the UK, the sources of demand and the factors
that significantly influence it. The second is critically to
explore the role of the property element of such schemes in
stimulating linkages between the academic world and industry.

Finally in this introduction it should be pointed out that we
use the term 'university' loosely to embrace both universities
and polytechnics (arguably some of the national research
laboratories should also be included). There are, as the ACARD
report has highlighted, some important differences between
universities and polytechnics in the kind of research undertaken, the way they are managed as institutions and the way
their relations with the business world are organised. But
there are strong common points too, and in a report as brief as
this it is convenient simply to refer to them as if they were
the same.

THE SOURCES OF SME DEMAND FOR UNIVERSITY SCIENCE PARKS

It is worth repeating that we are considering demand originating from SMEs or which takes expression through establishment
of an SME. Hence large projects of large companies -
exemplified by say the 1975 Syntex investment on the research
park at Heriot-Watt University or the current investment by
Wang at Stirling University - are not dealt with.

Within our context there are three principal categories of
potential demand by high technology SMEs for space on a
university based scheme:

Existing companies

There are two main groups within this category.

The first and, in our experience, quantitatively the more important group, are typically 'application engineers' (rather than 'leading edge technologists'), seeking larger and better quality premises to accommodate and facilitate their growth and to permit them to present a more prestigious image to the outside world. They are usually currently based within a convenient travel distance and time from the university, and there is evidence in some locations that enquiries are strongest from areas in which professional/managerial groups are a significant proportion of the population.

Our own experience is that this category of demand is dominated by companies in computer software and hardware, various applications of microprocessor technology, specialised scientific instruments, instrument engineering and the like. Such SMEs generally do little research of their own and only a modest amount of highly specific development work. Yet to remain competitive in what is far from a static market they must be able continuously to advance their product and process technologies.

The second group comprises local marketing/technical representatives of specialist suppliers based elsewhere in the country. A university campus location offers an appropriate marketing image; it may (on some schemes) offer shared secretarial and other business services that are extremely useful to somebody whose job involves a lot of travelling and does not warrant full time office support; and most importantly it offers potential access to technological expertise and typically excellent workshop facilities, in the solution of customer problems in using the specialist equipment concerned.

The reasons for both these groups seeking a university location do not generally stem from having had intensive or even much contact with the university to date. But they all have the potential to benefit from such links, whether directly in their own or in related technologies as well as in the development of new business opportunities, and their perception of this makes them feel that location on the science park will give easier access to the individual academics and the university's specialist facilities.

The cultivation of such linkages is not necessarily an automatic or easy matter simply by virtue of the scheme's being contiguous with the university. How such interaction can be stimulated is very much a function of how the scheme is marketed and its interface with the university managed, a topic returned to in its own right later.

New business formation arising out of academic ideas and inventions

Our experience is that there is no shortage in universities of ideas and inventions having possible business potential. It is only for lack of proper identification of such opportunities and, more particularly, of effective mechanisms for developing and implementing a comprehensive business plan for each that so few of them realise this potential.

There are basically two routes for carrying such ventures forward to commercial application:

(a) licencing the technology to an existing company. In all probability the company will not be located near the science park. Unless the project is at the very leading edge of its technology and the continuing close involvement of the academics concerned is vital for its success, there is no special reason why such a route should result directly in a demand for space on the science park. It is more likely that the project will be taken up on the company's own premises, for sound practical reasons;

(b) establishment of a new company to exploit the tech- nology, in which the academic plays a central role. Here clearly there are potentially compelling reasons for the business to be located on a science park.

Both of these routes, but particularly the second, require that the academic's technological skills be supplemented and complemented by business skills. Strategic thinking, practical business experience and negotiating skill are required on many interconnected topics: protection of intellectual property rights, marketing, capital funding and cash flow management, after-sales servicing, and so on across the whole range of business issues.

In the United States, for a variety of reasons peculiar to the prevailing business ethos, it is not uncommon for the academics themselves to become the entrepreneurs - this is now well documented (see e.g. Bullock, 1983; Rothwell and Zegveld, 1982). As yet in Britain this happens infrequently though there are a number of significant exceptions to this, notably in computer-related technologies in Cambridge. More generally, in the current climate we see significant evidence of changing attitudes and motivations in many higher educational institu- tions throughout the country that should, if properly

235

encouraged and assisted, result in a much higher incidence of academic entrepreneurs in the future.

No matter how exciting the medium term prospect in Britain, the fact remains that at present many academics even in the scientific and technological disciplines have little business experience and may even be suspicious of the commercial world. They also are likely to have little time to develop business skills (especially the outstanding academics who are inevitably heavily involved in research, teaching and university administration) and nor do they regularly come into contact with others outside the university who do have these skills. Moreover, it is so far only at few universities that this need has been properly recognised and that resources of the requisite quality and quantity have been devoted to effective commercialisation of the academics' know-how.

New business formation originating outside the university

These are typically companies applying or developing the leading edge of their particular technologies and hence needing access to specialised skills and facilities in the university that they cannot afford to have in-house at the early stage of their business development. They are either start up companies, in which case they are probably local and have been working with the university in development of the technology, or are special projects of larger companies that probably are not local but have been collaborating with the university previously.

We know of business projects in both these categories. Where suitable accommodation on or near the university campus concerned has been available, this has in most cases been seen as a significant benefit by the parties concerned and has contributed to getting the project off the ground. But not in all cases: there are some companies which, no matter how advanced their technology or how close their technological links with a university, actively prefer a location well away from the campus in order to project a proper business rather than ivory tower image to their clients.

FACTORS INFLUENCING DEMAND

The overall pressure of demand and its distribution among the three categories described above depend on many diverse factors. We have identified the following as being the most important:

- the nature of the local business environment

- the nature of the university concerned and of its policies and attitudes towards industrial involvement
- the characteristics of the premises offered and their financial terms
- the marketing programme undertaken, the terms of reference and the quality of management devoted to the scheme, and the support available from local public and private sector organisations
- the availability of finance

Each scheme is sui generis, reflecting differences in these factors as well as in the different personalities involved. Nevertheless, certain broad patterns as well as critical features exist and it is worthwhile commenting briefly on each of the above factors.

Local business environment. Taking an overall view of any local economy, it can be seen that the birth and survival rate of small firms and the types of small businesses formed are themselves a function of a variety of influences:

> past and present industrial structure, company size structure, skills and class structure in the labour force, the nature of the activities undertaken in the main companies and their procurement and business development policies, and the roles played by local institutions in the financial, education and government sectors.

These influences are partly demonstrated in the well-known Gudgin and Fothergill work that originated in a study of the East Midlands (Fothergill and Gudgin, 1982), as well as in the much earlier observations made by Chinitz on the comparative incidence of entrepreneurship among the steel communities of Pittsburgh and the garment workers in New York City (Chinitz, 1961). In the case of high technology SMEs the influences are much more sharply emphasised by the developments that have taken place around Boston and Stanford in the USA (see Bullock, 1983; Rothwell and Zegveld, 1982), and at Cambridge and along the M4 axis in England (see the Economist, 1983; Beaumont, 1982).

It is interesting to observe that in what would generally be held as the most successful breeding grounds of high technology SMEs, Boston and Stanford, the influence of the business environment has been essentially spontaneous and unplanned. Bullock (1983) demonstrates the vital role of the local financial sector in stimulating high technology SMEs in these two specific cases and this - together with the highly

supportive policies of MIT in the case of Boston, a quite
extraordinary series of events in the semiconductor industry in
the case of Stanford, and public procurement policies in high
technology fields that favoured small firms - explains far
better than would any conventional theory of regional economic
development why advanced technology SMEs have flourished there.

For a variety of well-known reasons it would be misleading to
seek to translate too directly the American experience to
Britain, and certainly the focus of this chapter is on circumstances and specific schemes here. Also, in the way interest
in new technology SMEs has evolved in the UK, public sector
agencies are playing a more prominent (and sometimes exclusive)
role in initiating policies and projects to promote such SMEs
than has historically been the case in the USA. It is nevertheless true that the private sector is playing an increasingly
active role on the high technology scene in the UK, especially
in new business development rather than property development
terms.

In any event, however, the emphasis of this chapter is on
planned efforts in promotion of high technology small firms
which deliberately seek to supplement (though not substitute
for) whatever 'spontaneous' developments may be taking place.

Nature and policies of the university. In virtually all the
universities in the country, linkages with industry are largely
determined by the inclinations and efforts of individual
members or perhaps specialist groups of the university staff,
rather than by particular actions taken by the central
administration. A central industrial liaison function has been
instituted only in the past 10-15 years. As the ACARD report
has observed, the impact of full time industrial liaison
officers has varied according to the policy commitment of the
university authorities, the calibre of the individual officers
and the resources available to them. In some universities the
function has waned, and in others no appointment has ever been
made.

Things are changing now as, one after the other, universities
are making new appointments sometimes at professional level of
men of high calibre and substantial business experience. There
is a much better prospect now than before that marketing the
universities' resources, adopting the right strategies towards
intellectual property rights and striking commercial deals
whether by way of contract research or new business formation
will be done in an effective, business like manner.

Yet the task is huge, even at the level of the individual
university. This is partly because most universities are

highly fragmented and often slow and bureaucratic in their
decision structures (this is one respect in which polytechnics
can differ significantly from universities), invariably have
little grasp of the complexities of the commercial world and,
no matter how good the new director of industrial liaison, are
understandably cautious as to how best to promote and protect
their corporate interests both as an academic institution and
as a quasi-commercial entity.

There is a nerviousness too as to how much freedom to give to
the individual academic to engage in commercial work, for fear
of the harm done to his regular teaching duties and also of the
consequences of the disparity of commercial opportunities as
between the different disciplines.

The enormity of the task arises also because there are so
many individual, highly specific matters demanding the
attention of the new industrial liaison officer. As already
observed, there is no shortage of academic ideas and inventions
having business and consultancy potential, and similarly no
shortage of contract research opportunities: the difficult
thing is to harness these resources and fully realise the
potential.

Just how effectively this potential is realised is of very
great consequence for a science park. Based on our experience
of universities to date, we are highly encouraged by the number
of business opportunities we see that if successfully
implemented would result in demand for space on a science park.
But by and large the mechanism, backed by the necessary finance,
is not yet in place to exploit this potential. To this extent
the question is one of phasing, the provision of space being
secondary in timing to the establishment of an effective
'commercialising' mechanism.

This discussion, being couched in very general terms, could
be taken to imply a degree of homogeneity among individual
academics in their links with industry that simply does not
exist. It is readily evident in any university that there are
individuals who already have excellent and mutually fruitful
links with industry - generally large companies - and who need
little if any assistance in furthering these links. But these
are the exceptions, certainly in numerical terms, and it is
equally evident that there is a vast body of academics, many
with excellent potential in the present context, who are
absolutely dependent on external support in this respect.

Property. Many variables must be taken into account in any
decision to supply property: the exact location of the site
and its accessibility; the quality of its overall development

(degree of landscaping, development density, development control standards); whether land is available freehold or leasehold, and if the latter the terms of the lease (or short term licence); whether property is custom built or provided speculatively, and if the latter what the unit sizes, design, quality, construction type, services and costs ought to be; the selling prices or rents to charge; and so on.

It is self evident that precisely how these variables are fixed influences profoundly the nature of demand subsequently forthcoming. For instance, new start companies invariably have quite different property requirements from, say, already well established small companies that are growing very fast and are increasingly conscious of their immediate physical environment as a factor influencing their own performance and their image to the outside world.

English Estates' high technology development at Bradford University usefully illustrates the point. Here the property is all speculative, originally in unit sizes ranging from 1,000 sq.ft. to 8,000 sq.ft., of an above average quality of design and finish, and fairly expensive in relation to the local property market. In the first six months of lettings, a low proportion of enquiries came from start up companies; enquiries were chiefly from already established local companies that wanted more space in a better quality environment (and that also had reasons for wanting a university location). English Estates' recent decision to provide on an experimental basis much smaller units, including 'rent-a-desk' facilities, available on easy in/easy out terms and with secretarial and other basic office services available on a shared basis, has demonstrably already widened the appeal of the scheme especially in attracting very young companies.

It is unnecessary to discuss in detail all the precise property features that are attractive to different market setments. But two general observations are worthwhile.

First, no matter how advanced their technologies, start up companies only exceptionnaly want special premises - it is typically only at the next stage of development that they seek, and can afford to pay for, more exacting requirements than a conventional unit can provide, and in the meantime they improvise if necessary to meet any special research or production needs.

Second, the most valuable shared services to offer such companies are those of a routine office character: telephone answering, photocopying, typing (word processing preferably) and the like. High technology start up companies seldom want high technology common services, and in any case since their special requirements are usually so specific to their own purposes it is unlikely to make financial sense to seek to supply such services. Of course there are exceptions to this: a reportedly very successful scheme in Philadelphia catering to the medical industry and professions has a high degree of shared equipment including computer hardware and software. And it will be interesting to see what pattern of demand emerges for the incubator building on the Warwick University science park, with its sophisticated in-built information technology systems.

Marketing, management and external support. It is relatively easy in physical terms to establish a science park. It is quite another matter for the scheme to attract not only tenants but tenants of the right sort, and also for it to achieve its technology transfer and university-industry interaction benefits. And yet it is precisely attainment of these wider benefits that will distinguish a science park from other property schemes no matter how high the quality of the real estate.

It cannot be emphasised too strongly that what has happened around MIT and Stanford in the USA and around Cambridge in the UK is as yet exceptional with respect to the synergy generated between the academic and business worlds and to the fact that it has evolved 'naturally' without special planning. It has also not been property-led, in that a specific physical development to house high technology projects can be said to have made a significant contribution to generating the synergy and to encouraging academics to set up in business. Indeed, in the cases of MIT and Cambridge new business ventures in high technology have got going in perfectly ordinary premises that happened to be available in the locality.

By contrast, the bulk of evidence from elsewhere is that fruitful and multiple university-industry links have seldom arisen naturally or even easily. Certainly, mere provision of physical facilities on their own has not been sufficient to ensure that the wider 'non property' objectives are achieved. To achieve these objectives - in the context of this paper, especially those to do with promotion of SMEs in advanced technology - requires a deliberate and conscious effort and cannot be left simply to chance.

Hence how well a science park is marketed and managed and how well supported it is by the university itself and other concerned local bodies are matters of the greatest importance.

With respect to marketing, a distinction can be made between

marketing the scheme to the outside business world and
marketing it within the academic institution itself.

As regards external marketing, our own experience so far
suggests that the most effective strategy comprises a combination of three main elements. The first is essentially routine
property marketing. Estate agents and local authority estates
and economic development units are continuously fielding
enquiries, and they must know about the science park in order
to be able to steer potentially suitable projects to it.

Second, there must be a sustained high level of general
promotional and public relations activity in order to stimulate
awareness of the scheme both inside and outside the university.
This involves getting regular attention in the local media,
covering the scheme in general and any special items that arise
such as the stories behind establishment of the high technology
enterprises that locate on the scheme. It also involves
assiduously cultivating the local network of public agencies,
accountants, chamber of commerce, business associations and the
like so that they can act as 'multipliers' of the marketing
effort and refer possible projects to the scheme. Finally, it
involves mounting seminars and other special initiatives, as
well as being a prominent participant in events organised by
others, so as to continue to draw attention to the scheme.

Third, and most difficult and time consuming, there is scope
for selective and targeted marketing. By this we mean taking
carefully tailored approaches to individual companies, perhaps
identified on the basis of their existing connections with the
university (which might be as seemingly tenuous as the owner
manager's being an alumnus) or of the individual academic's
knowledge of particular companies in particular fields. There
are many other possible ways of selecting target companies. We
do not as yet know which ways will achieve the best results, or
indeed what are the best ways of making the actual approach to
a selected company. But we can say with reasonable confidence
that broad-brush targeting - such as mail shotting companies in
a selected sector - is unlikely to be cost effective.

The internal marketing of a university science park - i.e.
marketing it to the academics themselves - is arguably more
difficult than the external marketing. It involves winning the
confidence of the academics, persuading them of the potential
benefits to themselves of having industrial companies on the
campus, and consequently of getting them to make a real effort
towards making the science park a success. Our observation is
that academic attitudes on these matters differ widely from one
institution to another, dependent in large part on the
enthusiasm and commitment of the vice-chancellor for the scheme.

But by and large, it is essential that the academics see real (probably financial) benefits to themselves as individuals (and not just in terms of the general concept of university-industry liaison or the prestige of the institution) if they are to want to contribute significantly to the success of the science park.

These marketing activities are inextricably associated with management of the scheme. Indeed, we would expect the major proportion of management's time to be devoted to marketing, both external (especially of the second and third categories discussed earlier) and internal. There are two further vital functions that management must perform. One is actively helping with business advice and support to very young companies, since as already noted it is on the commercial aspects of his project that the technological entrepreneur is most vulnerable. The other, closely linked to the internal marketing function, is fostering linkages between tenants and academics and helping the university effectively to deliver its specialist resources to the former.

It is clear that good management requires a wide range of talents and personal qualities. All the evidence from managed schemes of all kinds - industrial workshops, youth training workshops as well as innovation centres and technology incubator projects - is that the quality of management and the top level policy commitment to the scheme are together the most important determinants of how a scheme performs.

It is clear too that to achieve the requisite scale and quality of the marketing and management effort is expensive and unlikely to be justified in commercial terms. Who pays for them? The pattern of sponsorship varies from scheme to scheme around the country. Because of the potential significance of such schemes for local, regional and national economic development, we would expect to see a growing trend towards multiple sponsorship in which local authorities, central government (especially if the ACARD report's proposals are accepted), development agencies (such as English Estates and the Scottish and Welsh Development Agencies), the universities themselves and even private sector corporations join forces.

Finance. We have encountered two problem areas in the financing of high technology SMEs, both at the very early stages of getting ventures launched.

The first is where funding is required for additional development work before a business plan could usefully be prepared for commercial exploitation of the technology. Funding for a thorough survey of the market prospects for the technology, again prior to preparation of a full scale business

243

plan, may also be an issue. This is not a new problem and
various public monies exist, at both national and local levels,
that can be used for this purpose. There is growing evidence
that the private banks are willing to speculate with small sums
on individual projects if they believe the long term potential
is excellent, and of course the technologists themselves
usually have some resources of their own. There is no overall
answer to this development funding problem, and it probably is
inevitable that suitable financing is cobbled together for each
case on its merits.

The second problem area arises in the actual funding of new
ventures. There is not a shortage of funds per se, especially
now that the venture capital industry has started to develop in
the UK and a few (though so far only a few) of the venture
capital companies are seriously interested in supporting new
ventures in advanced technology.

The government has given an added stimulus to this through
the 1981 business start up and now the 1983 business expansion
financing schemes (though the latter might have the effect of
channelling more funds to established rather than new
companies). A number of public sector bodies now have venture
type funds at their disposal too.

And nor is it simply a question of getting propositions
organised in a form that is comprehensible and persuasive to
the funding bodies. This involves preparation of a rigorous
and realistic business plan, referred to several times above,
which technically speaking is not a difficult task to
accomplish.

Rather, the critical issue that we see is that a gap exists
between what most venture funds are willing and able to do and
what the projects need. On their side the financial institutions are reluctant to devote too many resources to appraisal
of an individual project and then to its ongoing business
development - in the latter respect they are typically prepared
to do no more than place a non executive director on the board
of the company (by contrast US venture capitalists tend to seek
a fuller 'hands on' role in management of their companies). The
institutions know from experience too that projects in
universities are likely to require a substantial input of their
own time and energy, for the various reasons discussed elsewhere in this chapter. Hence, with significant exceptions as
noted above, the UK venture funds tend to be cautious in their
approach to high technology investments and, if given a choice,
would generally place their money elsewhere.

THE ROLE OF PROPERTY

It follows from the foregoing discussion that we see provision of property as only one element in a package of possible measures for promotion both of high technology SMEs and of university-industry linkages.

In some respects it is a vital element. For instance, in terms of the market categories discussed earlier, the availability of suitable and acceptable property is undoubtedly a significant benefit in helping to foster interaction between a university and local 'applications engineering' SMEs and also formation of 'leading edge' companies spinning out of the university or set up in close association with it. It must be added of course that the physical scheme is not sufficient; active marketing and management in the ways described before are a necessary complement.

There are other, less tangible benefits potentially derived from the fact of a physical scheme. It constitutes a focal point and a meeting ground for university-industry activities. To the outside world universities are large and confusing institutions, and a readily identifiable location as the natural centre for such activities and which has a commercial rather than academic atmosphere is clearly an advantage. Also, once a university has its own science park or is explicity associated with one undertaken by others, the motivation is greatly enhanced for it to 'get its act together' with respect to linkages with industry - its wider reputation is at stake and will be vulnerable to failure of the scheme both in property and non property terms.

There are, nevertheless, potential dangers in a university's efforts to cultivate increased and more productive relations with industry being essentially 'property driven'. Planning and investing in the property necessarily consumes large resources of time and money, and even if the university is not itself the prime mover in this respect it must nevertheless responsibly play a significant role in the planning process. All too easily can there be correspondingly less attention paid to the non property aspects, even though some of them are prerequisites for realisation of the property benefits.

In addition, once it is built there will be powerful pressures to let space and generate rental income. These pressures may not always be compatible with the wider objectives that require securing tenants having very particular characteristics. (This is probably the main reason why financial institutions and universities have so far not found it easy to come to agreement on science park investments.) And

245

because of the understandable tendency to want to erect a high quality (and therefore expensive) building, rents are likely to be high which will suppress effective demand further.

None of these objectives is necessarily overriding. Their weight can be judged only in each particular case relative to the prospective benefits, to the likely strength of the market for the scheme, and to what other measures are included in the overall promotional effort.

As is invariably the case in economic development projects, provided the basic concept is sound it is the quality of its implementation that will determine the performance of a particular science park in contributing to promotion of high technology SMEs. There is no magic formula for success. But we would want to emphasise again and again that property is only one component in the promotional effort, and that either the other critical components must already be present or that substantial additional resources must be devoted to creating them if the property investment is to be justified.

NOTES

[1] This report was first drafted in August 1983 and was revised for purposes of publication in January 1984. In the intervening period there was a substantial continuing advance in the general body of knowledge and experience in this field, and of our own experience too. In addition to the projects mentioned in the main text of the chapter we undertook work (some of it still continuing) at University College Swansea and Biotechnology Centre Wales (for the Welsh Development Agency and the College, in connection with a proposed technology incubator scheme); Aberdeen (for the Scottish Development Agency, in connection with a proposed innovation centre linked to an HEI based science park); Cambridge (for a private and public sector consortium, in connection with the formation and growth of advanced technology firms); and the higher educational institutions and research establishments in the north west region of England (for the Department of Trade & Industry, in connection with formulation of a regional technology development strategy).

The new knowledge gained from this work has pointed to the complexity of many of the issues touched on in this chapter, but nevertheless has broadly endorsed our original observations and conclusions.

REFERENCES

Advisory Council for Applied Research and Development (ACARD), (1983), in association with the Advisory Board for Research Councils, 'Improving Research Links between Higher Education and Industry', HMSO, June.

Beaumont, J.P., (1982), 'The Location, Mobility and Finance of New High Technology Companies in the UK Electronics Industry', Department of Industry South East Regional Office, London.

Bullock, M., (1983), Academic Enterprise, Industrial Innovation, and the Development of High Technology Financing in the United States, Brand Brothers & Co, London.

Chinitz, B., (1961), 'Contrasts in Agglomeration: New York and Pittsburgh', American Economic Review, vol.51.

Department of Industry and Shell UK Limited, (1982), 'Helping Small Firms Start Up and Grow: Common Services and Technological Support', HMSO, May.

The Economist, (1983), 'British Small Business', 23rd July.

Fothergill, S. and Gudgin, G., (1982), Unequal Growth, Heinemann Educational Books.

Rothwell, R. and Zegveld, W., (1982), Innovation and the Small and Medium Sized Firm, Frances Pinter, London.

Competitive strategy through technology licensing for the small firm

JULIAN LOWE

INTRODUCTION

This chapter assesses some recent evidence on the use of
technology licensing by small and medium sized enterprises
(SME's) and discusses the extent to which technology licensing
has a role in the competitive strategies of smaller firms.
Competitive strategy concerns the combination of the ends for
which the firm is striving and the means (policies) required to
get it there. Technology licensing is just one part of the
firm's policy towards innovation and has to be seen in this
overall context.

  Technology licensing can be defined as the purchase and sale,
by contract, of product or process technology, designs and
marketing expertise. In many ways licensing is part of a
spectrum that may start with franchising, then assembly from
bought in components, then manufacture under the license and
finally in-house designed products/processes, which are spin
offs from previously bought in knowledge and may themselves
eventually be licensed out to others. There is a world wide
market in technical knowledge and product design and in 1978 it
is estimated that global international licensing payments

* This chapter arises out of a programme of research funded by
  the Leverhulme Trust.

249

amounted to $14 billion (Contractor, 1981). In the UK there
has been a four fold increase in licensing royalties received
between 1969 and 1979 and a similar growth in licensing
payments. Traditionally, technology transfer and the sale of
technology and knowhow under license has been dominated by the
transactions between subsidiaries of multi-national companies.
However, whilst licensing appears dominated by large firms,
there are various reasons for expecting it to have a
significant role for the SME.

THE SMALL FIRM AND THE PROCESS OF INNOVATION

The evidence on the role of SME's in the process of innovation
and new product development is not clear cut and varies
considerably between different countries, technologies and
product markets. In the USA for instance, it is estimated that
firms with less than 1,000 employees contributed to more than
40 per cent of innovations appearing in that country during the
early 1970s with only R & D inputs. In the UK however, the
contribution of small firms has probably been much less
significant (OECD, 1982; Pavitt, 1983).

 Neither the accepted Galbraithian wisdom of the role of large
scale economies nor the Jewkes and Stillerman view of the disproportionate impact of SME's on invention are views wholly
supported by empirical evidence. The sources of new products
are various but development through in-house research,
collaborative ventures with other companies (either large or
small) independently or under the auspices of various
programmes in the research associations, contract R & D, merger
and technology licensing are all important alternatives.

 The transience of technology may in fact lead to more
opportunities for small firms than in the past. Not only are
entry barriers to various industries reduced as changes in
technology make existing processes obsolete but the new
technologies themselves may reduce the minimum efficient size
of operation. Flexible manufacturing systems, for instance,
may allow short production runs at low unit cost and significantly reduce the competitive problems for some small companies
faced by large firm competition. Due to various technological
factors, changes in the competitive position of SME's have
occurred in a wide variety of industries such as brewing,
textiles, biotechnology and machine tools (Bollard, 1982).
However, from the point of view of in-house research in the SME
there are still substantial problems in various industries,
stemming from their lack of specialist knowledge and manpower.
Legislative progress in areas such as environmental control and
product liability may also make the research policies of SME's

untenable because they lack the post development resources for trials and product testing etc. The pharmaceutical industry is illustrative of this problem (Massan, 1981).

Collaborative research also presents opportunities for individual SME product development but interestingly one of the main avenues for this form of activity - the research associations - have, since the Rothschild report become more concerned with large firm collaboration than carrying out work for smaller firms which might, a priori, be expected to be the most suitable recipients for their services (Lowe and Crawford, 1984).

The existence of an R & D related size limitation for SME's does not rest purely with their inventive and innovative capability. Various commentators, for instance, have noted that SME's may be able to invent but may lack the resources to carry the process through to innovation and commercial development. This may be associated with the scale economies that exist in marketing and production or may instead be related to the trial/testing problems referred to above. Thus, many major inventions and innovations, whilst stemming from small firms, have had to rely on larger companies to take them to the market.

The position of SME's with respect to new product development presents an interesting paradox. There is a growing emphasis in their role in employment generation but success in this can only come about through having a suitable flow of new products with which to enter new markets and to challenge foreign producers. Whilst in some industries SME's have shown remarkable skill in the areas of both invention and innovation, it is unlikely, in the UK at least, that they will be able to rely solely on their own resources for the generation of new products. One possible solution, might be for SME's to rely, to an extent, on bought-in technology and manufacture innovative products under license and it is this which is the central theme of this chapter.

THE EXTENT OF LICENSING IN THE SME SECTOR

Theory

There are many reasons why the SME might find technology licensing an attractive facet of its overall innovation policy, although as with any aspect of policy their success may be limited by the cost of operating in technology markets, know-ledge constraints and a lack of an institutional infrastructure to deal with the specific needs of SME's. In this context for

251

small firms wishing to grow and expand, licensing may present some very real benefits. Firstly, licensing in and out, can, for the rapid growth small firm, present a means of expansion which would otherwise be unavailable. Recent studies of firms in this category have suggested that the rapid growers frequently have cash flow and liquidity problems. Certainly licensing out allows a firm, in this position, to capitalise on its industrial property by selling this to a licensee who effectively speeds up the flow of cash stemming from the exploitation of a market. The situation for inward licensing is similar, as new products and processes can be adopted quickly without necessitating original research programmes. To the small firm, with a narrow portfolio of research projects, inward licensing may help to reduce risks, at least at the development stages of the new product development process and it is perhaps not as risky as contracted out research since it only involves buying knowledge ex post. In addition a licensing 'package' may contain not only the engineering and production knowledge but also that concerned with marketing and distribution. This is, of course, why franchising is so popular with small firms and start up enterprises since it provides almost all the entry components (except an initial capital outlay) for a new enterprise. Another key area of risk reduction, where licensing is potentially able to make a contribution, is that concerned with product liability. As the legal interpretation of product liability moves towards caveat venditor the problem for small firms with inadequate test facilities increases.

In conclusion, inward licensing potentially allows small firms to compete technologically with larger rivals especially when they don't have sufficient resources for their own R & D effort. The next section of this chapter examines the extent to which this happens in practice and on the basis of this and other evidence we evaluate the practical role that licensing can play in the competitive strategy of firms.

The evidence

In order to put these factors into perspective we carried out an extensive survey of licensing in a stratified sample of firms across various industries. The full results of this are reported in Lowe and Crawford (1984b). Following an initial random survey it seemed that the total small firm involvement in licensing ranged from between 5 and 9 per cent to the total population of SME's.

Licensing and non licensing firms. Having defined those industries in which licensing appeared to be important we took a more stratified sample of firms for our main study. The industries analysed were those that we expected might exhibit a degree of licensing activity and covered chemicals, pharmaceuticals, plastics, electronics, engineering, packaging and paints.

In the analysis, summarised in tables 1, 2 and 3, the size of the company appeared to be a significant factor in the incidence of licensing. The sample was split, almost proportionally, between these firms in the 0-100 class, 100-200 and 200-500, employees classification. Table 1 shows clearly that as size of firm increased so also did the incidence of licensing. The most important and marked difference occurred between the 0-100 group and the rest with the smallest size group being least involved in licensing.

Possibly one of the principal reasons for non licensing by very small companies, was that the opportunity cost of finding and negotiating a license was too high. With the benefits of such an agreement being intangible and with various resource constraints operating, the small firm may have been unable to devote the necessary management time to this area. Larger firms with specialised licensing executives or patent agents were not subject to the same constraint. Additionally the small company was unable to provide an adequate market for licensors to generate sufficient royalties, since the gains to a prospective licensor were limited by the size of the small firm licensee's market.

Although difficult to define precisely, there seemed, for particular types of organisation, a minimum economic size necessary for licensing. This 'rule' cannot be universally applied, however, since some type of SEME's which were heavily research intensive, did have the required skilled manpower for finding and negotiating licences, whilst rapid growth SME's, in particular market segments, sometimes proved attractive to potential licensors. The two principal reasons (unskilled manpower and poor potential markets) for the relatively low level of licensing by the smaller of the SME groups are reflected in tables 2 and 3. From these it can be seen that firms operating with higher growth rates and in more diversified markets were also more likely to use licensing. In addition, in table 3 the research intensiveness of the firms, as measured by the ownership of UK patents and number of MSc/PhDs employed, was also related to the extent of licensing - a factor strongly supported by aggregate empirical analysis of licensing data across all industry groups (Lowe and Crawford, 1984b).

Finally, the study also tried to evaluate the impact of various environmental and cultural factors on the extent of

Table 1
Size of licensing/non licensing firms

Company Size	Total Sample		Licensing Companies		Non Licensing Companies	
	Nos.	%	Nos.	%	Nos.	%
0 - 100	55	(30)	16	(9)	39	(21)
101 - 200	69	(38)	42	(23)	27	(15)
201 - 500	59	(32)	47	(26)	12	(7)
TOTAL	183		105		78	

Table 2
Growth and diversification related factors

Firm Factors		Licensing Companies		Non Licensing Companies	
		Nos.	%	Nos.	%
Turnover Growth	<10%	24	(31)	21	(33)
	>10%	53	(69)	43	(67)
Operating in:					
Less than two markets		19	(28)	13	(35)
More than two markets		49	(72)	24	(65)

Table 3
Research related factors

	Licensing Companies		Non Licensing Companies	
	Nos.	%	Nos.	%
No UK patents	41	(39)	27	(64)
One or more UK patents	64	(61)	15	(36)
No Overseas patents	61	(58)	33	(78)
One or more Overseas patents	44	(42)	9	(22)
No qualified staff employed (MSc/PhD)	61	(58)	35	(83)
Employ qualified staff (MSc/PhD)	44	(42)	7	(17)

licensing in the total sample. Factors such as type of ownership and age of company were investigated to assess the extent
that these, as possible proxy variables for entrepreneurship,
might have had some impact on the licensing intensity of the
company. Whilst from case study evidence these factors
appeared important, statistical analysis of the whole sample
did not confirm a link between this factor and the extent of
company licensing activity.

Generally, both the questionnaire and case study analysis of
licensing versus non licensing firms showed that whilst
licensing was an activity in which the smaller company might be
disadvantaged, certain types of small firms had been able to
use licensing both as a substitute for in-house R & D and for
direct selling in export markets. The extent and success with
which SME's use either outward or inward licensing should
depend on various factors affecting the ease of technology
transfer and at the same time the need for licensing as an
alternative strategy to in-house development and direct selling.
In order to explore these factors, we broke our data down by
the type of licensing activity carried out and split the sample
into firms licensing-in (LI), those licensing-out (LO) and
those doing both together.

Licensing 'in' and licensing 'out' firms. A key finding of
this part of the research was that the LILO group were clearly
differentiated from the two other groups on the basis of
several of the measures that were used. They were, on average,
both older and larger than either the LI or LO firms. If
membership of the LILO group is evidence that licensing is
used in a more planned and less ad hoc manner within the firm
then it would seem that the size of company is an important
factor in this respect and that those firms in the very small
category are rarely involved in licensing in both directions.

The LILO's were also the most research intensive and hence,
by inference, the most innovative group of licensing companies.
This would again support the view that in such firms,
development and exploitation of technology is a much less ad
hoc process than in other groups. Development of a technology
strategy and recognition of licensing as a useful tool to be
considered in tandem with the alternative options of 'in-house'
development or contracted R & D may be important in the success
of such firms. Case study and interview data supported this
view and generally in LI and LO companies licensing appears to
be a much more reactive process. In the LILO group it did
appear to be a proactive process and this would be confirmed by
the fact that responsibility for new product identification and
policy making seemed a much more highly organised activity
than for the rest of the group. This latter factor is probably

linked to the overall larger size of firm in this group and would reinforce the point that whilst licensing can be used by the smaller company there are certain scale advantages which facilitate its operation in larger firms.

The licensing 'out' firms. The firms exhibiting the most rapid growth and the highest market share in their main markets were the firms in the licensing 'out' category. This might be consistent with an assessment of their position as quasi monopolists, first exploiting their domestic dominance and then extending this to an exploitation of their industrial property in overseas markets via licensing. However, even here, licensing had usually come about through the success of a particular product or group of products leading to an approach by a potential licensee, rather than being part of the strategy of the firm, in its exploitation of that technology. Since the average size of the LO firms was smaller than that of the LILO firms, much of the responsibility for selling and marketing domestically exploited technology was still in the hands of managers who had many other professional tasks other than licensing. Consequently even where potential outward licensing opportunities were recognised by small firms, exploitation of those opportunities was often dependent on considerable effort being expended by the licensee company. This might indicate that licensing to another small firm might be expected to be less successful than licensing to a large firm which would be more able to devote the necessary time and resources to absorbing and exploiting the technology. In cases where the small licensor firm had actively marketed its technology to large firms, it often received a raw deal due both to its inexperience in carrying out licensing negotiations and, in some cases, by the indifference of the larger firm to its approaches.

The licensing 'in' firms. The licensing 'in' firms were generally poorer profit and market performers than either the LOs or the LILOs (though more successful than the non licensing group). They were also, on average of smaller size than the other two groups of licensing companies. However, case study evidence did show that smaller firms can benefit from licensing 'in' even where the licensing is used in an unplanned manner. Many of the LI group had adopted licensing in an opportunistic or reactive way. In many cases licensing was only adopted because of a chance meeting or contact rather than as a result of a planned change in product policy. In some cases, licensing had been used as a panic measure to overcome product portfolio problems or those associated with an ageing product life cycle. For a small company wishing to extend its product line, such a course might seem a ready made solution, but in practice we found that unless the product could be demonstrated in a face to face context, and unless the licensee was wholly committed to the licence, the negotiations could easily fail.

Even where the licensee was committed to the licensing option, internal factors might mitigate against the success of the licence. Commitment by all levels of management, seemed to be particularly important, with the role of the managing director crucial. Delegation of the search process to junior employees or consultants led, in some of our case studies, to a lack of credibility of potential licensed products as they were presented to decision makers within the firm. The 'not invented here' syndrome seemed to be likely to cause problems unless the instigator of the licence had credibility within the firm. Where this was the case, successful licence agreements were accomplished in several instances, even where disparate technologies were involved and where synergy might not have been expected. Conversely, where the initiator of the licensed product lacked credibility, apparently suitable products failed to be successfully licensed. In some ways, the smaller company was at an advantage in this respect. Since there was little scope for a full time licensing executive, the task was often performed by a senior board member, a fact greatly facilitating the inward flow of external technology.

Even after the negotiation stage however, and with acceptance of the licensed product in principle, many of the licensee firms in our sample encountered problems in assimilating new technology. In some cases this was due to the NIH syndrome but in others, differences in materials, specifications, language and the availability of locally sourced components, mitigated against a successful transfer being accomplished. In some cases this led, after large expenditure, to the abandonment of the venture. In others it led to the failure of the licensed product to reach its full potential. The risks for a small company were substantial if such a venture went wrong.

Information sources. How firms came to license, and the sources of information used, are areas containing some important clues as to how the SME goes about licensing, since information sources may be one factor militating strongly in favour of big firms and large scale. In spite of this there was very low use of intermediaries and yet there are a large number of publications and licensing consultants whose stated function is to bring together buyers and sellers of technology, and it was a form of market organisation that might have been expected to be prominent in the sale of ex post knowledge for SME's. However, this sort of 'market facilitating mechanism' was only used in those cases where there was a low level of intra industry knowledge or where a licensing deal was being used as a way of helping the firm diversify. Less than 5 per -

cent of the survey sample of licensors and licensees had
recourse to technology brokers. This was interesting since it
suggested that whilst there was substantial scope for the
provision of information per se, it was insufficient of itself
to help facilitate the licensing process. Information required
by both buyers and sellers of technology had to be very
specific and detailed before a company would even invest in
further information search.

The analysis of the geographical location of licensors and
licensees with which smaller firms were associated, elucidated
some interesting facts. While licensee companies obtained
their licensed product from UK sources, in more than half the
cases studied, licensor companies found UK partners in less
than 10 per cent of cases. This is interesting, and can perhaps
be explained by the sort of sources for licensed products,
suitable for small licensee companies in the UK. With a large
UK public sector, which is relatively research intensive,
numbers of developments unsuitable to those corporations and
organisations are likely to be created. Several of the case
studies we drew up showed that the role of the public
corporations, in providing product technology for smaller
companies was important. In many instances, the small licensee
firms were suppliers or subcontractors to the public utilities
and moved into production of products, as a result of an
approach from the utility which had invented something for
which it had no direct use or for which it needed a supplier.
There was an increasing movement to license such inventions-out
with pressure both from government and from within organisations themselves. Also, larger UK companies seeking to place
an unwanted technology, often sought a local licensee for such
a technology rather than going abroad. Small companies are
especially attractive to larger companies seeking to license
this type of technology 'out' because they presented less of a
long term competitive threat.

Finally, one interesting and possibly important factor that
emerged from our analysis was that patents per se were not
necessarily the major property that was licensed. Even where
they were involved, companies quoted 'know how' and other
intellectual property (e.g. trademarks) as being equally or
even more important. In such agreements the characteristics of
the technology often provided its own protection. For the SME
this could present problems, if it entailed the tying up of key
personnel for too long in technology transfer.

It was clear that where licensing involved mainly 'embodied'
technology - in the form of a drawing, a piece of capital
equipment or some basic 'bought in' input, then the process of
transfer from one organisation to another was easier than where

such intangible skills and know how was involved - i.e., in disembodied technology. As well as presenting problems to the process of technology transfer per se, disembodied technology or know how was always something that was most difficult to deal with at the negotiation stage, because without a fair trial, the licensee could not evaluate the product adequately.

Return to licensing. The risks in licensing for the SME can be substantial and undoubtedly these risks account for the substantial number of companies who had considered licensing but had not gone through with it. However, the benefits can be substantial too. Whilst from questionnaire data it was difficult to assess exactly how successful the inward licensing had been, we were able to establish that in 54 per cent of our sample inward licensed products accounted for less than 10 per cent of turnover, in 40 per cent of the cases it accounted for between 10 and 50 per cent of turnover and in 6 per cent of cases it accounted for in excess of 50 per cent of turnover. These figures and other case study data suggest that there is considerably variability in the importance of inward licensing to firms, but that in the majority of cases licensed products make a significant contribution to the total turnover and profits of the company.

In addition we were also able, through a separate questionnaire, to establish the range of financial returns available to licensors. Taken as a percentage of total transfer costs (as opposed to R & D costs and transfer costs) returns ranged up to 17,000 per cent and averaged over 500 per cent. Since in nearly all cases firms had not considered licensing prior to commencement of R & D we considered it justifiable to calculate the return solely on licence trans- action costs as the basis for the rates reported. There were also problems of separating and disaggregating basic R & D data but in the few cases where we were able to do this, outward licensing was able to make a much more substantial percentage return than when compared to the basic return from R & D spending stemming from direct manufacture and sale of the products.

COMPETITIVE STRATEGY FOR THE SMALL FIRM

Our survey evidence suggests that licensing markets can work successfully for SME's but the process is far from frictionless and for certain sorts of firm, licensing cannot be used successfully. Nevertheless there can be do doubt about the potential role technology licensing has to play. In the toy industry, which in the UK is dominated by SME's, we estimate that over 50 per cent of firms are involved as either licensors or licensees and this has been the case for even the smallest firm in that industry. The key seems to have been that as licensing is a learned skill the negative impact of size lessens dramatically with use. For different reasons, intensive use of licensing has also occurred in other industries like pharmaceuticals and pollution control equipment, where demand pressures and ease of technology transfer have pushed licensing into a position of pre-eminence in inter firm strategic behaviour.

A framework of competitive strategy

In order to assess the role of licensing for the SME we need to first evaluate the context and framework of competitive strategy in general. Porter (1980) suggests that the basis of strategy should be seen in the context of the external and internal factors which both encourage and limit strategic behaviour and determine the development of the firms' competitive position. These external and internal factors can be described under the four headings of: (i) Internal strengths and weaknesses, (ii) Personal values of key implementers, (iii) Industry opportunities and threats and (iv) Broader societal expectations.

Internal strengths and weaknesses. The role of licensing in competitive strategy is clearly limited by what the firm can and cannot achieve with internal resources. In this context, licensing-in may well be important to the SME since its ability to develop new products and processes through in-house R & D, may be limited in particular product/markets because of various entry barriers, either at the research or development stage for smaller companies. The same applies to the SME wanting to consider the options of selling goods or technology, where its ability to adequately perform the former task may be limited by the necessary selling infrastructure required to cover markets in general and export markets in particular. Many of the firms referred to in our survey were involved in licensing for these reasons. However, it has to be recognised that licensing itself, may be problematical because of inadequate scale of operations. We found, on several occasions, that the SME was unable to compete adequately, because of a lack of skilled management or an aversion to use this scarce resource on some-thing which was often seen as a highly risky area or at least one where the return tended to be long term and uncertain. Lack of scale may limit licensing in the same way was it limits other forms of innovative activity. Finally, it must be emphasised that an in-house technical capability was still important merely to help the firm specify and receive the technology it required.

Personal values of key implementers. This represented the
other important internal limit to strategy formulation and was
manifested, to a very large degree, in the NIH syndrome in many
of the firms studied. This represented a clear barrier to the
use of licensing in firm strategy. However, it was not clear
that it was a particularly stable factor or that it was something related to the technical excellence of the firm. It was
a factor very much concerned with key individuals and
personalities within the organisation. Interestingly, the
personal values of these key figures may be just as important
in terms of positive progress in successful licensing. In the
majority of our licensing 'success' case studies, the drive and
commitment of individual managers to licensing was a key aspect
of successful projects. It was, however, important that such
individuals be influential and powerful within the firm. Under
these conditions licensing stood the greatest chance of success,
even when other external factors were less favourable.

Industry opportunities and threats. The external environment
can clearly limit the potential of licensing within the firm.
A large proportion of our respondents were shown to be
essentially reactive licensors/licensees, responding to threats
stemming from competition, the pace of technical change or
their own inadequate investments in R & D etc. and this 'me too'
approach was often successful. However, often licensing was
not the right strategy because it can take too much time and
for the firm with cash flow problems or collapsing markets
licensing may not provide the instant palliative sometimes
hoped for. Licensing negotiations could often take over a year
with production and marketing taking as long to come on stream
as well. Similarly with outward licensing where there was the
added problem of delayed royalties, in the absence of any
upfront payment, not materialising for several years. It
seemed very clear, from our case studies, that for licensing to
be most successful some element of longer term planning was
important.

Broader societal expectations. The broader environmental and
cultural background of society does impinge on innovation in
general. In particular, in our study, we noted how changes in
the law relating to the environment, health and safety at work
and product liability had a major impact on licensing in
particular markets such as pharmaceuticals and pollution
control equipment, where the impact of regulation was felt most
by the SME. Purchase of already proven knowledge and
technology from other sources, was a driving force behind
licensing in these sorts of markets.

The above factors are, of course, limits to the competitive
strategy of the firm as well as pointers to the direction the

firm should take. In the context of licensing and competitive strategy, licensing was a competitive weapon which could be sometimes used to help the firm adjust and minimise the impact of competition either from the existing rivals, potential rivals or indeed from suppliers and buyers. The SME is often at a disadvantage in many of these situations and licensing allows it a degree of control if it owns technology or if it wishes to purchase technology.

CONCLUSION

Porter (1981) has suggested that most firms adopt one of three basic generic strategies viz:

(1) Product differentiation, whereby the firm competes on the basis of actual or perceived differences in its products for particular markets.

(2) Low manufacturing costs whereby it competes on price in broad undifferentiated markets.

(3) Focus, whereby it segments the markets in such a way that it specialises in a particular segment.

Licensing can be crucial in getting product innovation for (1), process innovation for (2), and possibly a combination of these for (3). Importantly, it can be a means whereby the firm switches emphasis from one generic strategy to another. Licensing enables the firm to move more flexibly and with changing risk levels. Ultimately it has to be compared with other tools for achieving strategic goals such as acquisition and in-house development and some of our respondent firms were using licensing in this context. Our conclusion on the basis of evidence and this overview of strategy formulation must be that licensing has potential for the SME to operate success- fully against larger firms but that this potential is still limited by problems of scale in many situations.

REFERENCES

Bollard, A., (1983), 'Technology, Economic Change and Small Firms', Lloyds Bank Review.
Contractor, F., (1981), International Technology Licensing, Lexington Books.
Lowe, J.F. and Crawford, N.K., (1983), 'Technology Licensing and the Smaller Firm', European Small Business Journal, Summer.
Lowe, J.F. and Crawford, N.K., (1983), Innovation and Technology Transfer for the Growing Firm, Pergamon Press.
Massan, A.D.W., (1981), 'Product Liability: The Special Problem of Medicines', Managerial and Decision Economics, no.3.

O.E.C.D., (1982), <u>Innovation in Small and Medium Sized Firms</u>,
O.E.C.D.

Pavitt, K., (1982), Innovation in British Industry, <u>OMEGA</u>.

Porter, M.P., (1980), <u>Competitive Strategy</u>, The Free Press, New
York.

A study of the factors affecting the performance of independent retail newsagents

ELIZABETH CHELL AND JEAN HAWORTH

INTRODUCTION

There is a tendency to over generalise when discussing the small firm sector whereas no sector could be more heterogeneous. Curran and Stanworth (1982), for instance, have expressed optimism about the future of small firms, in contrast to Dawson and Kirby (1979) who were concerned that in Britain the retailing sector might be affected in the same way as the small scale retail sector of the US economy pre 1940, that is with high mortality rates and a short life expectancy. But even this was a reference to the grocery sector rather than retailing as a whole. The most noticeable change which had occurred in that sector was the demise of the corner shop and of personal, over the counter sales service.

The main contraction in small retail outlets occurred in the decade 1960-70. But, whilst the situation seems now to have stabilised, there is considerable variability in the distribution of small to large retail outlets across regions and towns (Census of Distribution, 1971). One major factor which has shaped the success and survival of the small retail outlet is that of location (Berry and Pred, 1965). There are planning implications of locating a shop on a new housing estate, for example, since it is not always a financially viable proposition to place the retail outlet in the centre of an estate, where there is little chance of them picking up passing trade (Butler, 1976; Dawson and Kirby, 1979).

The existence of competition from large multiples, super-markets and so on, has been questioned as the reason for the demise of the small retail outlet. It has been argued that the small shop neither attempts to compete in terms of price or range of goods with the larger supermarkets, nor does it serve the same purpose or need. Kirby (1976) has put forward the idea of a 'polarisation principle'. He argues that the small shop complements the large supermarket or superstore and suggests that, as the supermarket increases in size, so the small shop re-emerges as an integral part of the retail system: "Competition no longer appears to be one of the major problems facing the small shop in urban Britain. Certainly the shop keepers themselves see other problems as being of more importance". This is one of the conclusions drawn by Dawson and Kirby (op cit) and also echoed by Bates (1976) and Thorpe (1977) in their studies of independent retailers.

In the case of the independent newsagent, of which the vast majority are CTNs (Confectioners, Tobacconists and Newsagents) the extent of competition amongst themselves varies consider-ably from those who effectively have no competition (usually situated in a rural area) to those with considerable competi-tion (usually town centre shops). Thus, of those newsagents who may compete, it is not clear if the competition is perceived as such and what effects, if any, it has in a measurable sense on performance. Is the refitted shop with the modernised frontage on the High Street an example of a shop which is primarily competing for trade? Competition is such an overarching concept that when considering the survival and growth of the newsagency, or of any other retailing outfit, there are other factors which need to be taken into account. As Meyer and Goldstein (1981, p.158) have observed "Although adequate capital and managerial competence are indispensible for survival they are rarely sufficient in themselves to ensure it. They must be supplemented by other factors, such as motivation, hard work, persistence and flexibility" (our emphasis). It is an empirical question as to whether news-agents exhibit these qualities.

In addition to the issue of competition and the behaviour which can be identified as competitive, the independent news-agents form a small business sector which exhibits important visible, structural and organisational differences. One such feature is within the chain of distribution, where the importance of the wholesaler should not be underestimated (Cmnd 7214, 1978). In many parts of the UK the wholesaler has a monopoly; and in Scotland the monopoly of John Menzies is almost complete. Indeed between 1964-1976 a process of rationalisation ensured that wholesalers would monopolise a particular area of the country, thus reducing competition between wholesalers in supplying retail outlets. This practice has been investigated by the Monopolies and Mergers Commission (1978) who concluded that the apparent restriction on competition was justified and was in the public interest because it enabled the wholesaler to keep down distribution costs and thus the price of the publication sold over the counter.

The service which most newsagents offer is also distinctive. The important features of that service are early opening hours and a delivery service. Newspapers in particular have a very short shelf life; on the whole if they are not sold by mid morning on the day of delivery they are unlikely to be sold at all. It is thus essential that wholesalers deliver to the retail outlets in the early hours in time for the newsagent to parcel out the newspapers for door to door delivery, and that the newsagent's shop is open sufficiently early to catch passing trade and people on their way to work. These features promoted the wholesalers to put forward the argument to the Monopolies Commission that the existence of too many retailers serving an area would only result in a reduction in the need for early opening and for a delivery service. In the last analysis the service to the public would suffer and the price of periodicals and newspapers would rise to meet the additional distribution costs and reduced sales per retail outlet.

One of the problems facing publishers, wholesalers and retailers alike is that it is difficult to envisage any overall increase in the circulation of newspapers. An increase in retail outlets would serve only to spread the benefits more thinly and little or no advantage would accrue from the increased competition. Indeed total circulation of newspapers dropped markedly in the period 1970-77, and the price of national daily papers rose by 214 per cent (as compared with the retail price index which rose by 146 per cent in the same period (Cmnd 6810, 1977).

Perhaps one area where increased sales may occur is that of sales of periodicals and magazines. The shelf life of such items is much longer although with present practices newsagents rarely display a magazine for the full duration of its life. With such items, display and the extent of display, are important. In order to increase sales of magazines it is necessary to get customers inside the shop. Ironically, the idea of a delivery service, whilst ensuring a steady and secure sale of newspapers and periodicals, keeps the customer away from the shop and reduces the tendency for impulse buying. Further the range and stock of periodicals taken by the average

267

newsagent is low and unadventurous. The 'best sellers' - Radio
and TV Times, Woman, Woman's Weekly, Woman's Own, etc. - are
kept at levels which ensure all are sold, whilst special
interest periodicals need to be ordered. The average small
independent newsagent feels that he cannot afford to take the
risk of stocking a wide range of periodicals on the off chance
that interested customers may buy them on impulse. A way round
this problem may be to increase sale or return (SOR) on a wider
range of magazines. SOR increases the costs to the publisher
and to the wholesaler, it does not guarantee increased sales
and one aspect of the problem may be getting the newsagent
to promote that particular item. The sort of service the newsagent offers may not be compatible with active 'pushing' of
goods and so the only remaining factor which may influence
sales is the visibility of that item and the nature of the
display of magazines.

Many wholesalers particularly the 'big three' - W.H. Smith,
John Menzies and Surridge Dawson - have extended their business
into retailing. This move was welcomed by the publishers
because it overcomes some of the problems such as display,
professional managerialism, and siting of shops:

> Periodicals' publishers welcomed the participation of
> wholesalers in retailing because it led to larger and
> well sited shops which afforded better displays of
> periodicals, magazines and newspapers than those pro-
> vided by the average independent newsagent. It was
> also beneficial to the public because newsagents other
> than the larger multiples were unable to afford the
> more expensive high street positions where members of
> the Association must necessarily be represented.
> Wholesalers involved in retailing generally provided
> training facilities and opportunities for career
> development which attracted shop managers of a high
> calibre. They were also able to adopt, by management
> decision, promotional and service policies, which an
> independent wholesaler could only achieve by
> persuasion in the retail outlets he supplied. (Cmnd
> 7214, 1978, p.46)

The extension of the wholesaler into retailing is obviously a
potential area of threat to the small independent newsagent and
is comparable to the rise of the multiples and supermarket
chains which threatened and closed many small retail outlets
generally, in the wider retailing sector. Perhaps it is worth
remembering, however, that many of the wholesalers are themselves small businesses and to take over some newsagents may
not be the threat that it at first appears. The problem for
the wholesaler is how else might he raise the general standard
of performance of the newsagents he supplies if he can effect

little or no control over their businesses.

In the ensuing pages we describe a research project which focusses on factors affecting the sales of magazines of a sample of retail newsagents and the efforts made by the wholesale newsagent to affect their performances.

THE RESEARCH PROJECT OUTLINED

Preliminary considerations

The research problems we were faced with can be put in the form of a question:-

> Is it possible to identify and measure, with an acceptable degree of accuracy, the factors affecting newsagents' performance? If we can meet this objective then our findings should be of benefit to the publishers, wholesalers and retailers who operate within this particular industrial sector.

In addition a crucial problem seems to be that, according to Retail Business 175 (September 1972) (Special Report No.3):

> Most independent CTN owners have no wish to expand their businesses and this may weaken their ability to keep pace with competition from other types of outlet.

This raises two separate questions: firstly, to what extent are independent newsagents satisficers as opposed to profit maximisers? And secondly, just how significant is the effect of competition?

Methodological considerations

At a very early stage in the research, some of the key factors identified were LOCATION, SHOP CHARACTERISTICS, DELIVERY SERVICE, MARKET SHARE, COMPETITION and HUMAN FACTORS. Ways of 'measuring' these complex variables were conceived and data were systematically collected on each. In particular, a questionnaire was designed to measure the 'human factors' and was tested out in a small pilot survey. This gave us some useful insights for later modifications of the questionnaire and in terms of interpretation of the responses.

In terms of LOCATION factors, we eventually decided to control for many of these features by dividing the population into three, i.e. rural, suburban and town centre shops and analysing the samples from these populations separately. For each sub population, a regression model was applied to the data in an

attempt to explain the level of sales performance. The model
can be stated as follows:-

> SALES = f (ROAD, SI, PED, TOY BOOK, GR, PO, SOC, AGE,
>   M2 M3, DB, HD, OP, APP, SF, COMP, MS)

The variables in this model are defined below:-

SALES - Sales was measured in terms of the <u>money sales</u> of
periodicals and magazines over a four week period. We recognise that the mix of periodicals and magazines varies from
agent to agent and would have preferred to use data reflecting
the same product mix for each agent. However, these data were
not available.

ROAD - The type of traffic route on which the shop was
situated.

> ROAD = 1 - zero or very low traffic
>   = 2 - residential, access or side road
>   = 3 - secondary traffic route
>   = 4 - major traffic route

SI - shop index

This is a measure of 'attractiveness' which takes into account
the <u>number</u> and <u>type</u> of shops which are within 100 metres of the
newsagent. For example, a newsagent in close proximity to a
food shop or supermarket was believed to attract potentially
more customers than the one in close proximinty to a furniture
or clothes shop.

PED - pedestrian flow

An attempt was made to assess the flow of pedestrian traffic
past the shop. The obvious difficulties of obtaining this
measure were recognised and the results were finally expressed
on an 8-point scale.

TOY   TOY = (1 if newsagent also sells toys
               (0 otherwise

There are obviously some problems of definition with this
variable, viz how many toys does a shop have to stock before it
qualifies?

BOOK   BOOK = (1 if newsagent also sells books
                (0 otherwise

This is similarly problematic.

GR   GR = (1 if newsagent also sells groceries
           (0 otherwise

PO   PO = (1 if newsagent is also a post office
           (0 otherwise

SOC - social class

This was an attempt to measure the social class of the newsagent's customers. It was measured in terms of the copies of
'quality' daily newspapers sold, expressed as a percentage of
the total copies of daily newspapers sold.

AGE - age group of newsagent

Three age groups were originally used: the under 40's, 40-60
and the over 60's. However, the two under 60 age categories
were collapsed into one as they were never shown to be significantly different in their effects.

M2 and M3 - motivation of newsagent

Three classes of motivation were identified using a latent
class analysis (Haworth and Chell, forthcoming) and each agent
was assigned a probablility of belonging to each of the three
classes.

    M1 = probability of agent belonging to class 1 (low
         motivation)
    M2 = probability of agent belonging to class 2 (moderate
         motivation)
    M3 = probability of agent belong to class 3 (high
         motivation)

M1 is not included in the analysis because the total probability over the three groups always sums to unity.

DB - delivery boys

We felt that it was insufficient to record whether or not a
newsagent had a delivery service, but due to the 'sensitive'
nature of the item it was not possible to obtain accurage data
on the extent of the service e.g. in terms of the number of
houses delivered to. We therefore used number of delivery
boys as a proxy per size of service.

HD - the number of half days the shop was closed per week.

OP - opening hours

Originally data were collected on opening hours, but on

reflection it was thought to be not so much the length of time the shop was open but the time of day it was open. And so an attempt was made to differentiate between those shops which opened very early in the morning from those that did not open until 8.00 or 9.00; and at the other end of the day, those that stayed open until 7.00 or 8.00 at night as opposed to those that closed at 5.30 or 6.00.

APP - appearance of shop

This is measured on a 5-point scale assessing the inside and outside appearance.

SF - shelf feet of magazine display.

COMP - competition

The competition of agent i was assumed to be affected by the presence of any other agent j within an approximate 1 km radius of i. The competition measure was calculated as:

$$COMP_i = \frac{Shop\ Index\ for\ agent\ j}{j(distance\ i\ to\ j)^2}$$

MS - market share

Market share for agent i was calculated using the copy sales of the most popular selling titles (e.g. Radio and TV Times, Woman, Woman's Own etc) of all agents within a 1 km radius of i.

$$MS_i = \frac{Sales\ for\ agent\ i \times 100}{sales\ within\ 1\ km\ radius}$$

During the exploratory stage of this research, the following variables were measured, but were subsequently omitted, either because they were insignificant or they were highly correlated with other variables which were retained:- attitude to wholesaler; attitude to SOR; size of shop; years of experience; parking facility.

RESULTS

The results of the regression analyses are given below:

272

RURAL   n = 83   Mean = £294.2   Std. dev. = £26.92

$\widehat{SALES}$ = 102.1 + 6.073 SI + 37.78 PED + 100.7 TOY + 174.4 PED.TOY
             (1.422)   (46.82)   (42.69)   (67.9)

        - 56.92 PO + 55.16 M3 + 27.65 DB + 2.648 SF - 30.23 COMP
       (23.42)   (27.87)   (3.75)   (0.744)   (5.54)

        + 24.47 log SOC
       (13.17)

R^2 = 0.882 $\bar{R}^2$ = 0.866

TOWN CENTRE   n = 38   Mean = £1037   Std. dev. = £89.43

$\widehat{SALES}$ = -333.0 + 107.0 PED - 342.4 TOY + 16.17 SOC + 244.7 M2
              (24.3)   (92.54)   (3.95)   (117.4)

        + 275.8 M3 + 30.60 DB + 7.617 SF + 12.52 MS - 439.9 AGE
       (110.9)   (13.30)   (1.184)   (2.29)   (158.0)

R^2 = 0.865 $\bar{R}^2$ = 0.822

SUBURBAN   n = 67   Mean = £550.2   Std. dev. = £43.82

$\widehat{SALES}$ = -407.4 + 233.1 ROAD(2) + 325.0 ROAD(3) + 199.6 ROAD(4)
              (99.7)   (104.4)   (96.49)

        +2.743 SI + 90.48 TOY + 189.7 M3 + 26.97 DB
       (0.719)   (45.12)   (53.6)   (3.59)

        +6.291 SF + 0.9171 COMP + 3.881 MS + 136.5 AGE
       (0.982)   (0.390)   (1.027)   (61.7)

R^2 = 0.819 $\bar{R}^2$ = 0.782

NB. Figures in parentheses are standard errors.

The only variables which proved to be at all significant were the following: DB, SF, M2, M3, MS, COMP, SI, PED, TOY, AGE, SOC, ROAD, PO. Certain variables were important in all three areas, that is, in the town centre, the suburbs and in rural areas. These were delivery boys, shelf feet, toy shops and motivation 3 (highly motivated).

DB

This was an important variable in all three areas, being of least significance in the town centres as one would expect. However, there are problems with this variable in that it cannot be assumed that four delivery boys, for instance, represents twice the trade of two delivery boys.

SF

Shelf feet of display was also significant in all three areas but less so in rural areas.

M2 and M3

The highest motivation class (M3) is particularly important in all three areas. In the town centre M2 was also significant, but not so in the other two areas. The proportion of news-agents who were highly motivated were as follows: in the rural group, about one third (28/83 had a probability greater than 0.5 of being highly motivated; in the town centre, 45 per cent (17/38); and in the suburban group 45 per cent (30/47).

MS

Market share was found to be significant in the town centre and suburbs but not in the rural area.

COMP

Competition was significant in the rural and suburban areas. However, there is certainly some degree of correlation between this measure and market share. For instance, particularly in rural areas, where agents have no competition then by defini-tion they have 100 per cent of the market.

The effects of competition can, perhaps, be argued from two points of view: firstly, generally speaking, one would expect that competition would have a negative effect on performance because the greater the number of 'attractive agents' within the vicinity the lower any one agent's performance. Secondly, it could be argued that the existence of competition can provide a stimulus to the newsagent making him take a more

274

active interest in the way he runs the business. In this case,
competition would be expected to have a positive effect on
sales performance.

   The findings showed that in <u>rural areas</u>, competition had a
negative effect on performance, while in the suburbs, the
reverse was the case. In the majority of rural shops there was
no competition and in the few that had, there was competition
from only one or perhaps two other shops. These agents were
competing for a fairly fixed static market and we would suggest
that the existence of another agent in the vicinity is unlikely
to have a stimulating effect. In addition, the newsagency side
of the business often represents a small proportion of their
total business than is the case in the other two location
groups and in some cases it was viewed as merely providing a
service to the community.

   In the suburban shops, the effect of compeition was positive
which may be explained by our second proposition concerning the
stimulating effects of competition. However, we must confess
to being a little surprised at this result but observe that the
size of the effect (compared with the size of the effect in the
case of the rural areas) was relatively small; we therefore
view the result with a certain amount of reservation.

SI

This was significant in the rural and suburban areas, but not
in the town centre. This is probably because town centre shops
are likely to be more homogeneous in terms of this measure.

PED and TOY

Pedestrian flow was significant in rural areas and the town
centre, but in the rural areas it was found to interact
significantly with whether the shop sold toys or not. This
probably relects the fact that with this group of shops those
selling toys are located in the busier areas and are likely to
be the larger shops. We do not think that the mere fact that
the shop sells toys has any direct effect on their sales of
magazines. In other words, the toy variable, in particular, is
acting as a proxy for some other measure. Toys however, are
significant in the other two areas. In the town centres toy
shops have a substantial negative effect, whereas in the
suburban areas they have a positive effect. Therefore in rural
and suburban areas toy shops appear to be better newsagents,
whereas in the town centres they are the worst. However, we
have already stated that we have reservations over the
definition of this variable.

AGE

Age was significant in two of the location groups: for those over 60, it has a fairly negative effect in the town centres, whereas the over 60's have a positive effect - albeit of lower significance - in the suburban area. This is very difficult to explain.

SOC

The social class measure was significant in the town centre shops. Included in this particular category was a small city centre which could be contrasted with outlying towns, some of which were industrial and others which were market towns.

In addition we found that log SOC was also of marginal significance in the rural areas. This would reflect the considerable variability in such areas, reflecting social class differences.

ROAD

This was only of importance in the suburban areas. This finding makes sense in that the suburban areas are more hetero-geneous in terms of their location and with respect to the type of road. Road obviously reflects other variables. For example, in the case of secondary amd major traffic routes, secondary traffic routes have a greater effect on performance, probably due to the fact that there may be fewer parking difficulties. Secondly, road is also related to the amount of passing trade and, thirdly, to other location factors, such as the existence of a housing estate or of a shopping precinct.

PO

Post Office was only significant in the rural area. Again this was in line with expectations as the rural PO frequently doubles up as the newsagents-cum-village store. In these situations there is a tendency for the newsagency side of the business to be somewhat secondary and in many instances it has been the post office that has attracted the vendor who has become a newsagent almost by default.

CASE STUDIES

It would be unrealistic to think that we had identified and measured every conceivable factor which has some impact upon the sales performance of the newsagents sampled. A useful exercise in trying to understand the limitations of the

Table 1

Profiles from a selection of newsagents from the three location categories

LOCATION GROUP

NEWSAGENT	Town Centre				Suburban		Rural	
VARIABLE	A	B	C	D	E	F	G	H
ROAD	4	3	3	2	4	2	2	4
SI	148	157	141	123	9	90	9	9
PED	4	7	7	4	2	4	1	1
TOY	0	0	0	0	1	0	0	0
BOOK	0	0	0	0	0	0	0	0
GR	0	0	0	0	0	0	1	0
PO	0	0	0	0	0	1	0	1
SOC	13.5	9.5	2.1	8.3	10.0	2.3	7.7	11.1
AGE	1	1	1	1	1	1	1	1
M2	0.98	0.00	0.00	0.02	0.00	0.0	0.01	0.03
M3	0.00	1.00	0.00	0.98	1.00	1.00	0.99	0.97
DB	4	6	0	6	10		10	10
HD	1	1	0	2	0	2	0	1
OP	3	3	3	3	5	1	3	1
APP	1	2	1	3	4	4	3	2
SF	0	40	20	15	70	50	60	35
COMP	0.0	346.8	256.8	262.5	5.3	0.6	0.0	0.0
MS	100.0	35.1	4.9	27.3	25.6	55.3	100.0	100.0
ACTUAL SALES (£)	1,646	2,099	228	1,487	570	703	466	725
PREDICTED SALES (£)	1,927	1,773	663	1,144	911	792	636	521

277

performance model and the results that it has produced, is to examine those cases which fell below or above the predicted or expected level of sales performance, and explain why this may have been so. In the following pages we have selected groups of newsagents within each location category which are comparable on most of the dimensions measured but whose performances differ somewhat. The profiles of these agents are listed in Table 1. The question to ask is whether some factor has not been identified which might explain the apparent discrepancy in their performance and if so whether these can be measured or not.

Town centre shops

A selection of four town centre shops were chosen because three of them (B, C and D) are sited in the same small town and because their performance levels may be contrasted sharply.

If we examine shops B and C we find that they are both positioned on the High Street, yet B is performing above what might be expected of him given his circumstances, while C is performing below par. This is at first sight puzzling because both shops have many location characteristics in common: their positions are good; they have similar, very high Shop Indices; and they have a high Pedestrian Flow of 7. But, in the case of Shop B, the owners also have another newsagency in a rural area some four miles away. We know that this particular newsagent does, on occasions, divert some of his supplies from one shop to the other, but we do not know the extent or direction of this. The implication is that his 'true' sales figure may well be less than the recorded figure of £2,099; and he may not be out performing his High Street competitors quite to the extent that it appears. However, newsagent C, in contrast, lacks motivation, has no delivery service and the social class of his customers is below that of the others. These factors are already taken into consideration by the model to arrive at his <u>predicted</u> sales performance, which is almost a third that of B. However, his actual level of sales is significantly lower than that predicted and this difference can be partially explained by other entraneous information. We know that this particular agent is devoid of commitment to the business and is rather extreme in his lack of motivation and effort. These factors taken together almost certainly have several implications for his business. For instance, it would appear from his social class measure that he could possibly sell more 'quality' news-papers if he were to stock them. Similarly, he could well be understocking in many other major titles. Furthermore, we wondered to what extent the self presentation of the proprietor and the run down appearance of the shop deterred custom. These are factors which we have obviously not been able to measure.

Shop D is disadvantaged compared with B and C on the High Street as it is located on a side road just off the main thoroughfare. On the other hand, we know that D has built up the reputation of being a 'good' shop over many years and it is quite likely that some of the differences can be explained by customer allegiance. Again this is a variable which we have been unable to measure.

Shop A, on the other hand, may be contrasted with the others. It is located in a different town and on a major traffic route. It has a high SI, and is therefore located in a group of attractive shops, but has relatively low pedestrian flow. Although there are other differences that we will come to, the main distinguishing feature for A is its lack of competition (and the consequent fact that it has 100 per cent of the market). However, given such apparent advantages A is performing significantly below expectations. We know that this shop is situated in a fairly affluent market town. It is somewhat old fashioned in appearance with many features similar to those in rural areas. These findings raise two questions:

1. If this newsagency was managed by a person who was more highly motivated and had a more positive attitude and the shop had a refit, how might sales be affected?

2. If this agent suddenly found himself in a competitive situation, how might his performance be affected? Certainly, as things stand, he does not appear to have taken advantage of his monopolistic situation by exploring his market potential.

Suburban shops

Shops E and F pose an interesting comparsion because both are situated in the same suburb, approximately 200 metres apart and are owned by the same person. E is situated on its own on a main road and captures early morning and evening commuter traffic, whereas F is situated round the corner amongst a small row of shops and is also a Post Office. Both are operating below expectations, E significantly so and F barely so. One explanation for their relative differences could be that E has a more important newspaper trade in terms of customers entering the shop because of its location. On the other hand, F is likely to perform better in its sales of periodicals and magazines because its customer flow is more even throughout the day with customers having more time for browsing. Furthermore, we suspect that there could well be some substitution between the supplies to these two shops and that they could be operating as one in some respects. They obviously compete with one another to some extent and the owner uses shop E as his delivery base. Had these two shops been owned by different people, it is possible that both would offer a delivery service and the market would divide between them in a different way than is shown by our data. We suggest that because of the likely 'contamination' of the results particularly for shop E, they be treated with great reservation.

Rural shops

Newsagents G and H have reasonably similar profiles although H is a Post Office whereas G is a grocer. H performs significantly above expectations. It is possible that he is not typical of the PO's in the rural location who generally, it will be recalled, under perform. We have strong grounds for believing that this agent is in fact achieving his sales potential. This is based on the fact that he was a participant in the wholesaler's SOR experiment (which we describe later) and the result for this agent was that the scheme had little effect on his level of sales. Newsagent G has performed significantly below expectations. We know of no reason for this except we note that he is also a VG grocer, and we suspect that the grocery part of the business may predominate.

Concluding remarks on the case studies

It is a useful exercise to be able to pinpoint those newsagents who are either under or over achieving according to our model of performance. However, we are not really in a position to offer any explanations in those cases where performance is significantly greater or less than expected. Our task, we feel, is to provide the best model we can, given the data and their various inadequacies, and it is then up to the wholesaler who knows his customers to search for any explanations. Initially, his greatest interest is in trying to raise the level particularly of those agents who are under achieving. The question which must be asked is: are the agents whom we have identified as under and over achievers in fact so? The wholesaler may know of some particular factors to explain this which we have not been able to include in our model. In the cases where he can offer no explanation of under achievement, we hypothesise that in the majority of instances the low level of performance is due to the extent of understocking and in some other instances is due to a lack of customer potential. The latter is particularly so in rural areas.

AN EXPERIMENTAL 'SALE OR RETURN' (SOR) SCHEME

Some of the factors which were shown to affect the sales
performance of the newsagents are difficult to control from the
wholesaler's point of view. However, one way in which he may
be able to influence and raise the general level of performance
of the agents he supplies is through an SOR scheme. In June
1982 we presented the wholesaler with a list of newsagents who
repeatedly appeared as outliers across a number of regression
calculations. We considered it 'safer' to categorise these
agents according to whether they appeared consistently to
perform well above average, above average, below average or
well below average, given their circumstances as dictated by the
data. The agents not included in this list were classified as
average performers. The SOR shcme was applied to a sample of
these agents.

Some of the practical problems for the wholesaler arose from
the need to balance his supply from the publisher to the anticipated demand from the newsagents. For instance, the agents
had to be given deadlines for reporting their stock position on
the SOR titles so that the supply for the following week could
be adjusted accordingly. But the ordering of weeklies from the
publisher has to be done two weeks in advance. This inevitably
led to a certain amount of speculation on the part of the
wholesaler and to a further problem of controlling his wastage.
In addition he has the problem of trying to maintain the
interest and cooperation of the newsagent.

The performance and response of the agents to the scheme also
had its practical problems. Weekly reports from the agents of
their current stock position frequently proved to be somewhat
inaccurate and resulted in the wholesaler unwittingly making
inappropriate adjustments to the supply for the subsequent
period. However, these problems apart, at the end of the
scheme, it was shown that the sales of the chosen titles for
the majority in the experimental group of agents increased
dramatically vis a vis other agents who were not on the scheme.
This goes some way to supporting our hypothesis that much of
the under-performance is due to understocking and is highlighted by the fact that there was considerable sales potential
on the best selling titles.

CONCLUDING REMARKS

It is clear that the newsagency business is a specialised
sector of retailing which has many features and characteristics
which contrast sharply with, say, the small grocery outlet.
Essentially, the newsagent is not threatened by competition -

partly because this is restricted by the wholesaler - although as we have seen, the extent of his competition may vary from zero to being quite considerable, depending upon his location. In addition, the newsagency business, despite the current economic climate, is quite buoyant and, as we have demonstrated, there is scope for considerable expansion of sales of weekly and monthly magazines. Part of the problem for the wholesaler in attempting to educate and encourage the newsagent to raise his horizons, is that the newsagent is a satisficer rather than a profit maximiser. Whilst some are highly motivated, few take it upon themselves to explore their market potential. Perhaps there is a case for the smaller wholesaler to enter the retail sector by not just setting up newsagencies in the expensive High Street positions, but also in other locations, where he can identify a potential for a new retail outlet. (This was amply illustrated in our discussion of the case of shop A.)

The research has enabled us to assess the newsagents' actual sales performance relative to that which was expected given their circumstances and to identify some of the variables which are significant in determining their performance. Although the wholesaler would eventually want to raise the level of perform-ance of all agents, in the first instance he concentrated on the under achievers. To this end he conducted an experiment to enable the newsagents to explore their market potential on a selection of magazine titles and thus raise their level of sales. The next practical problem to be faced was to persuade such agents to maintain their stock of these magazines at the new level once the SOR scheme was withdrawn; all too often they have been found to revert to their original ordering levels. This suggests that SOR schemes on their own will have little lasting effect without: (i) the necessary back up in terms of closer personal relations between wholesaler and newsagent, (ii) more extensive training and education of the small shop-keeper and (iii) a general change in attitude to the business as a whole. This would result in:

- greater professionalism on the part of the newsagent;
- a willingness to invest in the business in terms of modernisation of the shop and increasing the area for display of magazines;
- a need to demonstrate greater flexibility in adjusting his order levels week by week;
- a keeness to explore his market potential and take advantage of SOR schemes and other promotions;
- and perhaps even a willingness to move into the computerisation of those aspects of the business which lend themselves to it, such as the monitoring of stock levels.

Generally speaking, we feel that there is a great deal that the newsagent could do for himself to improve his business.

We must not lose sight of the fact that under no circumstances of which we are aware are we ever talking about the
entire business of the newsagent. In some instances, the newsagency side of the business ranges from being inconspicuous in
a store which may sell a variety of goods - from tools to
stamps - and may be part of the 'service' which this shop
offers to a relatively small village community, to representing
the major portion of the business. This suggests that
different functions are served by different newsagencies in
different localities. Additionally, the extensiveness or
otherwise of the newsagency side of the business must affect
the newsagent's perception, and awareness, of local competition.
Where the newsagency is such a small part of the business the
newsagent may not anticipate competing with a shop which has
made the selling of newspapers and magazines a predominant
feature of its business. Such expectations of his competitive
position vis a vis other shops, or the total absence of any
competitive stance where no other local newsagents exist, help
to shape the newsagent's attitude to his business and his
motivation to raise his performance standards and his market
share. Moreover, the newsagent may also be constrained in this
regard by his expectations of his customers and their
expectations of him. Thus, for example, in rural areas the
relationship between the absence of existing competition and
the apparent complacency of the newsagent with regard to that
aspect of his business is not direct. It would appear to be a
function of a constellation of intervening variables, that is,
those characteristics which shape that particular type of
business in the situation in which it is located.

We feel that this research has highlighted areas where more
extensive research is justified. One such area is competition -
'real' and perceived. We attempted, albeit somewhat crudely,
to measure 'real' competition, but we were not able to
ascertain in any usable way whether the newsagent was fully
aware of his competitors and what effect, if any, that knowledge had on his performance. In addition, we would have liked
to have included more questions in our interview schedule which
would have enabled us to measure additional dimensions of
motivation. This may have included the use of performance
criteria which may have served as independent measures of
motivation thus lending a degree of external validity to the
latent class measure that we derived from the questionnaire
survey. Furthermore, as this study has deliberately excluded
any investigation of the multiples, we feel that a comparative
study of the performance of the multiples and of the independent newsagent would reveal some very interesting and valuable
information.

There are various practical constraints to any piece of research - not least of all to the present one. However, acknowledging these we felt that we have been able to arrive at a useful model for measuring the sales performance of the newsagent. This has enabled the wholesaler to pick out the under achievers and attempt to raise their performance. But our recommendations go beyond this; we believe that this exercise is ultimately about an interdependent relationship between wholesaler and newsagent, and about the ways in which the relationship can be fostered. It is about the cooperation and trust and the willingness to modify attitudes on both sides to achieve what perhaps should appear as a common objective - the increased sales performance of the independent retail newsagent. The mechanism for arriving at this goal is clear, but it is the willingnes to travel along the path which is the key to success.

ACKNOWLEDGEMENTS

We would like to thank Thos. Swift & Co. Ltd who have given generously of their time and resources in pursuit of this research. It is clear that without such assistance this research project would not have been possible. In addition we would like to give special mention to Mr. Mark Rowlands, an employee of Thos. Swift & Co. Ltd, for his assistance and collection of some of the data, and for some helpful discussions on various aspects of this work.

REFERENCES

Bates, P., (1976), The Independent Grocery Retailer, Manchester Business School, Manchester.

Berry, B.J.L. and Pred, A., (1965), Central Place Studies: A bibliography of theory and applications, Regional Science Research Institute, Philadelphia.

Butler, P., (1976), 'A study of local shopping in Newcastle upon Tyne', in Jones, P. and Oliphant, R., (eds), Local Shops: Problems and Prospects, URP1, Reading, pp.45-61.

Cmnd 4811, (1971), Report of the Committee of Inquiry on Small Firms, Chairman, J.E. Bolton, HMSO, London.

Cmnd 6810, (1977), Royal Commission on the Press, Final Report, Chairman, O.R. McGregor, HMSO, London.

Cmnd 7214, (1978), Wholesaling of Newspapers and Periodicals, The Monopolies and Mergers Commission, HMSO, London.

Curran, J. and Stanworth, J., (1982), 'The Small Firm in Britain - Past, Present and Future', European Small Business Journal, vol.1, no.1, pp.15-25.

Curran, J. and Stanworth, J., (1982), 'Bolton Ten Years On: A
   Research Inventory and Critical Review'. Paper presented at
   The Small Business Research Conference - Bolton Ten Years On
   - Polytechnic of Central London, 20th-22nd November.
Dawson, J.A. and Kirby, D.A., (1979), Small Scale Retailing in
   the U.K., Saxon House, Farnborough.
Dawson, J.A. and Morgan, R.H., (1976), 'Shopping in Carmathen',
   University of Wales, Saint David's University College,
   Department of Geography Working Paper.
Haworth, J.M. and Chell, E., 'An Application of Latent Class
   Analysis of the Measurement of Motivation'.
HMSO, (1971), Census of Distribution.
Mayer, K.B. and Goldstein, S., (1961), The First Two Years:
   Problems of small firm growth and survival, Small Business
   Research Series, U.S. Government Printing Office, Washington.
Thorpe, D., (1977), The Independent Toy Retailer: A study of
   his characteristics and problems, Research Report No.28,
   Retail Outlets Research Unit, Manchester Business School.

SECTION III
POLICY IMPLICATIONS
AND QUESTIONS

Issues in small firms research of relevance to policy making

DAVID REES, CELIA FRANK AND ROBERT MIALL

INTRODUCTION

This chapter is intended to provide an indication of the areas
connected with new and small firms where policy makers would
find it useful to have further research or analysis undertaken.
Equally, it suggests, by specific reference or omission, the
areas where further work by academics is not seen at present as
having a significant return for policy purposes. In general,
it has not proved possible for reasons of length to probe all
issues of interest in great depth, and sometimes only a sketch
has been attempted and bald questions raised.

   The chapter begins by outlining the policy objectives towards
small firms as developed in recent years and describes some
recent policy measures. Then, since we are concerned not
just with the simple acquisition of data but also with its
analysis for very practical purposes, it uses the Loan
Guarantee Scheme to explore the nature of the questions that
need to be answered when evaluating the success of any policy.
The main body of the chapter then presents guidelines to the
issues regarded as important, linking these where possible to
declared policy aims. The final section draws together some of
the underlying themes from a small firms policy perspective.

   Before discussing these issues, two points need to be made.
First, in much of what follows reference is made to 'small

firms' without further elaboration. It is of course appreciated that small firms are not homogeneous and the need to take account of diversity within the small firms sector, which is itself only capable of being arbitrarily defined, should be taken to be implicit. Secondly, although government departments are interested in a wide range of small firms and other research, we would only expect to fund research into a few of the questions raised by this paper. It can also be noted that there is now a new Small Business Research Trust. This is an independent research organisation, launched in May 1983, with the objective of advancing knowledge and educating the public in relation to small and medium sized enterprises.

OBJECTIVES OF SMALL FIRMS POLICY

The small firms sector is recognised by the Government as having a vital part to play in the development of the economy. It accounts for a significant proportion of employment and output, and is a source of competition, innovation, diversity and employment. There are also social reasons for wanting a sector in the economy which provides the opportunity both for the self employed and for new and small firms to assert their independence.

The Department of Trade and Industry has overall responsibility in Whitehall for small firms policy, and its policy objectives in this area can perhaps best be viewed in relation to the strategic aims of the old Department of Industry. The Department considered its central aim to be that of achieving "a profitable, competitive and adaptive productive sector in the UK". This is to be approached in three main ways. The first is to promote a climate for UK industry which is as conducive to enterprise as that in any other industrialised country. Applied to small firms, this has several aspects:

(1) To foster more positive attitudes towards self employment and entrepreneurship and a better understanding of business opportunities in the community as a whole; and to provide assistance to small firms in their buying and selling practices.

(2) To improve tax incentives and rewards, and to promote the flow of finance to small businesses.

(3) To identify legislative and administrative burdens affecting small businesses and to remove obstacles to their formation and development; to ensure an adequate supply of small premises; and to contribute to European Community policies on small firms without constricting the UK's freedom to pursue its own policies.

The second way of achieving the Department's central aim is through promoting "industrial efficiency, through the selective use of the power of government to achieve international competitiveness". For small firms policy, this means Government should:

(1) Provide an information and business advisory service for small firms; ... increase the provision of management education and training for small businesses, especially its relevance and accessibility; ... encourage communication and cooperation between organisations concerned with small firms; ... encourage large firms to provide assistance to Enterprise Agencies and Small Business Clubs.

(2) Test whether a finance gap exists for small firms by evaluating the pilot Loan Guarantee Scheme.

Promoting "opportunities for innovation, with the technology available applied on the scale necessary to ensure UK competitiveness" is the third approach. In the case of small firms, this involves encouraging "the transfer of technology from large firms and academic centres of excellence to small firms, and to provide small firms with assistance in using microcomputers".

ISSUES RELEVANT TO A SMALL FIRMS MEASURE

One example of a measure introduced in response to research findings, and which is subject to continuing evaluation not only as part of normal government monitoring but also because it is a pilot scheme, is the Small Business Loan Guarantee Scheme. The proponents of the scheme argued that banks and other financial institutions were rarely willing to finance viable, but risky, small firms, and then only on terms which were a severe disincentive to the businessman; in particular it was claimed that the banks would only support the more marginal small business projects if the borrowers were able to offer security in the form of a legal charge on personal assets. This, it was claimed, constituted a finance gap. The banks on the other hand argued that there was no shortage of finance for good, viable small firms. The Wilson Committee (1979), which found no reason to believe that there was a bias, in the sense of unjustified discrimination with respect to charging for financial deals, concluded that a bias might exist in banks' assessment of risk in that they might be excessively cautious. Since the evidence was inconclusive, they recommended that a publicly underwritten loan guarantee scheme, with a limited subsidy element and some part of the risk retained by the banks, should be set up on an experimental basis.

The Loan Guarantee Scheme (LGS) was introduced in June 1981 as a pilot measure designed to encourage participating banks and financial institutions to make additional loan facilities available to small businesses when they would not otherwise be prepared to do so. Under the scheme, the government guarantees to repay 80 per cent of the outstanding loan to the bank in the event of default. The original allocation of £150 million of bank lending over three years was used up in only twelve months and a similar amount was made available for the second year. The ceiling of bank lending covered has since been raised by a further £300 million, following a review of the scheme. This means that the total ceiling on bank lending within the pilot scheme has been raised to a total of £600 million.

Succcessful identification of a finance gap through experience with the LGS must hinge on two aspects: additionality and viability. The scheme is intended to provide finance to firms which would otherwise find it difficult or impossible to raise finance from conventional sources, rather than diverting them from existing sources of funds to the LGS. That is, such borrowing must be 'additional' - it would not have happened at all, or on the same scale, without the government guarantee. Additional small firm projects financed by the scheme must also prove to be viable in the longer term, otherwise the banks' original claim that there was no shortage of finance for good viable small businesses would be shown to have been correct. It is clearly too early to make any final judgement about the viability of the small firms receiving scheme loans, and the evaluation so far has concentrated on additionality and related issues.

The work done to estimate additionality is a good illustration both of some of the methodological problems involved in assessing the effect of government measures and of the value of such studies in providing information or recommendations which can be used to improve the particular measure or to inform wider policy decisions. It also illustrates the combined use of expertise inside and outside government. A report, by chartered accountants Robson Rhodes has examined some early calls on the guarantee. It was based on case files and interviews with the banks and in some instances the businessmen responsible for the failed projects. Robson Rhodes have also commented on the second of two telephone sample surveys carried out by DTI economists (Robson Rhodes, 1983a, 1983b; Department of Industry, 1982).

The assessment of additionality, for lack of suitable aggregate data on lending to small firms with and without the LGS, relied exclusively on the survey results. Interpretation of such material is not easy. The replies represent opinion, not fact, and even when honestly given (it might not appear to be in the self interest of the interviewee to say that the loan was not additional) may not be correct. Interviewer bias may also be a problem. However, the DTI economists who conducted the survey were encouraged by the quality of the interviews, and felt their estimates of additionality were fairly robust. It was judged that about 80 per cent of scheme borrowers would either not have been able to raise finance without the scheme on any acceptable terms or only by pledging personal assets. At least 60 per cent would not have obtained finance without the scheme on acceptable terms, if those who might have been able to raise finance by pledging personal assets are not counted.

The definition of additionality used here is clearly quite narrow. In evaluating a measure, an estimate of the net effect on the national or local economy is necessary. Additionality of finance does not necessarily mean that the output of the firms financed can be regarded as additional to the UK economy since it may be displacing output of existing UK large or small businesses. Estimating this displacement at either a local or a national level, other than impressionistically is a challenge, and perhaps impossible. Some idea can be obtained by looking at the industries and markets involved: Is the output tradeable over a wide area? Do the markets seem new? The length of time considered is also relevant. Even if displacement is total – and we would expect that many small firms measures will have high displacement – there could still be a positive effect on the economy in terms of increased efficiency and dynamism. These are key issues in the evaluation of any small firms measure and ideas for ways of evaluating both local and national displacement and for assessing what types of activity are more likely to lead to displacement than others are needed.

Research into the LGS also came up with other findings of relevance both to the running of the scheme and to those involved more generally in small firms' finance. For example, from their analysis of the failures, many of which appeared to have been from their case files extremely fragile, Robson Rhodes emphasised the need to establish simple but robust appraisal and monitoring procedures for such businesses and the important part that outside advisers might play in this.

ISSUES FOR FURTHER RESEARCH

New firm founders

One government objective is to improve the climate for entre-preneurship and to foster more positive attitudes towards it.

In pursuing this aim it is necessary to have a good understanding of the characteristics of actual and potential
entrepreneurs. A number of studies have investigated the
characteristics of new firm founders, and we have found them
helpful. They have tended, however, to be limited in terms of
the characteristics they have investigated, or in terms of
either their spatial or sectoral coverage and there may be
scope for a more national approach, which could still make
distinctions by region or type of area. Any further research
in these areas could also seek to throw light on the reasons
for the apparent increase in business start ups in recent years
and whether the characteristics, motivations and attitudes of
new firms founders have changed in recent years. It would, for
example, be very interesting to know whether 'push' factors
have become more significant in recent years as a motivating
force. In this context it is relevant to note that Storey
(1982) reported that in the late 1970s about 25 per cent of new
entrepreneurs were 'pushed' into starting their own business,
principally because of unemployment or job insecurity, while
recent research on new manufacturing firms in Nottingham
(Mitchell and Binks, 1984) suggests a figure of around 50 per
cent. Any further research might also throw light on whether
the Government's encouragement of 'entrepreneurship' has helped
to generate more positive attitudes. A further issue concerns
the activities chosen by new firm founders. Earlier research
has suggested founders tend to establish businesses in the
activities in which they were previously employed. It will now
be interesting to see whether this tendency has strengthened
during the recent recession, or weakened with there being more
diversification of activity. The latter would probably be of
greater significance to the process of economic change. The
early results of the Nottingham area study (Mitchell and Binks,
1984) suggest, however, that only a minority of 'first time'
founders have tried to establish themselves in industries in
which they have no previous experience and still fewer have
succeeded in introducing product or process innovations.

Success or failure of small firms

The proposed research discussed above should help our understanding of the process of new firm formation. It would be
helpful, however, to know more about the chances of different
types of business, or businessman, 'succeeding', 'failing', or
just continuing to exist. Thus, while it would be unrealistic
to expect research to come up with an identikit whizzkid
entrepreneur, research to establish the distinctive
characteristics of those running successful, growing businesses
and the characteristics of those running static or declining
businesses, and of the businesses themselves in each category,
would be a useful extension of the topics sketched in the

previous paragraph. Some work has already been done in this area but there is scope for more comprehensive analysis, which could for example be helpful to people making decisions about where to channel advisory services.

In assessing the success of Government schemes to aid small business, information on the proportion of firms in a normal population which would be expected to achieve a particular performance level (including failure) is often desirable. Yet information in some of these areas is very vague and often anecdotal. Well researched data, distinguishing between types of small firm and possibly variations in macro economic conditions, would certainly be very helpful.

Finance

Concern about the type and availability of finance for small firms has been expressed for many years. The Bolton (1971) and Wilson (1979) Committees devoted considerable attention to these issues, and while both concluded that small firms operated at a disadvantage in obtaining external finance, neither inquiry found that this constituted an unwarranted bias. The difficulties experienced were considered to be the natural result of the high cost of lending to, and investing in, small firms, together with the high risk of default and problems of investment marketability. Following the Wilson Report and largely building on a number of suggestions in it, recent governments have, as outlined earlier, made considerable efforts to improve the financial institutional framework confronting small firms. There has also been an associated expansion in the number of agencies, in both the public and private sectors, which have been designed to advise and assist small proprietors to set up, finance, manage and develop their businesses.

Nowadays there is considerably less public concern about the issue of small firm finance than there was two or three years ago but it remains an area of particular interest to us. There are, however, a number of issues worthy of research. Evaluation of the various government measures is important. The chapter has already discussed the evaluation of the Loan Guarantee Scheme, and it should be noted that the Enterprise Allowance Scheme is being assessed by the Department of Employment, the Manpower Services Commission and ourselves. Fresh approaches to the assessment of these schemes are, of course, always welcome! There has, as yet, perhaps not surprisingly, been little assessment of the relatively new Business Start-Up (or Expansion) Scheme. There are two broad groups of questions that might be posed here: first, the effect of the schemes on attitudes and behaviour and, secondly, the cost effectiveness of the schemes. On attitudes, why has the response been so slow? Is it because of complexities, lack of certainty, poor marketing, opposition from the professions? Or are there more fundamental factors involved? On cost effectiveness, one could consider whether an analysis involving the schemes could establish how far the investment undertaken is genuinely additional and what happens to growth and performance.

A recurring theme of concern is whether small firms should be encouraged to relinquish more equity. General evidence on small firms gearing as compared with other firms in the economy, is neither very good nor conclusive. Indeed research commissioned by Wilson on this did not show small firms as being very far out of line, if directors' loans were counted in as being part of equity. This is something which might be investigated further. What are typical levels of debt/equity for different kinds of small firms? Do different financial structures relate in any way to the performance of the company? Is it true/inevitable that growth seeking small businesses resist conceding minority equity participation or if firms are really interested in growth is there a need for them to take more equity in any case. Will this be eroded by the very attractive tax concessions now available? Have government moves to allow firms to buy back their own shares, for example, had any observable effect on small firms' traditional reluctance to accept external equity?

Venture capital may be taken as a related special case. Is gearing important for new firms, especially in high technology areas where a good return is unlikely in the short term? There has been a considerable growth in the supply of venture capital in the UK, though the supply is often unfavourably compared with that in the USA. Is this criticism still justified? (It can be noted here that the evidence so far from the Nottingham (Mitchell and Binks, 1984) study suggests that the innovative entrepreneur cannot attract reasonably priced funds, while his non-innovative counterpart is enjoying the fruits of the recent changes in the lending practices of financial institutions). One further problem is that only a few of the 'venture' capital companies in the UK are prepared to put the 'necessary' management skills into a new firm - i.e. a 'hands on' approach. This is in contrast to US venture capital firms which usually do. Why is this?

There are various policy issues concerning the shares of small firms. It is common ground that their shares are less marketable than those quoted on the Stock Exchange or the USM. But how much less marketable, especially taking into account the growing Over-the-Counter (OTC) market in the UK? Is there scope for further relaxation of the rules governing the Unlisted Securities Market (e.g. opening it up to private companies) to give it a role nearer to that played by the US OTC market?

Concern is sometimes expressed about the degree of understanding of the peculiar problems and needs of small businesses possessed by providers of finance such as banks and finance houses. In view of this, and of the high cost of evaluating and subsequently monitoring small firms projects, is it possible to devise relatively simple, standard financial evaluation and monitoring procedures which would reduce these costs? It would also be interesting to analyse the perceptions of financial institutions about the chances of different types of business or businessmen succeeding or failing. Are the professions adequately equipped to deal with the complexities of tax law and raising funds for small businesses? If not, how can their performance be improved?

Finally on finance there may be scope for some evaluation of the increasing role various public agencies are playing in lending money to small firms. For example, what gaps are they filling, are the loans leading to 'additional' finance? What is the subsequent performance of the companies which receive the loans?

Urban policy and small firms research

Perhaps the basic question for small firms research in relation to the urban problem is to what extent small firms can make a significant contribution to meeting the employment needs of inner city residents. There are several interesting questions which arise from this basic question. It is important to know more about the type of activity which is relatively well suited to urban areas (e.g. manufacturing or service activities, small or large firms) and what role they might play in providing employment for residents of these areas. The Department of Environment are interested in the role that the non manufacturing sector could play in providing jobs for inner city residents. We ourselves are sponsoring work on the costs faced by various manufacturing and service industries according to whether they have an urban or a more rural location. There would certainly seem to be scope for further work on the relative costs and benefits of an urban location for firms of different sizes and types.

The Department of the Environment, with their responsibility for encouraging economic activity in inner city areas is interested in the extent to which assistance to firms, particularly small firms, results in additional employment for inner city residents and whether certain types of small firms are more likely to do so than others. Do small firms draw on labour from the local area more than large firms - this might be the case if small firms tended to require the sort of skills possessed by inner city residents. These are important points as a major requirement in the design of policies for urban economic regeneration is to identify policies which are likely to increase the employment of disadvantaged residents who are the intended beneficiaries.

Some researchers have argued that because many small firms tend to have a fairly narrow market area, any increase in small firm activity is likely to displace other, principally small firm, activity within a fairly narrow area. To the extent that this is the case, encouraging small firms in selected parts of urban areas may stimulate activity at the expense of other firms within the same conurbation (see Lloyd and Dicken, 1982). This may be quite acceptable to the extent that inner city residents are better off as a result, but referring back to the last paragraph, there would be little advantage in shifting activity around in conurbations if those employed still came from the wealthier parts of the area. Displacement is there-fore another important issue in urban policy. Is it possible to throw more light on the types of small firm activities which (a) are likely to employ inner city residents and (b) do not displace other activity in the local area?

Having gone into some detail on some of the questions on which more research might help to provide understanding of whether encouraging small firms is an appropriate urban policy objective, some other issues will be more briefly considered. First, if small firms do have a role to play, how much should be expected of them? Evidence from the job generation literature suggests that new firms only offer the prospect of significant employment gains in the medium to long term. This suggests that policies intended to encourage new firm formation have only a relatively minor part to play in urban areas. But there may be scope for fostering the existing small business sector in urban areas. This raises a number of issues. Are there impediments to small business development in urban areas and how could they be removed? What are the most cost effective policy responses? There has already been a good deal of research by Fothergill and Gudgin (1982) on the importance of premises to the decline of manufacturing employment in urban areas. The Department of Environment has also looked at the question of whether the provision of premises, especially small units, is a cost effective way of increasing the employment of inner city residents in Tyne and Wear (Cameron, 1982) but intends to continue and to extend this work to compare its relative cost effectiveness of providing inner city employment with other policy measures.

Local government and small firms

The Department of the Environment (DoE) are interested to know
more about the impact of local government policies and services
on small firms (e.g. the effects of planning policies and
rates). One area, in particular, where further work would be
beneficial is the planning system. Research undertaken at
Middlesex Polytechnic (1982) suggests that planning control is
not a particular problem for small firms but there is a need
for a more detailed consideration of the extent to which small
firms experience difficulties in getting planning permission
for their activities. The DoE have advised local planning
authorities to be sympathetic to the needs of small firms (DoE
Circular 22/80) and have it in mind to commission research
which will make a systematic assessment of the ways in which
local planning authorities deal with applications from industry
and small business.

Premises and small firms

A number of government initiatives have been concerned with the
provision of premises for small firms. Our own analysis of the
effects of the Industrial Building Allowance showed that this
incentive had a major impact. It would, however, be useful to
have a better understanding of the operation of the market for
small premises. One possibility is that there is a natural
'gap' in the market for small premises, because of the
reluctance of the institutions to finance and, more importantly,
manage, a large number of small premises. This may interact
with a further reluctance to invest in inner city areas, to
make the supply of small premises in most urban areas a
particular problem. It may be of interest to note in passing
that we are ourselves sponsoring work to evaluate the impact of
the public provision of advance factories for regional policy
purposes (which increasingly in recent years has been
orientated towards small premises) on the private sector
provision.

Firm size and employment change

There has been a lot of interest expressed recently in the
employment generating capability of small firms. There have
been two main empirical approaches to the relationship between
size of firm and growth. The first, starting from a long
standing interest in increasing concentration in the UK economy,
analysed data for samples of firms, divided into fairly broad
size bands. Studies of samples of firms in the UK since the
1950s have shown a weak positive relationship between firm size

and growth (i.e. bigger firms grow faster) (Macey, 1982); but that the variance of growth rates of firms is inversely related to size of firm (i.e. typically, small firms have been more likely to exhibit both high rates of growth and of decline than large firms, and have therefore been more likely to die). These studies have, however, tended to ignore very small companies and they reflect the effects of the take-overs.

The second, more recent approach has been to examine the components of employment change by size of establishment (not by firm because of data limitations). There have been several UK studies which have been limited either by geographical area or short time period (Fothergill and Gudgin, 19 ; Storey, 19 ; Scottish Economic Planning Department, 1980). These studies have to be interpreted carefully. A particularly thorny issue is whether the results should reflect the impact of new openings, or whether one should simply analyse the employment change of establishments in existence at the start of the period under examination. The various results using the latter approach are shown below.

All studies suggest the smallest establishments have the most favourable employment performance, but there is no consistency in the results beyond this. It should in any case be noted that the data for the smallest size class is typically not comprehensive and may be more representative of growing and surviving establishments than of declining ones - the size of this bias is not known. We are naturally rather interested in our results which suggest there was an inverse relationship between size and employment growth for the 1975-78 period, but not for 1972-75. This apparent change in the findings is also reflected in more global analysis which shows an increased share being taken by small manufacturing firms and establish- ments in total manufacturing employment.

We feel that it is probably easier for government officials with larger data bases to carry out national components of change analysis and would certainly not wish to encourage the establishment of new data bases for this purpose. Furthermore, while components of change analysis is interesting, its explanatory powers are limited. We suggest outside research in this area could more usefully concentrate on the reasons for the relationships found and we would be particularly interested in further insights as to the reasons for the changing results over time. David Storey (1982), for instance, has put forward various arguments to explain the findings. He argues that the emergence of newly industrialised countries in the 1970s, producing 'standard' industrial goods, has meant that developed countries have had to shift towards more specialised goods where they cannot reap the same economies of scale. He further

Table 1

Net employment change by size of establishment – various studies
(Establishments in existence at beginning of period only)

EMPLOYMENT SIZE BAND	0	10	20	25	50	100	200	500
East Midlands[a] (1968–75)			+12.6		-3.2		-14.9	-14.8
Cleveland[b] (1965–76)	+56.0			+16.3	-28.3	-20.9		-26.2
Scotland[c] (1969–74)		n.a.	-1.0	-11.0	-12.0	-15.0		-12.0
UK (1972–75)[d]		n.a.	+1.3	-6.4		-7.6	-6.8	-6.1
UK (1975–78)[e]		n.a.	+7.5	+3.1		-1.4	-4.7	-7.3

Note: Figures are expressed as a % of initial employment in size band.

Sources: (a) Fothergill and Gudgin (19)
          (b) Storey (19)
          (c) Scottish Economic Planning Department (1980)
          (d) Macey (1982)
          (e) Internal Department of Trade and Industry paper (unpublished)

argues that the increase in energy prices has affected plant
level and distribution economics in favour of smaller
establishments. It also contributed to the post 1974 world
recession and recessions tend to be periods in which small
firms prosper rather better than large firms. Finally he
argues that increases in wealth lead to a relative increase in
demand for 'one off' products which are likely to be produced
by small firms.

International dimension

The evidence, summarised by Ganguly and Povey (1982), suggests
that the UK as compared to other countries continued to have
relatively few small manufacturing firms in the 1970s. (This
finding was not universal for all industries, but was not
'explained' by a different mix of industries in the UK compared
with other countries.) There are obviously a number of reasons
for the relative paucity of small firms in the UK and a number
of commonly held hypotheses about the reasons. Clearly,
however, any fresh insights about the reasons and the
consequences are of interest. Are wage levels relative to
large firms significant? What is the relationship between the
size of the sector and the performance of the economy? It is,
for example, sometimes argued that the large size of the small
firm sector is a major reason for Japanese success in
manufacturing. This strong claim, however, contrasts rather
strongly with Rothwell and Zegveld's (1982) figures which
suggest that postwar Japanese small firms make a negligible
contribution to innovation, an essential part of Japanese
success.

   The role and effectiveness of government policy in other
countries is of interest. Allen and Yuill's (1982) work on
European industrial aids suggests that small firm expenditure
(in grant equivalent terms) is high in Germany, the Netherlands
and France but is of relatively little significance in the
other countries. This is not to say that other countries
(including the UK) do not consider small firm development
important. It is simply that they do not have significant
financial aid schemes on offer which are specifically targetted
to small firms. We are always interested to learn more about
the effects of other countries' wider assistance packages to
small firms e.g. policies towards loans. What are the most
successful ways of tackling a particular problem? What is the
perceived cost effectiveness of individual measures or the
package of measures offered elsewhere? Providing answers to
these questions does, of course, pose severe methodological
problems.

Other government policies

There is a clear and continuing need for evaluation of
objectives, existing measures and potential measures. This
chapter has already discussed evaluation of certain small firms
measures but there is clearly scope for further work on other
measures. For example we always welcome insights about the
effectiveness and coordination of the various services the
government provides to small firms e.g. the Small Firms Service
and the Small Firms Technical Enquiry Service. The DTI has
itself commissioned a consultancy study of firms' views of
existing and possible new schemes e.g. for marketing. As part
of this study some 500 companies will be approached, and it is
hoped that the study will guide the Department as to the demand
for and effectiveness of existing services and the demand for
further services. The Manpower Services Commission are
interested in whether it could do more in its training capacity
or via Open Tech to further small firms policy objectives.
What is the role of education and training in developing small
firms? Can 'entrepreneurial' thinking be taught?

It is possible that industrial aid schemes are biased against
small firms in some way which can reasonably be rectified. For
example, public purchasing procedures are thought to have been
burdensome in some cases and have been altered in the hope of
redressing this. We are now commissioning a study of the
experience of small firms in the field of defence contracts to
broaden our view of the influences on their access to contracts,
and one purpose of the study will be to see whether the changed
procedures have made much difference. Experience in other
fields would be of interest, and we would always be interested
to know whether there are further ways in which government
pruchasing policy could usefully follow best practice in the
private sector.

With the declining mobility of industry, the emphasis in
regional policy in recent years has shifted towards the
development of indigenous potential. This does not exclusively
mean small firms, but it is evident that such firms have a
significant part to play. We are therefore always interested
in research which highlights any special problems faced by
small firms in the assisted areas and which can provide
additional material to help the design of more effective
regional policies. Conversely, is there any danger as Storey
(1982) has argued that small firms policies tend to conflict
with regional policy objectives?

Concluding remarks

The issues for further research discussed in the previous pages can be related to certain general concerns of policy makers in the small firms area. It may be of interest if these under-lying themes are set out explicity as they may provoke others to suggest further themes or particular ideas for research relevant to small firms policy.

Several of the ideas in the 'issues' section of this chapter are suggestions for improving our understanding of new firm formation and the role of small firms in the economy. For example, it has been suggested that the need is now to develop and test theories which explain the results typically obtained by job generation studies, rather than more components of change analysis of firm size and employment change. In general successful policy making clearly must be founded on an under-standing of how new firms come to be founded, who forms them, the motive for firm formation, and of the strengths, weaknesses and potential of new and small firms in relation to the general objective of improving the performance of the economy of the UK and its constituent countries and regions.

Knowledge of the strength and weakness of small firms is of course insufficient to indicate or determine the appropriate policy response, if any response is called for. If weaknesses are to be overcome, or strengths built on, it is necessary to have an understanding of the underlying causes of the strengths and weaknesses of small firms to indicate the constraints on their performance which cause the weaknesses or which prevent full realisation of potential. Policy makers are clearly particularly interested in constraints on performance which are amenable to public policy action, but it is also useful to know when there is no scope for policy to remove constraints.

In a world of limited resources it is not enough to know what the constraints on performance are and what policy action would remove them. Knowledge of the prospective costs and benefits of particular policy responses is also needed; ideally the cost benefit outcome needs to be known relative to some generalised alternative use of the resources involved and also relative to the costs and benefits of achieving the same policy objective in some other way.

Although these points will be familiar, it is worth restating them as it is as well for researchers looking to influence policy to have them in mind even when their research is inevitably too narrowly focused for all the considerations to be of direct relevance.

However good the information on which a policy was formulated, its costs and benefits also generally need to be evaluated after some time. A final theme is therefore the estimation of

the effects of policy measures and their evaluation both
against their stated objectives and in terms of whether those
objectives are relevant and appropriate in the current state of
knowledge. The importance of further work on evaluation has
been stressed at several points in this chapter.

Research into particular aspects of one or more of these
themes will need to face and solve difficult problems. It is
perhaps inevitable that the questions policy makers want
answered are the difficult ones; the answers to the easy
questions are either obvious or have been researched already.

ACKNOWLEDGEMENT

The authors are grateful to helpful comments from a number of
colleagues, in particular Ian Elliott and Michael Back (ICD
Department of the Environment).

REFERENCES

Allen, K. and Yuill, D., (1982), Industrial Aids in the
    European Community, report to the Department of Industry.
Bolton, J.E., (1971), Report on the Committee of Inquiry on
    Small Firms, Cmnd 4811, HMSO.
Cameron, S.J., et al, (1982), Local Authority Aid to Industry:
    An Evaluation in Tyne & Wear, Inner Cities Research Programme,
    Report no.7, DOE, April.
Department of Industry, (1982), Interim Analysis of the Small
    Business Loan Guarantee Scheme, Department of Industry.
Fothergill, S. and Gudgin, G., (1982), Unequal Growth,
    Heinemann Educational Books.
Fothergill, S. and Gudgin, G., (1979), 'The Job Generation
    Process in Britain', Centre for Environmental Studies,
    Research Report no.32.
Ganguly, A. and Povey, D.A., (1982), 'Small Firms Survey: The
    International Scene', British Business, 19th November.
Lloyd, P. and Dicken, P., (1982), Industrial Change: Local
    Manufacturing Firms in Manchester and Merseyside, Inner
    Cities Research Programme, Report no.6, DOE.
Macey, R.D., (1982), Job Generation in British Manufacturing
    Industry: Employment Change by Size of Establishment and
    Region, Department of Industry.
Middlesex Polytechnic London Industry and Employment Research
    Group, (1982), Monitoring Manufacturing Employment Change in
    London 1976-81.
Mitchell, J.E. and Binks, M.R., (forthcoming), Growth
    Constraints on New Manufacturing Firms, Small Firms Unit,
    Nottingham University, (SSRC Report).

Robson Rhodes, (1983a), A Study of some early claims under the Small Business Loan Guarantee Scheme, Department of Industry.

Robson Rhodes, (1983b), Small Business Loan Guarantee Scheme, Commentary on a telephone survey of borrowers, Department of Industry.

Rothwell, R. and Zegveld, W., (1982), Innovation and Small and Medium Sized Firms, Frances Pinter Publishing.

Scottish Economic Planning Department, (1980), 'Small Units in Scottish Manufacturing', Scottish Economic Bulletin, Spring.

Storey, D.J., (1980), 'Job Generation and Small Firms Policy in Britain', Centre for Environmental Studies, Policy Series no. 11.

Storey, D.J., (1982), Entrepreneurship and the New Firm, Croom Helm.

Wilson Committee, (1979), The Financing of Small Firms, Interim Report of the Committee to Review the Functioning of Financial Institutions, Cmnd 7503, HMSO.

A complete version of this chapter by David Rees, Celia Frank and Robert Miall was published in Regional Studies Vol.18 No.3, June 1984. Sections entitled 'Recent policy measures towards small firms','Technological Change', 'Administrative burdens', and 'Interaction between large and small firms' have been deleted for reasons of space from this version. Crown copyright, published with permission.

Small business management training in European business schools and management centres

GAY HASKINS

INTRODUCTION: CONFUSION - NOT CONCLUSION

For many European Business Schools and Management Centres, small business management training is a comparatively infant area. Nonetheless, it is an area in which a good deal is going on and in which interest is clearly burgeoning.

   With this in mind, the European Foundation for Management Development (EFMD) carried out, in the summer of 1983, a questionnaire survey of its member (or affiliated) business schools and management centres, to learn of their activities towards small enterprise.

   Forty six responses were received (see Table 1). It is the feedback from these questionnaires, together with information gained at the 1982 EFMD European Small Business Seminar on the theme of Management Development, Training and Education, the May 1983 meeting, co-hosted by the Union des Industries de la Communauté Europeenne (UNICE) and Manchester Business School on the Training and Counselling of Small Firm Entrepreneurs and Managers, together with telephone interviews and documentation from EFMD member files that form the basis of this report. In addition, useful supplementary material was obtained from a recent study of higher education and small business in France effected through the Comité d'Etudes sur les Formations d'Ingenieurs (CEFI, 1983).

Table 1
EFMD questionnaire on small business programmes:
organisations responding

	QUESTIONNAIRE A: Undergraduate/ MBA	QUESTIONNAIRE B: Continuing Education Programmes	
		Start-up programmes	for existing business mgrs
1. Anglian Management Centre	V	V	-
2. Ashridge Management Centre	-	-	-
3. Associacao Industrial Portuguesa, Lisboa	-	-	-
4. University of Aston	V	-	V
5. Bath University	V	V	-
6. Universita Luigi Bocconi	-	-	V
7. Universität Bonn	-	V	V
8. University of Bradford	V	-	-
9. Centre de la Petite Entreprise, Lille	-	V	V
10. CIFAG, Lisboa	-	-	V
11. Cranfield School of Management	V	-	-
12. University College, Dublin	V	-	V
13. Durham University Business School	V	V	V
14. School of Small Business - Danish Employers' Confederation	-	-	V
15. Ecole Européenne des Affaires, Paris/Oxford/ Dusseldorf	V	-	-
16. EADA, Barcelona	-	-	V
17. EDHEC, Lille	V	-	-
18. ESADE, Barcelona	V	-	V
19. ESSEC, Cergy Pontoise	V	-	V

20. Rijksuniversiteit te Gent, Interfacultair Centrum voor Management	V	–	V
21. Helsinki School of Economics	V	V	–
22. Hernstein Management Centre, Vienna	–	–	V
23. INSEAD	V	–	V
24. IPA, Univ. de Lille	V	–	V
25. IESE, Barcelona	V	–	V
26. IMI, Geneva	V	–	–
27. ISA, Jouy-en-Josas	V	–	–
28. Instituto Superior Ciencias Trabalho e da Empresa, Lisboa	V	–	–
29. Interuniversitaire Interfaculteit Bedrijfskunde, Delft	V	–	–
30. ISTUD, Italy	V	V	V
31. Foundation for Business Administration, Delft	–	–	V
32. London Business School	V	V	V
33. Manchester Business School	V	V	–
34. University of Montpelier I Applied Management Centre	V	–	–
35. Nijenrode Business School, NL	V	–	V
36. Norwegian Employers' Confederation	–	–	V
37. Polytechnic of Central London	V	V	V
38. Robert Gordon Institute of Technology	V	V	V
39. St. Gall Graduate School of Economics, Law, Business & Public Administration	V	–	–
40. Scottish Business School (University of Glasgow Division)	V	V	V
41. Stockholm School of Economics	V	–	–

42.	Sundridge Park Management Centre	-	-	V
43.	Swedish Institute of Management	-	V	V
44.	Trent Polytechnic	V	V	V
45.	Ulster Polytechnic	V	V	V
46.	University of Warwick, School of Industrial Studies	V	-	-

The EFMD questionnaire was in two parts. Part A looked at small business courses in undergraduate and MBA (or equivalent) business/commerce programmes. Part B investigated continuing education programmes both for small firm start-ups and for existing enterprises.

Obviously, this chapter does not represent an exhaustive piece of research. Nor does it offer any conclusive findings. Much information but more confusion is the name of the day. Additional information, feedback, comment, correction and eventually, perhaps, clarification on the state of small business management development education and training in Europe is, therefore, invited.

THE UNDERGRADUATE AND MBA LEVELS

While small business courses still receive scant billing in most business school brochures, the importance of entrepreneurship, risk taking and creativity is increasingly emphasised. This may be a reaction to criticisms that business school courses tend to mitigate against entrepreneurship, it may be in reaction to the 'small is more beautiful' movement, it may represent an awareness of the important role played by small business in our economies, it may be in response to unemployment or even in response to student demands for small business options.

Thirty three business schools responding to the EFMD questionnaire offered undergraduate and/or MBA programmes and, of these, only five do not offer small business elective courses at some point (generally towards the end) of these programmes. Most frequently occurring small business course electives are in the areas of: Small Business Start-Up: Developing a Business Plan; New Firm Management; Small Firm Management; and Advice and Counselling to Small Business.

In most cases, only one or two small business electives are offered. Of the schools responding to the EFMD questionnaire survey, the following appear to offer the greatest number of small business electives (i.e. three or more) at the undergraduate/MBA (or equivalent) levels: Cranfield School of Management, DUBS, ESSEC, IIB, ISA, London Business School (LBS), Stockholm School of Economics (SSE) and Trent Polytechnic (TP). The CEFI Study mentioned previously indicates a range of course offerings also at ESCAE Rouen and ICN (CEFI, 1983). And certain schools, such as the St. Gall Graduate School of Economics, Law, Business and Public Administration, emphasise that small business is integrated in <u>all</u> courses.

At four schools - Escuela Superior de Administracion y Direccion de Empresas (ESADE), The Helsinki School of Economics, Manchester Business School (MBS) and Robert Gordon's Institute of Technology - small business projects or electives are compulsory. That at MBS has been in effect for some years now: called the <u>Entrepreneurship Project</u>, it is compulsory for all second year MBA students. This course began as an option and was made compulsory by popular demand some ten years ago. Groups of between three and six students work full time over an eighteen day period either on a business initiation project or with an individual or new firm to an agreed brief on a problem central to the existence and future success of the business (Watkins, 1976).

These types of project-based/action-learning approaches are not infrequent and very much advocated in small business training. At ESC Lyon for instance, students in the small business option work one day a week over a six month period to assist a small business manager with a specific problem. At EDHEC in Lille students are offered a course on <u>Small Business Management</u> which comprises initial classroom preparation followed by a ten week period in a small firm under the supervision of the school. Several other French schools (ISA, Hautes Etudes Commerciales (HEC), ESCP, ESCAE de Dijon) offering small business start-up courses also use a project-based approach.

Course offerings, then, are increasing. But what of the demand? Student demand for small business courses in undergraduate and MBA programmes appears generally high and evaluation of these courses apparently positive. However, little research seems to have been effected to date on how many students of these courses end up either working in or owning their own small firms. One school which has carried out an evaluation in this area is the Ecole des Hautes Etudes Commerciales du Nord (EDHEC) in Lille. They have found the following:

- from the '<u>création d'entreprise' course</u>': little

start-up activity upon leaving the school but results later on;

- from the 'small business management course': has been appreciated by the twelve firms which have received students over the past three years and the students themselves are more motivated and less apprehensive towards small business.

In addition, a recent report at the Stockholm School of Economics concluded that 20 per cent of the students taking the small business option between 1977 and 1982 have started their own firm. A similar study at Cranfield School of Management showed that of the 50 students taking the first credit course offered on Entrepreneurship and Small Ventures, about half subsequently opt for the longer follow-up option on the same topic. Of those who participated in the longer option between 1976 and 1980, 25 per cent are running businesses which are the same or similar to those presented in their Entrepreneurship and New Ventures proposals during the course, 7 per cent are running their own businesses in different fields and 68 per cent are ex-students not running their own businesses. In the latter group, about three quarters said that they intend to run their own businesses one day (Harper, 1981).

Despite the high demand, small business programmes and courses are not so easy to introduce or develop in universities and other business schools. Frequently mentioned problems include:

- acceptance, respectability and fit: small business teaching requires a specialist staff which cannot easily be categorised into a traditional, function- ally oriented faculty structure; difficulties may arise in getting small business accepted into the curricula; small business training lacks academic respectability and gives no clear cut career path, hence a risk of alienation from the rest of the faculty.

- course content and focus: a great deal of time and care is required to develop appropriate course content and focus and to show how the content of other undergraduate and/or MBA courses may be applied to the small business context.

- teaching materials and methods: different teaching materials and approaches are required and while project-based learning is desirable, it may be difficult to identify good projects and/or to find

faculty willing to give the significant time
required to supervise them; good cases are needed
but the local community is frequently reticent to
supply them.

- assessment: small business course performance is
difficult to assess along traditional lines; and,
where group projects are carried out, it is
frequently difficult to assess individual performance in groups.

- faculty supply: it is frequently difficult either
to identify appropriate faculty and/or to get
existing faculty to 'think small'.

START-UP PROGRAMMES

At least among the centres offering continuing education
programmes which responded to the EFMD questionnaire, there
appears (with the notable exception of the UK respondents) to
be a greater involvement in programmes for existing small
business managers than in programmes for small business start-
ups. On the other hand, several of the respondents to the EFMD
questionnaire expressed the desire to get into this area as
long as financial support is made available.

Several interesting start-up courses are presently offered
through the UK Manpower Services Commission at business schools
and management centres throughout the UK:

- The New Enterprise Programme (NEP) for people wanting
to start up their own business. Each programme lasts
sixteen weeks and involves sixteen unemployed
participants. (Participants receive standard training
grants and help with expenses incurred in the
training.) During this period, every participant
undertakes a feasibility study of a new business idea
and begins, if appropriate,to implement it on a
commercial basis.

- Small Business Courses for those wishing to start
smaller scale businesses than in the NEP, perhaps
employing the family only. These are generally
between six and ten week, full time courses: for
instance four weeks of lectures and six weeks' project
work. Student numbers range from about 12-16.

- Cooperative Enterprise Programmes, typically of four
months duration and through which potential founders

of producer cooperatives may examine the feasibility
of their ideas, acquire basic management expertise
and begin trading. As with the NEP, there are
typically 16 participants in all with each cooperative represented by two participants.

- Skill into Business, a ten day programme for skilled
  or semi skilled unemployed workers who wish to
  explore the possibility of using their skill to work
  for themselves.

While UK business schools and management centres would appear
to be ahead of the pack in the provision of these types of
programmes, this may be because small business training is more
frequently carried out by these types of institutions in the UK
than in other parts of Europe. In West Germany, for instance,
training programmes are most frequently administered through
the local Chambers of Commerce and Handicrafts and/or the
Rationalisierungs-Kuratorium der Deutschen Wirtschaft (RKW)
rather than through the education sector. In Belgium, where
there exists a special Ministry for the Middle Classes (i.e.
small and medium businesses and independent workers), most of
the training for small business is carried out through the
Institute for the Permanent Education of the Middle Classes
which has training centres across Belgium with small firms as
their exclusive market. Thus, while many interesting and
innovative initiatives are underway in the UK's education
sector, it may be premature to judge these without a more
exhaustive study of what is offered elsewhere in Europe through
different mechanisms.

A number of start-up training initiatives were, for instance,
mentioned by schools and centres in the Nordic countries. In
Finland, a number of new free start-up courses have been
recently introduced as employment generating initiatives. One
such course, offered through the University of Jyvskyla,
comprises twelve hours of teaching per week over a nine month
period for people who have just started their own firm or are
about to do so. In addition, each participant can benefit from
50 hours of counselling. Short information courses (1½-2 days)
and longer programmes (5-10 days) are also offered to would-be
entrepreneurs in Sweden with subsidies through the regional
development funds.

In Ireland, an interesting new course has recently been
introduced. Directed at would-be high technology entrepreneurs,
it has been designed by Shannon Development in cooperation with
Dr. P. Marshall Fitzgerald of the National Institute for Higher
Education, himself a partner in a successful Californian
electronics firm (Curtin, 1983).

In France, programmes offered through the Centre d'Enseignement Supérieur des Affaires (CESA), boast particularly high success rates. Over the last six years, twelve start-up programmes have been offered apparently leading to the creation of 105 enterprises and 1,000 jobs (Clement, 1982). In Italy, the management school in Belgirate, the Instituto Direzionali SpA (ISTUD) has recently introduced a twelve week programme in cooperation with the Confederazione Generale dell' Industria Italiana. This programme is split into four two week blocks over a six month period and is aimed at young men and women who have recently undertaken or are about to undertake an entrepreneurial activity. Training is given both in the functional areas of control, finance, marketing, organisation and strategy and topics related to the entrepreneurial function such as innovation and the creative process, the role and social responsibility of the entrepreneur, and the management of a family business.

Such then is the focus of the ISTUD programme. But which areas were felt to be in need of focus among other respondents to the EFMD questionnaire? Not surprisingly, finance, accounting, marketing and legal rules and regulations were frequently mentioned. But also - and in line with the ISTUD programme - a need for an emphasis on the essentials of entrepreneurship and entrepreneurial ability was underlined. (What does entrepreneurship require? Do you have it?) In addition, a validation of the business idea and the development of a plan which explores the business and its resource needs were seen as highly important in start-up programmes.

PROGRAMMES FOR EXISTING SMALL FIRM MANAGERS

Having briefly described some small business start-up programmes, let us now turn to programmes for existing small firm managers.

In this area, a variety of offerings were cited by those responding to the EFMD questionnaire. Despite the variety, however, there seemed to be general agreement that programmes for existing small firm managers should be organised in modules or discrete blocks (e.g. nine days spread over a four month period, once a week over a certain period of time, as one or two day workshops). That type of modular organisation is favoured in particular in response to the fact that small businessmen are generally very pressed for time and unwilling/unable to spend long periods away from their firm for training purposes.

Agreement as to course costs is, on the other hand, less

apparent. UK respondents to the EFMD questionnaire tended to stress the need for low cost programmes. However, courses offered by Bocconi University in Italy, INSEAD in France and the Irish Management Institute all charge comparatively high course fees and (yet) seem to attract a reasonably high participation.

The Bocconi University course (<u>Corso di Sviluppo Imprenditoriale</u>) runs for six days in three two day blocks over a three week period for a fee of It. Lira 1.500.000 (approx. £630) and has attracted some thirty participants on the two occasions run in 1982-83. A factor contributing to its success may be that its content and course materials are based upon interviews with some sixty entrepreneurs in the Lombardy Region. Accordingly, its three parts cover: 1) signs and causes of success and failure; 2) improving economic and financial results in the short/medium term; 3) medium/long term perform- ance and how to improve it.

The INSEAD course (<u>Direction de l'Entreprise Moyenne à Vocation Internationale</u>) is, perhaps not surprisingly,given the school's image, an up-market course for companies with sales of US $10-100 million and typically comprises a class of ten students for a high, and unsubsidised fee of FF 20.200 (£1,700). Here emphasis is placed upon: the identification and penetration of new markets both at home and abroad; launching new products; maintaining financial independence and financing growth; and the development of responsible management within the firm.

The Irish Management Institute's <u>Business Development Programme</u> is remarkable in that it runs over a lengthy eighteen month period, a duration seen as critical to its objectives. As its Director, Chris Park states:

> The BDP is not about skills. It's about changing attitudes. You cannot condense something like that into six weeks, but over eighteen months, attitudes begin to change. (O'Toole, 1983)

The format is a two day residential workshop each month, emphasising experience sharing and the use of participant company models. A primary aim is to get the entrepreneur to draw up a development plan for his/her company. This residen- tial aspect is seen as very important in getting the partici- pants to know each other well and therefore to be willing to share information. Also important is the appointment of counsellors to work with the participating entrepreneur one day each month in his/her company:

> ... not acting as a management consultant but rather as

a _catalyst_ to listen to the entrepreneur and to bounce
ideas around. (O'Toole, 1983)

Not surprisingly this course is very costly to run and has
required sponsorship to the tune of some £100,000 Irish on each
of the three occasions run to date over and above the course
fee of £1,800. A notable development is that past participants
are now beginning to sponsor future courses, albeit in a modest
way.

Elsewhere, courses are typically less costly than those
described above. In Scandinavia, various programmes have been
developed based on the Swedish Employers' Federation's well-
known manual '_Look After Your Firm_' which enables the user to
pinpoint the strengths and weaknesses of his business and
himself. In fact, the Employers' Confederations play an
important and active role in each of the three Scandinavian
countries. In Denmark, for instance, the Danish Employers'
Confederation's School of Small Business has been organising a
locally run _Small Firm Management Course_ for some time now. It
runs one afternoon per week over a period of five weeks for
classes of up to sixteen participants at a subsidised fee of
dkr 1,050, approx. £70.

Small business clubs and chambers of commerce and/or handicrafts also play an important role in many parts of Europe.
Typically, small business clubs offer _club evenings_ with guest
speakers offering an attractive informality and peer group
contact for the small businessmen. In addition, certain
chambers of commerce and/or management centres have organised
à la carte programmes in which small businessmen can take their
pick of a variety of courses specially designed to meet the
needs of small firms.

As well as describing their programmes, respondents to the
EFMD questionnaire were asked to list the topic areas they felt
to be in particular need of emphasis in programmes for small
businessmen. These are shown, in approximate order of
frequency of mention below:

(1) Marketing and selling
(2) Finance, accounting, budgetting and forecasting
(3) General management
(4) Strategy and planning
(5) Personnel management, especially team work,
    delegation and personal planning (e.g. time
    management)
(6) New technologies/R & D
(7) Export management
(8) Legal contracts

Not surprisingly, new technology is receiving increasing (but probably still insufficient) emphasis. Certain centres have and are developing special courses on Computers and the Small Firm. In Austria, for instance, the Hernstein Management Centre offers a two day course EDV: Einsatz in Klein und Mittelbetrieb which seeks to address the question, 'What advantages can a computer bring me?' The course fee is AS 3800 (£130) and, like other Hernstein courses, is subsidised by the Vienna Chamber of Commerce.

Also receiving increasing emphasis, particularly in reaction to the high rate of small firm failures, are Growth Programmes. In the UK, the Manpower Services Commission is subsidising small programmes at, for instance, the Durham University Business School (DUBS) and the Scottish Business School. These courses take place in short sessions spread over a four to six month period. Their objective is to 'provide encouragement for owner managers to take a systematic approach towards exploiting new product, process and market development. The recruits are, therefore, companies with interest and estimated capability to develop and grow' (Gibb and Dyson, 1982).

But not only are the topics and emphasis of such programmes important. Also critical to their success are the teaching methods used. Particularly frequently mentioned by respondents to the EFMD questionnaire was the need for:

- A practical focus: focus on business problems or opportunities rather than on the conventional subject areas shown above - learn the theory through practical examples;

- A mixture of cases, theory and linkage to the specific problems of the participants;

- An atmosphere that would encourage participation and 'getting to know each other'; and

- Where possible, an integration of training and counselling.

But even with well designed programmes, the small businessman is not an easy participant to attract. Indeed, 'Getting small businessmen to courses is reminiscent of selling refrigerators to the Eskimos, or shoes to the Africans', wrote one respondent to the EFMD questionnaire. For there is no doubt that there are some challenges to be overcome when developing and marketing programmes for existing small firm management particularly if no subsidy exists from government, chambers of commerce or employers' associations. While some comparatively expensive courses may succeed, this would not appear to be the norm. What then are the challenges? Respondents to the EFMD's questionnaire mentioned the following:

- Reaching the client: potential clients are both
  difficult and costly to reach.

- Promotion: as a result of the above, a wide variety
  of promotional tools are needed including: direct
  mail; newspapers; TV and radio; government ministries,
  chambers of commerce, banks and other professional
  referral systems; small firm networks; word of mouth
  and referrals from previous participants and small
  firm visits. In short: 'use as many channels as
  possible'.

- Demand: while there was no clear consensus as to the
  demand either for start-up programmes or for programmes for existing entrepreneurs, the demand for start-
  up programmes did appear to be rated as somewhat
  higher, particularly when programmes were offered free
  to the unemployed or to redundant managers. As
  already mentioned, most small business entrepreneurs
  are not motivated towards training nor do they attach
  a very high premium to attending courses, particularly
  if theoretical in content. In the CEFI report
  referred to previously, for instance, small business
  owner/managers not surprisingly attached far more
  importance to experience than qualifications (although
  there appeared to be a correlation between size and
  sector and the importance attached to diplomas - the
  larger the size, the greater the importance, with the
  service sector attaching a somewhat greater importance
  to diplomas than their industrial and commercial
  counterparts). Nonetheless, the same small business
  owner/managers affirmed that they looked systematically
  for continuing education opportunities for themselves
  and their staff, particularly in financial management,
  marketing, sales techniques, personnel and production
  management. (CEFI, 1983)

- Time and cost: given the problems outlined above and
  the fact that many of the programmes for small enterprise are new, significant time is required in their
  development and refinement. In addition, unless
  sponsored or subsidised, it can be very difficult to
  ensure the profitability of these courses.

- Pricing: Linked to the above is the problem of
  pricing. Both would be and existing entrepreneurs are
  generally unwilling and/or unable to invest a great
  deal of money in training programmes. It may be

difficult (but perhaps, as the previous section has
indicated not altogether impossible), therefore, to
charge a fee which covers all course costs (let alone
guaranteeing a reasonable profitability). Sponsorship or subsidy is frequently required.

- Scheduling: as already indicated, the small businessman prefers courses which are scheduled not to conflict too much with his working day. As a result,
  programmes for small businessmen are frequently
  scheduled in the evenings, or on Fridays and
  Saturdays, times which may well conflict with the
  preferences of the staff teaching the course.

- Teaching skills: again as already indicated, a down
  to earth, practical, non academic approach is
  required in teaching small firm courses, not always
  evident in universities and business schools.

- Image: the question of the 'image' of the organisation running the course is also important.
  Universities, for instance, are frequently seen as too
  academic by small businessmen: for them, academics
  are to be avoided 'like the plague'. Other business
  schools/management centres are seen as too up-market,
  catering to big business needs, but lacking credibility and expertise in the small business sector.
  Nonetheless, as UK business schools like Durham,
  Manchester and London and post experience centres
  like IFL, the Swedish Institute of Management (which
  has been running six programmes a year for small
  businessmen for several years now) have shown, it can
  be done.

CONCLUDING COMMENTS

Confusion, not conclusion, is the name of the day: so ran the
statement at the opening of this chapter. Nonetheless, the
information obtained to date does permit some preliminary
insights into the activities of Europe's business schools and
management centres towards small enterprise, as well as
stimulating a great many thoughts and questions. These
include:

Basic education

If, as certain experiences mentioned in this chapter appear to
indicate, you can 'educate for entrepreneurship', surely this
education should start at the school level. Furthermore, while

family background, characteristics, work and attitudes are important influences on career orientations and decisions, basic education also plays an important role in this regard.

This appears to be recognised more in some countries than in others. In Germany, for instance, there is a government committee on 'Schule und Wirtschaft'. Also in Germany, some 50 per cent of all leavers from compulsory schooling take apprenticeships, mostly in small Handwerk firms (Economists Advisory Group, 1980). In Britain, however, school curricula has traditionally done little to motivate interest or ability in this area. Four years ago, a report of The Economist Advisory Group lamented:

> ... the educational system in Britain ... seems to our-
> selves and to many observers to be more remote from the
> influence of the wealth creating sector of society than
> it is in other countries ... The practical arts of
> baking bread, filing and drilling metal or even photo-
> etching are seen in the British education process as
> activities for the academic failure, not as an import-
> ant part of the learning process, and as a means to a
> satisfying and probably more creative alternative to a
> desk job. (Economists Advisory Group, 1980)

While things may be changing somewhat, these types of criticism are still frequently raised and may well have some credibility elsewhere in Europe. Where links between basic education and the realities of today's (and tomorrow's) career opportunities seem particularly weak, might not those involved in management development and training play an active role in trying to overcome these discrepancies? Is not greater effort required to attract school children to entrepreneurship? Furthermore, particularly in the UK are not closer links needed between those involved in basic education, vocational training and management training?

The undergraduate/MBA levels

If the responses to the EFMD questionnaire can be taken as fairly representative, it would appear that many undergraduate business and/or MBA programmes now offer one or two small business courses. But if small business is to be seen as a really serious option to a large firm career, might not greater prominence and publicity be given to this in undergraduate and MBA brochures through, for instance:

- A more clearly marked special highlighting of small
  business options. (At present they appear generally
  to be hidden among a long list of course electives,

sometimes amid the marketing electives, and at other
times amid the policy/strategy options or elsewhere);
and/or

- Displayed quotations from those who either have gone
  into business for themselves or have chosen to enter
  a small/medium firm after graduation; and/or

- Listing both small and large firms in publicity on
  'firms which have hired our graduates/undergraduates'.

In addtion, there appears to be a clear need for more
evaluation of these programmes in terms of the results of these
courses: Do they change student attitudes towards small
business as an option? Do they help them to assess their
potential (or otherwise) for a small business career? (We are
not all 'born entrepreneurs', nor should we necessarily all be
entrepreneurial.) How many have actually started up their own
firm, or joined a small enterprise? How many now anticipate
starting or joining a small firm in a few years time? And so
on.

It would also be of interest to hear of:

- Initiatives aimed at identifying small/medium firms
  who were interested in hiring small business graduates;

- Specific examples of the integration of small firm
  material into the rest of the curricula (accounting,
  finance, marketing, personnel, strategy, production
  courses, etc);

- Small firm case studies available from the case
  clearing houses (and the demand for them);

- New faculty chairs designated in this area
  (increasing its academic respectability and
  visibility); and

- Other instances of compulsory small business courses/
  entrepreneurship projects and their results.

Start-up programmes

Start-up programmes are clearly receiving increasing attention,
particularly as unemployment increases. If, as seems to be the
case, schools and centres in the United Kingdom have developed
a significant expertise in this area, efforts should be made to
ensure that these experiences are shared with people now
establishing such programmes elsewhere. Perhaps too, greater
attention needs to be paid to the different 'market segments'
for start-up programmes, segments which may range from the
professional manager with a clear business idea to the

unemployed person without any idea at all. Clearly differing programmes are required for these and other market segments. Are we as yet sufficiently addressing these differences?

Programmes for existing PME's

Similarly, while a variety of offerings were noted in the section on programmes for existing small firms, are there certain areas which are under serviced and/or in need of greater emphasis? Are present programmes giving sufficient attention to the firm at various stages of growth - and, in particular, to that stage of growth when too much entrepreneurial flair and too little management can become a danger, when the owner/manager has to start delegating and build a management team? Is more attention needed to the causes of small business failures (of which there are inevitably a high number of cases each week, let alone each year)? Are the small (under 50 employees) firms catered for better than their medium-sized counterparts? Do present programmes cater too much for the owner/manager and not enough for other managers in small and medium-sized firms? Could there not be an increasingly developing market for those who have done an MBA or equivalent, know the 'business basics', would like to be, or are, in business for themselves and require quite sophisticated specialised knowledge - and is this market catered for? Is the market for 'specialised' small business areas (computers, bio-technology, other high technology areas, import/exporting) adequately covered - and, if not, should management schools (particularly those linked to technological institutes and/or science parks) be more active in these areas?

A dangerously sexy area ...

Finally, let us stress that small business management training is, as one respondent to the questionnaire stated, 'A dangerously sexy area' - full of allure, but very risky! Some management centres have deliberately chosen not to place a high focus on small business. Indeed, think hard - don't rush into it, would seem to be wise advice. Are we committed to this area? Does it complement the image we have already developed? Have we looked into the challenges of establishing these programmes? Is our faculty (a) motivated; and, (b) equipped to carry them out? Are we willing to train our existing staff and/or hire a team (or at least one highly committed and energetic individual) to build the area up? If small business training requires special materials, approaches and methods, do we have the interest, time and money to develop them? Given the difficulties in 'reaching the small businessman', do we also have the time and money to use the variety of marketing channels required to promote these kinds of programmes? Is government or other sponsorship available for small business programmes, or will we have to 'go it alone' ... These are just a few of the questions that schools and centres might ask before 'taking the plunge'.

Sharing our knowledge

More information is needed if a comprehensive picture of small business management training in Europe is to be obtained. There is clearly an ever increasing number of programme offerings in this area, but information is still required on:

- programmes offered at centres other than those mentioned in this paper;

- start-up programmes offered outside the UK;

- new programmes in new areas; and

- programme results.

EFMD is a network. As such, we can play a useful role in disseminating information and facilitating contact and information sharing between those involved in management development across Europe. Those schools and centres which are, for instance, new entrants in small business start-up programme delivery are, we know, most eager to learn of other, more tried and tested, initiatives in this area.

So keep us informed of your activities. In that way, we can pass on this information to those known to be interested, put you in touch with others involved in small business research, training and development and, in a modest way, contribute to the sharing of knowledge in this interesting and rapidly developing field.

REFERENCES

Clement, J.P., (1982), 'Les Critères de Selection d'un Projet de Création d'Entreprise', Conference Paper, EFMD European Small Business Seminar, Lille.

Curtin, T., (1983), 'Now You Can Learn How to be a High-Tech Entrepreneur', Management, (Journal of the Irish Management Institute), July/August.

Comité d'Etudes sur les Formations d'Ingenieurs (CEFI), (1983), Les P.M.E. et l'Enseignement Superieur, Les Cahiers du CEFI, no.3, March.

Economists Advisory Group Ltd., (1980), The Promotion of Small Business: A 7-Country Study.

Gibb, A.A. and Dyson, J., (1982), 'Stimulating the Growth of Owner Managed Firms', July, available from Durham University Business School.

Harper, M., (1981), 'Entrepreneurship and New Ventures, a Course at the Cranfield School of Management', Venture Capital Report.

O'Toole, A., (1983), 'Third Business Development Programme', Business and Finance, 28th April, vol.19, no.33, p.20.

Watkins, D.S., (1976), 'Education for Entrepreneurship: Is it Possible?', paper prepared for the 6th European Small Business Seminar, Milan, September, p.7.